Hunting and Fishing Military Lands

J. L. Spinks

Foreword by Christina U. Ramsey
Director, Environmental Planning, Department of Defense

Stackpole Books

Copyright © 1991 by Stackpole Books

Published by
STACKPOLE BOOKS
Cameron and Kelker Streets
P.O. Box 1831
Harrisburg, PA 17105

All rights reserved, including the right to reproduce this book or portions thereof in any form or by any means, electronic or mechanical, including photocopying, recording, or by any information storage and retrieval system, without permission in writing from the publisher. All inquiries should be addressed to Stackpole Books, Cameron and Kelker Streets, P.O. Box 1831, Harrisburg, Pennsylvania 17105.

Cover photos: background photo courtesy Fort Hunter Liggett, California; inset photos courtesy Arnold AFB, Tennessee
Cover design by Mark Olszewski
Photo credits: pp. 4, 147: U.S. Air Force photos courtesy Arnold Air Force Base, Tennessee; p. 22: U.S. Army photo by SPC T. James Stickel, Fort Huachuca, Arizona; pp. 35, 81, 108, 137, 191, 223: U.S. Army photos courtesy Fort Hunter Liggett, California; pp. 65, 155, 203: U.S. Army photos by Alan Dyck, Fort Pickett, Virginia; p. 122: U.S. Navy photo by James A. Harris, NAS Meridian, Mississippi. All other photos by the author.

Printed in the United States of America

First Edition

10 9 8 7 6 5 4 3 2 1

Library of Congress Cataloging-in-Publication Data

Spinks, J. L. (Johnnie L.)
   Hunting and fishing military lands / J.L. Spinks. — 1st ed.
       p.   cm.
   Includes index.
   ISBN 0-8117-3018-2
   1. Hunting—United States—Guide-books. 2. Fishing—United
States—Guide-books. 3. Military bases, American—Guide-books.
4. Military reservations—United States—Guide-books. 5. United
States—Description and travel—1981- —Guide-books. I. Title.
SK41.S65   1991
799′.02573—dc20

91-11284
CIP

CONTENTS

FOREWORD

Those who now endeavor to advance conservation programs may forget that there was a time when wild things were something to be overcome, not respected and purposefully managed. The growth of environmental awareness in the 1960s stimulated the public will to reform attitudes and actions of man toward nature. It spawned the first broad, major effort in the United States to reorient responsibilities of government—the National Environmental Policy Act. Public polls in the past two decades have shown continuing concern and strong support for a healthful and productive environment.

In the 1930s, some people (notably Aldo Leopold) recognized a need to interject wildlife values into the planning of various land and water developments and uses. Several federal laws were enacted, including the Fish and Wildlife Coordination Act, which advanced wildlife conservation to varying degrees. Other pollution laws sought to maintain the geophysical characteristics required for sustained productivity. In 1973, the Endangered Species Act set forth a comprehensive federal wildlife conservation effort that emphasized habitat protection and management.

While a number of wildlife populations have been restored since the early 1900s as a result of increased awareness, laws, and advancing technologies, many need more attention. The increasing number of threatened and endangered species affirms a need to be concerned. We continue to amass sound information upon which to base management of wildlife and other natural resources. We have available to us a wealth of all types of information, but wildlife will always be threatened when we do not use that information to avoid habitat degradation.

The Department of Defense manages millions of acres of land in the United States, containing every conceivable landform and type of habitat. As this book indicates, these well managed lands provide environments in which fish and game animals flourish. Across the country on our military installations, there are numerous hunting and fishing programs that are regulated to benefit wildlife and to provide sporting opportunities for both civilian and military sportsmen.

In this era of more enlightened natural resources management, the Department of

Defense is striving to make a significant contribution to the public's desire and need for wildlife-oriented land and water uses. We recognize wildlife to be a national treasure that deserves the best management attention we can give it.

Christina U. Ramsey
Director, Environmental Planning
Department of Defense

INTRODUCTION

I've written this book to give sportsmen, both military and civilian, the best information possible about hunting and fishing on the millions of acres of government land controlled by the Department of Defense. Nearly 150 military installations in forty states are included in this volume.

Some of the installations contained in this book are open only to military personnel or DOD employees, others are open to the public. Most of these installations have excellent wildlife and fisheries programs. Some are even better managed than those of the states in which they are located. The Department of Defense is serious about conservation and wildlife management.

When hunting or fishing on any of these installations, keep in mind that the primary mission of these installations is military activities. Consequently, the mission may dictate that certain restrictions apply to outdoor activities. Seasons may not match those of the state. Installations may be closed at certain times. Restrictions on how many hunters or fishermen are allowed or where and how they may hunt or fish may come into play. Many of these installations require hunters to sign in and out before going afield.

In 90 percent of the cases, these restrictions are primarily for safety reasons. Believe me, you don't want to be out hunting quail in a field that doubles as an artillery impact area. The results can be, literally, earth shattering. In the remaining 10 percent of the cases, security is a primary reason for the strange rules and regulations. Some of the equipment and programs on these installations are vital to our national security. While you may not be a spy, others out there are. So, if some of the rules you have to adhere to while hunting and fishing on DOD lands may be frustrating, remember, they are necessary for both your personal safety and your freedom.

When hunting on a military installation, it's possible that you will come across some live ordnance. If you do, *leave it alone*! This stuff was designed with one thing in mind—to kill! Even duds are dangerous. Sure, it might look good on a shelf back home, but it's not worth dying for. If you find anything resembling ordnance in the field, mark it somehow and report your find to a game warden or the law enforcement office on the installation. Above all, don't mess with it!

Certain areas on installations are permanently closed. They are closed for a reason. Stay out of them. These areas may be minefields, artillery impact areas, or may even contain hazardous chemicals. Again, it's nothing to fool with. If a sign says "DAN-GER—KEEP OUT," do just that. Not only could you get yourself hurt, you could also cause the installation to be closed to the rest of us. Sometimes, all it takes is one bad incident to close an installation for years. Enjoy these lands but be careful and abide by the regulations.

Most of the installations contained in this book do not allow off-road vehicles (ORVs) or all-terrain vehicles (ATVs). Unless specifically mentioned, you can assume that the installation does not authorize the use of ATVs, trail bikes, or any ORVs. When they are authorized, a general summary of the requirements is included with that section.

The point of contact for obtaining more information on hunting and fishing opportunities is listed at the end of each installation's segment. Contact these people before you visit an installation for the latest information available on outdoor activities.

Good luck and good hunting and fishing.

ALABAMA

Alabama is a state people dream about for hunting or fishing. It has one of the largest herds of white-tailed deer and one of the longest deer seasons in the United States, and the limit is a generous deer a day in most areas of the state. Unfortunately, Alabama is also mostly privately owned. If you don't belong to a hunting club, have permission to hunt on private land, or have a deer lease, you can either crowd into one of the state wildlife management areas or pay big bucks to hunt on one of the commercial hunting preserves in the state.

Fortunately, there are other options. Another 118,000 acres are available on DOD lands in Alabama.

Army Installations

ANNISTON ARMY DEPOT

- 12,000 acres open to hunting and fishing
- Closed to the public
- Installation permit required
- White-tailed deer, turkey
- Fishing

Hunting   This installation is not open to the general public, but it is open for big game hunting to depot employees, active duty military personnel, and some of their dependents. At any given time during the season, up to 12,000 acres may be open to deer and turkey hunting.

1

Hunters on the depot must have a valid state or county license and a depot permit. The permit is free, but it is available only after a prospective hunter has completed the depot safety/orientation course.

Hunters must sign out for a specific area at the main gate the day of the hunt. The hunter's name and identification are checked against a master list of those eligible to hunt on the installation. The ratio of hunters is maintained at one hunter to forty acres for shotgun hunters and one to twenty for bowhunters.

Anniston Army Depot is open only to shotgun and archery hunting for deer and turkey. Shotgunners must use slugs for deer and shot for turkeys. Archers must use equipment that meets state requirements. There is no small game hunting authorized on the depot.

According to Billy Burns, the depot forester, the average annual take of whitetails is roughly 100, between archers and shotgunners. Anniston also supports an exceptional population of eastern wild turkeys.

Fishing The only fishing on the depot is for bass and bluegill in the thirty-five-acre impoundment on the installation.

For more information, contact: Provost Marshal, Anniston Army Depot, Anniston, AL 36201-5047.

FORT McCLELLAN

- 1 hour east of Birmingham
- 39,000 acres open for hunting and fishing
- Installation permit required
- White-tailed deer, turkey, small game
- Fishing
- Restricted camping and boating

Hunting White-tailed deer are the only big game animals on the post. Cottontails, squirrels, quail, dove, raccoon, opossum, wild turkeys, snipe, woodcock, and waterfowl make up the small game population.

Fort McClellan uses a priority system to determine eligibility for hunting on the post. The system allows a hunting area to be reserved up to three days in advance if you're on active duty, a dependent of active duty personnel, retired, an unmarried widow or child of an active duty servicemember, in one of the military academies, an ROTC cadet on active duty, or a Medal of Honor recipient or surviving spouse or family member of a Medal of Honor recipient. Military personnel of foreign nations and their family members may reserve a hunting area two days in advance, as may American Red Cross workers, cadets of the Coast Guard Academy, surgeons under contract to the DOD, DOD appropriated and nonappropriated fund employees of Fort

McClellan, DOD contractors, their technical representatives, employees of Fort McClellan banks and credit unions, and others as determined by the commanding general of Fort McClellan. The public may reserve a hunting area up to one day in advance. Additionally, all registered hunters are authorized one guest.

It may seem as though you'll never get a reservation to hunt on Fort McClellan, but that isn't the case. There are forty-two hunting areas open on the post proper and another forty on the Pelham Range. Areas 1A through 10B and 22A through 24C are on Pelham Range. Areas 14A through 20C are on the main post. As many as 761 people can hunt on any given day in all the wildlife areas combined. The hunter-per-acre goal is roughly forty acres each during the firearms deer season and twenty acres per hunter during the archery deer season and small game seasons. Some areas are small and can accommodate only three or four people. Others may have up to twenty-one hunters at a time.

While the seasons on Fort McClellan follow those of Alabama and Calhoun County, there are a few additional restrictions on the fort. All hunters wanting to hunt on Fort McClellan must attend a Fort McClellan hunter's safety course and receive a hunter's safety card prior to purchasing a post license. The course is one hour and held weekly on Thursday nights. It is offered from the third Thursday in July through the third Thursday in September. Sometimes, additional classes are held in October, November, and December, depending on requirements.

All hunters age sixteen or over on Fort McClellan must have a valid Alabama hunting license prior to purchasing a Fort McClellan permit. People sixty-five or older may purchase a post permit for $1. In addition to the state license, you must have proof of age, residency, and the hunter safety card prior to purchasing a post hunting license. The post hunting license is inexpensive at $9 per year or $12 for both hunting and fishing. The licenses are valid from August through July 31. The Fort McClellan hunter's safety course is a one-time requirement.

Children under sixteen may hunt on Fort McClellan under direct adult supervision. Although they aren't required to have a state license, the young hunters must have a post license and must have taken the hunter safety course.

Whitetails may be taken on Fort McClellan with 20-gauge slugs or larger, black-powder rifles .40 caliber or larger, or archery equipment. Shotguns can only be used in those areas open during the general firearms season. Black-powder rifles may be used during the general firearms season or the primitive-weapons season. Archery gear is legal during any of the seasons.

Archery equipment legal for deer on Fort McClellan is restricted to compound, recurve, or longbows with a draw weight of thirty-five pounds or greater. Arrows must be a minimum of twenty-four inches long and tipped with a broadhead of not less than 100 grains or seven-eighths inch wide. Crossbows are not legal.

Upland game may be taken by any of the above methods during the season. Additionally, hunters after rabbit, squirrel, or raccoon on Pelham Range may use .22 caliber short, long or long-rifle standard, or high-velocity ammunition in their .22 rifles. Hyper-velocity ammunition such as Stinger, Viper, Yellow Jacket or Mini-Mags is not authorized. Bowhunters after small game cannot use broadheads but must use a small game head such as the Judo Point or blunts. Small game hunters must not have buckshot or slugs in their possession while hunting.

Hunting permits are issued on a daily-by-area basis. Upland game hunters are

issued one permit per party and the permit is for the area and type of game to be hunted. Though only one permit is issued to the entire hunting party, all members of the party must present their post licenses when checking in. Small game hunting parties are limited to no more than four adults or adults-and-children groups of six or fewer.

Deer-hunting permits during the general firearms season are only for the area selected. Unlike upland game permits, each member of a deer-hunting party must have his own permit. Hunting group size for deer hunting is limited to no more than two adults or four adults and children. Permits may be obtained up to three days in advance. Each day's hunting permit must be turned in no later than 7:00 P.M. Daylight Savings Time or 6:00 P.M. Central Standard Time. Permits may be turned in at either Gate 3 on Pelham Range or at the Game Management Office on the main post.

Permits can only be obtained in person from the Game Management Office on Fort McClellan. No more than four different days' hunting permits may be in a hunter's possession when afield. In addition to deer and small game permits, other permits are available for special activities such as coon hunting at night, predator hunting, and training bird dogs. Dogs may be used on Fort McClellan for upland game and raccoon. They are not allowed for deer or turkey hunting.

Fishing Fishing on Fort McClellan is excellent. The post has numerous bodies of water containing largemouth bass, bream, catfish, and crappie. The only waters on post permanently closed to fishing are the water hazards on the golf course. All others are open. Individuals wishing to fish on Fort McClellan must have a post fishing license, available at the game management office for $5 per year for adults age sixteen and over and $1 per year for people over age sixty-five. You must have a valid Alabama fishing license before getting a post license.

In most cases, daily permits aren't required to fish on Fort McClellan. The exceptions are Pelham Range and Three-Mile Pond. The duck pond is closed to fishing for everyone over the age of fifteen. Children twelve and under must be accompanied by an adult while fishing on Fort McClellan.

You can fish on Fort McClellan by just about any method you choose. The only things not allowed are using minnows for bait, unattended trotlines, and bowfishing or spearfishing for game fish.

Miscellaneous   There are several boating restrictions on Fort McClellan. Gas-powered motors are not allowed in any waters on the post. Boats using electric motors can be used on Cane Creek, Pelham Range, Reilly Lake, Yahou Lake, and Lake Contreras as can boats under paddle power. All boats must have a flotation device for each person aboard.

Camping is allowed on Fort McClellan for certain eligible individuals. Topographic maps covering Fort McClellan are Fort McClellan and Pelham Range.

For more information on hunting and fishing on Fort McClellan, contact: Game Management Office, 2nd Avenue, Fort McClellan, AL 36205-5000, phone (205) 848-5663 (8:00 A.M. to 4:30 P.M., Monday through Friday).

FORT RUCKER

- 30 miles northwest of Dothan
- 61,000 acres
- Installation permit required
- White-tailed deer, turkey, small game
- Fishing
- Restricted camping

Hunting   Fort Rucker is open to military and civilian hunters. Both must have valid Alabama licenses and post permits. The cost of the post permit to service-members varies depending on rank or pay grade. The post seasons follow those of the state.

Deer are abundant on Fort Rucker. Both gun hunters and bowbenders are successful. Like most Army installations, Fort Rucker is divided into separate hunting areas. Some are open only to bowhunting during the entire season; others are open to both bow and gun during the gun season. Not all areas are open on any given day but are open as training on the fort allows.

Small game hunting is popular on Fort Rucker. The hardwood bottoms along the creeks and sloughs on the post harbor a bumper crop of squirrels every year. Those same hardwoods also feed a healthy population of wild turkeys. One might also stumble across raccoons, possums, quail, coyote, or bobcat at this southern fort.

Fishing Bass fishing is good in this part of Alabama. From early spring through the first of June it's not uncommon to hook into some real monsters in the waters of Fort Rucker. The Florida strain of largemouth found here grows to impressive proportions.

Fort Rucker also has healthy populations of bream, crappie, catfish, and striper/white bass hybrids. All are lots of fun to catch and they're definitely good eating.

Miscellaneous Both Fort Rucker and Maxwell AFB have recreation areas in Florida. These areas are six miles east of Niceville on Choctawhatchee Bay, off State Highway 20. These recreation areas are open only to active duty, retired, and DOD civilian personnel and their dependents. See the entry for Maxwell AFB for more information.

Military ID card holders may camp on Fort Rucker. ATVs are not allowed on the installation.

For more information, contact: Outdoor Recreation, Box 367, Fort Rucker, AL 36362, phone (205) 255-4305/5768 (Thursday through Monday, 7:30 A.M. to 4:15 P.M.).

REDSTONE ARSENAL

- Near Huntsville on the Tennessee River
- 26,000 acres open to hunting and fishing
- Closed to the public
- Installation permit required
- White-tailed deer, turkey, small game
- Fishing
- Restricted boating

Hunting Redstone Arsenal remains in the forefront of missile development. It is also a great place to hunt and fish. It is situated along the north shore of the Tennessee River. Parts of the Wheeler National Wildlife Refuge are within Redstone boundaries.

There are 26,000 acres of land and water open to hunting and fishing on Redstone. Due to the nature of the work done there, Redstone is not open to the public. Yet members of the public may hunt and fish on Redstone Arsenal as guests of military personnel authorized access.

According to Redstone Arsenal regulations, military personnel are defined as "active duty U.S. military personnel and members of the reserve components while on active duty but not while on weekend drill status, allied forces personnel assigned for duty with U.S. forces when authorized U.S. Army support, and retired U.S. military personnel. Family members must possess a valid military ID card."

DOD civilians employed at Redstone and DOD contractor employees may fish on Redstone Arsenal and participate in the specially designated military/civilian deer hunts. Additionally, two family members (maximum hunting party of three) of military personnel may hunt when accompanied by their sponsor. Family members eighteen or over are also authorized to hunt unaccompanied during the military/civilian deer hunts. Younger hunters must be accompanied by their sponsor at all times.

All hunters sixteen or older on Redstone Arsenal must have a valid Alabama or Madison County hunting license. Additionally, they must attend the Redstone Arsenal hunter safety course. Hunters under sixteen must complete a state-approved hunter safety course prior to hunting on any Wheeler National Wildlife Refuge lands within the Redstone Arsenal reservation. The Redstone Arsenal license costs $3 for military members and $5 for guests. Licenses for hunters over sixty-five are free.

White-tailed deer are abundant on Redstone Arsenal. During the 1989–90 season, 471 whitetails were taken on arsenal land. Periodically, the herd reaches almost unmanageable proportions that require special deer hunts and drives to keep it within manageable limits. The deer season coincides with the state season for Madison County. The deer hunting is well managed, with a limited number of hunters per area. By limiting the number of hunters per area, the overall quality and safety of the hunt is improved.

Deer hunters may reserve a hunting area the day before they plan to hunt during the general gun season. On weekends, they can reserve areas on Friday for Saturday and Sunday hunts. Permits for the area must be picked up no later than 7:00 A.M the day of the hunt. All hunters must check in with the outdoor recreation office to receive their permit and badge prior to going afield.

Hunters participating in the general deer season must wear 500 square inches of hunter orange while traveling to and from their stands. Additionally, hunters are required to wear hunter orange while traveling to their stands during the spring turkey season. Bowhunters must also wear hunter orange caps to and from their stands.

Redstone Arsenal does not allow the use of centerfire rifles or handguns during the hunting season. Shotguns 20 gauge or larger with slugs and black-powder rifles .40 caliber or larger are the only legal weapons. No weapons are allowed that have a muzzle velocity greater than 2,300 feet per second.

Bowhunters after deer must use recurve, compound, or longbows with draw weights of forty pounds or heavier. Broadhead cutting widths of seven-eighths inch or larger and weighing a minimum of 100 grains are required. Arrows must be at least twenty-four inches in length. Crossbows are not allowed.

As you might imagine, small game abounds on Redstone Arsenal. Hunters will find cottontail rabbits, squirrels, quail, doves, woodcocks, snipe, raccoons, and waterfowl on the reservation. Though technically not small game, the reservation also contains a healthy population of wild turkeys, bobcats, coyotes, groundhogs, and crows. The check-in and permit requirements for small game are the same as for big game. Again, Redstone's seasons match the local, state, and county seasons.

Small game hunters may use any gauge shotgun with shot smaller than #2. Small game hunters may not have slugs or buckshot in their possession while hunting. Black-powder rifles are legal for small game hunting. Bowhunters after small game may not use or have broadheads in their possession while hunting. Dogs are allowed on Red-stone for small game and bird hunting but not for deer or turkey hunting.

Redstone Arsenal has a very aggressive hunter safety program. Alcohol consumption before or while hunting is strictly forbidden. Even having a beer in your vehicle during the hunt can cost you your hunting privileges on the reservation.

Fishing Generally, fishermen on Redstone Arsenal must have a reservation license except for the recreation areas along the Tennessee River. The fishing license eligibility requirements are the same as for hunting licenses. There is no restriction on the number of fishermen on the water at the same time. Fishermen aren't required to check with Outdoor Recreation prior to going afield except when going to Bradford Sinks, Swan Pond, and Finance Pond.

Game fish on the reservation are largemouth bass, bream, crappie, and catfish. As is the case all over the South, rough fish such as gar, carp, and buffalo are also found in the reservation waters. The legal means of fishing on Redstone Arsenal are the same as those for the state of Alabama.

Miscellaneous No gas outboard motors are allowed on the Arsenal. Boaters must use electric motors or paddle power when fishing the arsenal's waters. All persons aboard must *wear* Coast Guard-approved personal flotation devices.

The topographic maps for the Redstone Arsenal are the Farley, Huntsville, Triana and Madison, Alabama, quadrangles in the 7.5-minute, 1 : 24,000 series.

The office responsible for all hunting and fishing activities on Redstone Arsenal is the Outdoor Recreation Branch. For more detailed information, contact: Commander, U.S. Army Missile Command, ATTN: AMSMI-RA-CF-CR-OR, Redstone Arsenal, AL 35898, phone (205) 876-4868 (Monday through Friday, 8:00 A.M. to 4:00 P.M.).

Air Force Installations

MAXWELL AIR FORCE BASE

> • Near Montgomery
> • Closed to the public
> • Fishing

Miscellaneous Both Maxwell AFB and Fort Rucker have recreation areas in Florida. Both areas are located off State Highway 20, six miles east of Niceville, on Choctawhatchee Bay. The recreation areas are open only to active duty, retired, and DOD civilian personnel and their dependents.

Fishing is good in Choctawhatchee Bay for saltwater species, especially speckled sea trout. The recreation area also offers boating, camping, swimming, and beach-combing.

Reservations are advised. Air Force personnel may make reservations through the Maxwell AFB Recreation Office at AV 875-5496 or commercial (205) 293-5496/97. Army personnel may make reservations through the Fort Rucker Outdoor Recreation Office. The address and phone numbers are: Fort Rucker Recreation Center, ITT Office, Box 516, Fort Rucker, AL 36362, phone (commercial) (205) 255-5816 (AUTOVON) 558-5816.

ALASKA

Wildlife thrives in the wilderness of Alaska. Caribou herds stretch for miles across these northern plains, rivaling the bison of old in herd size. Old *Ursus horribilis* is found throughout the state. The world's largest deer, the Alaska-Yukon moose, leaves its prints in practically all parts of the state.

Fishing is a dream come true in The Great Land. Giant rainbow trout, king salmon, Dolly Varden, arctic char, ferocious northern pike, and the fragile arctic grayling are but a few of the species found here. Some of the lakes and streams in Alaska have never seen a fishing lure!

There are three major Army installations, three major Air Force installations, and one large naval air station in Alaska. The Army installations alone cover over 1,644,400 acres of mountains, tundra, and water. Most are accessible by automobile, preferably four-wheel drive. All offer reasonably good hunting and fishing, though some restrictions apply.

Army Installations

FORT GREELY

* 80 miles south of Fairbanks
* 639,000 acres
* Installation permit required
* Big game and small game
* Fishing

Hunting   Fort Greely lies in Alaska Game Management Unit 20A. As such, it is technically open to big game hunting for moose, black bear, grizzly bear, caribou, and Dall sheep. The pickings for sheep and caribou are pretty slim in this area but the moose and bear hunting is quite good.

All hunters on Fort Greely must have a post permit. The permit is available at no charge from the Provost Marshal's office and is valid for a year. Bowhunters on post must follow state requirements for archery tackle.

Big game hunters on Fort Greely must use the buddy system when going afield. This area, like much of Alaska, is true wilderness. The land here is not forgiving of even small mistakes. One mistake can cost you your life. Besides, it's a lot easier for two people to get a moose out than one.

Small game hunters on Fort Greely can expect willow and rock ptarmigan, varying hare, squirrel, spruce grouse, and ruffed grouse. Varmints and furbearers found on the post include lynx, wolf, beaver, muskrat, wolverine, marten, fisher, porcupine, and mink. Fur-bearing animals may be taken on a general hunting license but may not be taken for sale on such a license. Fur animals taken for sale must be taken on a trapping license.

Fishing   The fishing on Fort Greely is quite good. There are several lakes on the installation that are stocked with rainbow trout, grayling, and silver salmon. The creeks and rivers on post contain burbot, grayling, pike, and, at certain times of the year, salmon.

A valid Alaska fishing license and a post permit are required to fish on Fort Greely. Fishing is open year-round, but it may take a snowmobile to reach some of the lakes in winter.

Off-road Vehicles   This is a true wilderness area. As such, some areas are pretty well inaccessible unless you have a strictly off-road vehicle. Three- and four-wheeled ATVs are very popular all over Alaska and are the primary means of transportation in some remote villages and towns. There are special regulations that govern their use on the military installations in Alaska.

Prior to operating an off-road vehicle on the post, the owner must furnish proof of state registration and completion of a safety course. Additionally, there are certain areas on the installation where travel by ORV is prohibited. Be sure to check with the provost marshal before operating an ORV or a snowmobile on post.

For more information, contact: Provost Marshal, Fort Greely, AK 98733, phone (907) 873-3108.

FORT RICHARDSON

- Near Anchorage
- 62,500 acres
- Small game hunting closed to the public
- Installation permit required
- Big game and small game

Hunting   The terrain of Fort Richardson is mostly rolling hillsides covered in birch and spruce with little tundra. There are quite a few moose and bear on the post.

Fort Richardson is a special-use area as defined by the Alaska Department of Fish and Game. Big game hunting for moose is open on the installation, but you must receive a permit through a lottery.

The other major restriction to moose hunting on Fort Richardson is that it is only open to muzzleloading rifles and bows and arrows. Because the installation is located in a fairly urban area, high-powered rifles are too dangerous. The chances of a ricochet or missed shot hitting someone are quite high.

Bowhunters after moose on Fort Richardson must have a valid Alaska hunting license and the appropriate hunt/moose tag. Additionally, they must have completed the International Bowhunter Education Program course. Part of the course is a shooting competency test.

Moose hunters must check in and out with the provost marshal prior to going to and upon returning from their hunt. The reservation is divided into separate hunting areas so pressure is spread fairly throughout the installation.

Fort Richardson, despite its proximity to Anchorage, has a respectable population of small game and fur-bearing animals. Small game hunting with shotguns and archery equipment is allowed. Trapping is also allowed on post.

Small game hunting on Fort Richardson is open only to active duty military, retirees, their dependents, and DOD civilians. Hunters under the age of sixteen must be accompanied by a parent or guardian.

Fishing Fort Richardson is open to sport fishing. A post permit and a valid Alaska fishing license are required prior to fishing on post. Species available include rainbow trout, arctic grayling, northern pike, salmon, and burbot.

Miscellaneous ATVs and snowmobiles are allowed on Fort Richardson but must meet special licensing and permit requirements before they may be operated on post.

For more information, contact: Wildlife Manager (or) Provost Marshal, Fort Richardson, AK 99505-5320, phone (907) 864-1199.

FORT WAINWRIGHT

- East of Fairbanks
- 656,250 acres
- Installation permit required
- Big game and small game
- Fishing
- Wilderness camping

Hunting Though still over 100 miles south of the Arctic Circle, this part of Alaska often has temperatures colder than those found above the circle. Lows to minus

80 degrees Fahrenheit have been recorded. On the other end of the spectrum, highs during the long summers have reached 100 degrees.

Fort Wainwright is spread out across 656,250 acres of spruce-and-birch-covered hills, river bottoms, and tundra. Part of the fort lies across the Tanana River from the main post where access is strictly by boat, floatplane, or, in the winter, snowmobile.

Fort Wainwright is located in some of the best moose country in the world. Additionally, grizzly and black bear roam all over the post. Fort Wainwright, including the Yukon Training Area, is open to the public.

The cantonment area of Fort Wainwright holds a respectable population of moose. It also lies within the Fairbanks Management Area and is open only to bowhunters. Bowhunters must have taken the IBEP course and have passed a shooting exam.

All big game hunters on Fort Wainwright must have a valid Alaska hunting license and a post permit, and weapons used for hunting must meet the standards set by the state of Alaska. Hunters must use the buddy system when hunting for moose in any of the nonarchery-only areas, and all hunters under sixteen must be accompanied by an adult. Bear hunting over bait is authorized in certain areas.

Small game hunting is also good on Fort Wainwright. Snowshoe hare, ruffed grouse, ptarmigan, squirrel, spruce grouse, and waterfowl can all be hunted on this post. Small game hunters must have the appropriate federal, state, and post permits and stamps. All seasons match those of the state.

Fishing Fort Wainwright has miles of water open to fishing. The Tanana River splits the post almost in half. The Chena River flows through the cantonment area. The Wood River forms the eastern boundary of the reservation.

The grayling fishing is excellent in some of the more remote parts of the installation. Some of the lakes on the reservation contain northern pike that reach impressive proportions. Salmon fishing is open in some parts of the Chena River on post. The Chena and Tanana both are excellent places to take burbot.

Fishermen on Fort Wainwright must have a valid Alaska fishing license and a post permit. The post permit is free.

Miscellaneous ORV, ATV, and snowmobile use is allowed on Fort Wainwright. The vehicle must be registered with the post and the state. Drivers and riders must have proof of having taken a safety course prior to riding the vehicle on post.

Wilderness camping is authorized on Fort Wainwright. Additionally, the post has several camping pads in their FAMCAMP areas with RV hookups.

For more information and maps, contact: Wildlife Management Office, Fort Wainwright, AK 99703-5000, phone (907) 353-7426.

Air Force Installations

CLEAR AIR FORCE STATION

- South of Nenana
- 9,000 acres
- Closed to the public
- Installation permit required
- Small game
- Fishing

Hunting Unfortunately, big game hunting is not allowed on the 9,000 acres that make up Clear Air Force Station, and it is not open to the public. The only people authorized to hunt on Clear are military members, retirees, their dependents, and the site's civilian employees.

Small game hunting on Clear Air Force Station is good. The area abounds with snowshoe hare, grouse, ptarmigan, squirrel, and waterfowl. Like hares everywhere, the snowshoes follow a seven- to nine-year population cycle. When they reach their peak, you can just about kick a rabbit out from under every bush.

Ptarmigan and grouse generally follow population cycles as well, though their populations don't fluctuate as markedly as the varying hare's. Waterfowl hunting is seasonal at Clear, usually opening the first of September. The shooting can be fast and furious for a couple of weeks as all the waterfowl begin their fall migration to warmer climates.

Those wishing to hunt or fish on Clear must have a valid Alaska hunting or fishing license and a Clear AFS Form 3. Children under the age of sixteen must be accompanied by an adult over twenty-one when hunting.

Clear, like most installations, is divided into separate hunting areas. Some areas are open only to shotgun or archery hunting. Others are open to any weapon legal for hunting in the state.

Fishing   The fishing is excellent at Clear. Many times I've traveled the eighty miles from Fairbanks to try to entice five- and six-pound rainbow trout from the station's cooling ponds. The limit is three per day, and this may be the best place in interior Alaska to catch a rainbow trout over five pounds.

Grayling can also be found in the waters of Clear. The limit on these "sailfish of the North" is five per day, fifteen in possession. Anything except live fish and corn can be used as bait to take rainbows and grayling from Clear.

Fishing on Clear can be a real adventure. Black bears abound in this area, so be careful. In 1980, I was fishing in one of the ponds on base and counted thirteen different bears in as many hours.

Black bears normally aren't dangerous, but it never pays to take them lightly. Everyone talks about how bad the grizzly is, but the truth is that while you may be mauled by an irate grizzly, you're more likely to be killed and eaten by a black bear. Don't mess with them!

Miscellaneous   ORVs and ATVs are allowed on Clear AFS. They must be registered with the base and the state. The rider/driver must have proof of completing a competency course before operating the vehicle on the installation.

All ATVs/ORVs must stay on trails, if you can call them that. As rough as most of these trails are, there's no need to create your own.

For more information, contact: 13th Missile Warning Squadron/SPAI, Clear AFS, AK 99704-5000, phone (907) 585-6474.

EIELSON AIR FORCE BASE

- South of Fairbanks
- 54,392 acres
- Installation permit required
- Big game and small game
- Fishing
- Camping and boating

Hunting Eielson is adjacent to Fort Wainwright and covers 54,392 acres. Eielson also controls an additional 34,000 acres across the Tanana River on the Blair Lakes Range. The hunting on Eielson proper is excellent for small game. The only big game hunted on the base itself is moose, and that is archery only.

Eielson and the Blair Lakes Range are both open to the public. All hunters over sixteen must have a valid hunting license and a base permit. Children under sixteen are not required to have a state license but must have the base permit. Bowhunters after moose on Eielson must pass a shooting competency test to receive the "Bow and Arrow Qualified for Moose" stamp on their base permit.

The test consists of shooting three out of four arrows into the kill area on a moose silhouette at an unknown range less than thirty-five yards. It doesn't sound very difficult, but it is. The kill zone is not marked so you must know your moose anatomy as well as be able to shoot.

Moose hunting on Eielson is excellent, with several bulls that surpass Pope and Young minimums on the base. Hunter success is not high, but they don't call it bow "hunting" for nothing.

Small game hunting on Eielson is also great. In high population years, it's not unusual to take twenty or thirty snowshoe hares in an afternoon's hunt. Likewise, ruffed and spruce grouse are readily available to shotgunners and bowhunters. High-powered rifles are not allowed on Eielson proper but are legal on Blair Lakes.

Eielson is also an excellent area for waterfowlers. It is a stopover for tens of thousands of ducks and geese on their migration southward. It is one of the few places in the United States where a bowhunter has a reasonable chance of taking a Canada goose with bow and arrow.

Ptarmigan are also found in good numbers on the reservation. These chameleons that change the color of their feathers twice a year are not terribly hard to hunt but are excellent table fare.

The spruce trees on Eielson are home to more than ptarmigan and grouse. They are almost overrun with gray squirrels. These little tree rodents are not terribly bright but they provide excellent sport for bowhunters and young shotgunners.

The Blair Lakes portion of Eielson supports a reasonably good population of moose. Unfortunately, it is located on the Tanana Flats and is extremely difficult to hunt unless you are in great shape. Walking across tundra is like walking across a half-filled waterbed. It's an experience you have to feel to believe.

There are also lots of black bears and a few grizzly bears on the Blair Lakes Range. You can hunt them in this area.

Fishing Eielson has seventeen ponds and lakes and two creeks open to fishing. Almost all of the lakes are stocked annually by the Alaska Department of Fish and Game. One of the creeks, Piledriver Slough, is also stocked with rainbow trout. The other lakes and ponds are stocked with a variety of fish including rainbows, silver salmon, northern pike, burbot, grayling, arctic char, and white fish.

Fishermen on Eielson must have a valid state fishing license and a base permit. Children under sixteen and adults over sixty do not need a state license but must have a base permit. Nonresident children under sixteen must have a state license and base permit.

Fishing in Piledriver Slough for grayling and rainbow trout is limited to artificial lures and flies only. The other bodies of water all follow state regulations.

Boating is permitted on all the lakes, ponds, and streams. In fact, floating Pile-driver Slough, just off the Richardson Highway, is an excellent way to introduce float-fishing to a kid. The water is not dangerous and the fish are usually cooperative.

Miscellaneous Camping is allowed on base in the FAMCAMP area run by outdoor recreation. Primitive camping is not authorized in any of the hunting areas.

Eielson allows ORV/ATV use on the installation. The categories of vehicles allowed are trail bikes, snowmobiles, lightweight ATVs (three- and four-wheelers), medium-weight ATVs (Cushman Trakster), and heavyweight ATVs (Bombardier, Sno Cat).

The registration requirements for all are the same. The owner must present proof of ownership when registering the vehicle with the Security Police Pass and Identification Section. Additionally, street-legal trail bikes, snowmobiles, and lightweight ATVs must be registered with the state. Operators of two-wheeled vehicles and lightweight ATVs must also complete a certified safety course.

Eielson Air Force Base also operates a recreation camp on Birch Lake, thirty-five miles south of the base. The recreation area offers cabins, boat rentals, RV pads, and primitive camping. Fishing for stocked rainbows is good at Birch Lake and there is a small base exchange. The recreation area is open to active duty military, retirees, their dependents, and DOD civilians in Alaska.

Eielson AFB and Blair Lakes are covered by the Fairbanks C-1, Alaska 1:50,000 Sheet 345011 Series Q701, Edition 4-DMA; and Big Delta C-6, Alaska 1:50,000 Sheet 3550111 Series Q701, Edition 2-AMS, topographic maps.

For more information, contact: Natural Resources Office, c/o 343rd Civil Engineering Squadron, Eielson AFB, AK 99702-5000, phone (907) 377-5182 (7:30 A.M. to 4:30 P.M., Monday through Friday).

ELMENDORF AIR FORCE BASE

- Near Anchorage
- 13,166 acres
- Closed to the public
- Installation permit required
- Moose
- Fishing

Hunting Elmendorf Air Force Base is in an area rich in game, and 5,600 acres of prime moose habitat was opened for the first time in thirty years during the 1990 moose season. Permits were granted on a lottery basis to hunters who had passed a hunter safety course and competency test prior to going afield. Hunter success was expected to be almost 100 percent for the first season.

Like Eielson, the only weapon allowed for moose hunting is bow and arrow.

Hunting on Elmendorf is restricted to DOD civilians, active duty military, retired military, and Alaska National Guard employees. Licensing requirements are the same as for the state. Permit applications must be received by the end of May each year. No small game hunting is allowed on Elmendorf.

Fishing With 250 surface acres of water stocked with rainbows, landlocked king salmon, and Dolly Varden, fishing on Elmendorf is pretty good.

Fishermen must have a valid state license. No base permit is required. Any form of bait, except minnows, and all artificial lures are allowed on the base.

Miscellaneous Aside from the waters on Elmendorf proper, there are several world-class salmon streams within an hour's drive of the installation. The base runs a fishing camp out of the seaside port of Seward. The camp is open to ID card holders, and it even offers party-boat fishing.

Elmendorf authorizes the use of ORVs and ATVs on base. The requirements are basically the same as for Eielson. The types of vehicles are divided into separate classes with basically the same licensing rules for all classes (see ORV section for Eielson AFB).

Elmendorf is covered by the Anchorage (B-8) SW and SE and (A-8) NW and NE quandrangles in the Alaska Series.

For more information on outdoor activities on Elmendorf Air Force Base, contact: 21CSG/DEEVW, Elmendorf AFB, AK 99506-5000, phone (907) 552-2282/2436 (8:00 A.M. to 5:00 P.M., Monday through Friday).

Naval Installations

ADAK NAVAL AIR STATION

- In the Aleutian Islands
- 66,000 acres
- Installation permit required
- Caribou, ptarmigan, arctic fox
- Freshwater and saltwater fishing

Hunting Adak NAS covers 66,000 acres of the 181,000-acre Adak Island. The island is volcanic hill country covered in tundra. Getting around on land there can be a real adventure. Adak is open to the public for hunting. In this case, the public is defined as "island residents." It is also open to active duty military, retirees, their dependents, and DOD civilians on the island. An Alaska hunting license is required, except for active duty military hunters on military lands. In either case, a hunting permit from the Navy is required. Adak NAS is not open to non-Adak residents, except for those on official installation business.

Adak Island supports a large caribou herd. Caribou are the only big game animals found on the island. The limit is two by registration permit only. The island also supports a healthy population of ptarmigan and the ptarmigan's natural predator, the arctic fox. Hunting regulations for these two species are the same as for caribou.

Fishing   The fishing on Adak is open to all. This part of the Alaska Maritime National Wildlife Refuge has excellent fishing for sea-run Dolly Varden and good saltwater fishing for salmon and halibut. The license requirements are the same as for hunting.

Miscellaneous   Adak Island is part of the Alaska Maritime National Wildlife Refuge but is open to hunting for small game and caribou as well as to fishing. It is an excellent place to view seals, sea lions, and killer whales. Camping is allowed on the island, though not on Adak NAS.

The Adak, Alaska, topographic series covers this part of Alaska.

For more information on Adak NAS and this part of the Alaska Maritime National Wildlife Refuge, contact: Refuge Manager, U.S. Fish and Wildlife Service, Aleutian Islands Unit, Alaska Maritime NWR, Box 5251, NAS Adak, FPO Seattle, WA 98791, phone (907) 592-2406 (Monday through Friday, 8:00 A.M. to 5:00 P.M.).

ARIZONA

Arizona has some of the best hunting and fishing in the West. It's home to monster mule deer, elk, javelina, desert bighorn sheep, and even that diminutive desert white-tail, the Coues. Unlike states farther east, Arizona has an abundance of public land. It also has an abundance of hunters and fishermen. Fortunately, Arizona has over 2.7 million acres of military property.

There are two major army installations in Arizona. Together, they cover 89,000 acres of some of the best big and small game habitat in the state. In both cases, the installations are open to hunting by authorized personnel only. Fishing is open to the public. The Barry M. Goldwater Air Force Range is open to the public.

Army Installations

ARIZONA ARMY NATIONAL GUARD NAVAJO DEPOT ACTIVITY

- 12 miles west of Flagstaff
- 16,000 acres
- Closed to the public
- Big game, turkey, small game
- Fishing
- Camping

Hunting   The Navajo Depot is open only to members of the Arizona National Guard and civilian employees of the depot. National Guard members have access to about 8,000 acres of prime hunting real estate, while the depot's civilian employees can roam over the installation's full 16,000 acres.

National Guard members and civilian employees wanting to hunt on the depot must have a valid Arizona hunting license and proof of a state- or National Rifle Association-certified hunter safety course. All hunters must attend an installation orientation.

The northern part of Arizona has always boasted healthy mule deer and elk herds. The Navajo Depot is no exception. The hunter success rate for big game on the installation is 60 percent. Like Fort Huachuca in the south, the hunter success rate on the installation exceeds the state's.

Small game hunters on the Navajo Depot can hunt cottontail rabbits, waterfowl, wild turkey, and the Abert's tree squirrel. Again, hunter success on these animals is higher than the state overall.

Varmint hunters can have a field day on the Navajo Depot. There are massive prairie dog towns and lots of coyotes. The hunting provisions for small game are the same as those for big game.

Fishing   The only fishing on the Navajo Depot is for stocked rainbow trout. Fishing is allowed year-round and, like hunting, is only open to Arizona National Guardsmen and depot civilian employees.

Miscellaneous   Camping is allowed on the reservation, but all camping is primitive. There are no campgrounds. Eligible personnel can pitch a tent in any authorized area.

The topographic maps for the Navajo Depot are the Garland Prairie and Bellemont quadrangles.

For more information on the Navajo Depot Activity, contact: AZXA-AS-F-F, Natural Resource Manager, Navajo Depot Activity, Bellemont, AZ 86015-5000, phone: (602) 774-7161, ext. 274.

FORT HUACHUCA

- Near Sierra Vista
- 77,000 acres
- Hunting closed to the public
- Fishing open to the public
- Installation permit required
- Big game and small game
- Camping

Hunting Fort Huachuca sprawls over 77,000 acres of southeastern Arizona. Seventy-three thousand of those acres are open to hunting—for authorized personnel only.

All active duty and retired military personnel world-wide and their dependents over ten may hunt on post. Fort Huachuca civil service employees may also hunt on the installation. All hunters eligible to hunt on post must have a valid Arizona hunting license and the appropriate big game tags. All hunters must have proof of a hunter safety course prior to purchasing a Fort Huachuca hunting permit, which costs $6 per year and is valid January 1 through December 31.

Getting a big game tag for Fort Huachuca is more complicated than it sounds. You have to apply through the Arizona Game and Fish Department for a specific hunt number to get a tag. The tags are issued via a lottery drawing. Fortunately, there are usually enough to go around.

Like most military installations, big game hunting on Fort Huachuca is very well managed. The post employs five full-time wildlife biologists to manage the 73,000 acres open to hunting. Hunters after big game on Fort Huachuca must sign in and out for specific areas with the post military police prior to going to and upon returning from the hunt. The areas are managed so that there is one hunter to approximately forty acres during the firearms hunts, and one hunter to twenty acres during the archery-only seasons. Fort Huachuca has several archery-only areas that are open to bowhunters during the general season.

Unlike many installations, there are no weapons restrictions on Fort Huachuca. Any weapon legal for hunting in Arizona is legal on Fort Huachuca. The same holds true for archery-only hunts and areas. Crossbows are not legal during the archery-only seasons but may be used in the archery-only areas during the general firearms season.

Fort Huachuca is one of those installations I've had the good fortune to hunt. The big game hunting is outstanding. White-tailed deer, mule deer, javelina, and antelope can be found on the post. The numbers speak for themselves. Deer hunters on post averaged a 60 percent success rate during the 1989 season. Statewide, the average was 15 percent for deer. Javelina hunters also beat the odds with a 30 percent success rate versus 28 percent for the state. Antelope hunters hit 100 percent on post!

I hunted Fort Huachuca during the January archery-only deer and javelina season. I saw more javelina during the two days I hunted at Fort Huachuca than anywhere else during the rest of the season combined. Deer were abundant, too. I saw forty-three whitetails and seven mule deer during the two days I hunted. Unfortunately when you're bowhunting, seeing them and getting close enough for a shot are often two entirely different things.

Fort Huachuca is also open for black bear hunting. The season is open only during the spring and, again, you must apply through the state.

All big game gun hunters on Fort Huachuca must wear hunter orange. Bowhunters are not required to in either the bowhunting-only areas or during the archery-only seasons. If they hunt in a gun area during the general season, then they, too, must wear hunter orange.

Upland game hunting on Fort Huachuca is exceptional. The rolling hills are covered in grass and are home to all three species of Arizona quail: Mearns, Gambel, and scaled. Fort Huachuca is one of those places just made for quail hunting with a dog. The hunting grounds are fairly open but covered with knee-high grass.

Quail aren't the only birds on Huachuca. The post is also host to all three species of dove found in Arizona. Fort Huachuca is also one of the few remaining places where one can hunt the band-tailed pigeon. There are several ponds spread out across Fort Huachuca. During the waterfowl season, it's possible to catch a few stragglers from the Pacific Flyway using them.

Since Fort Huachuca is mostly rolling hills covered in grass and oaks, small game hunting for other species is great. Cottontails are abundant on the post. Jack rabbits, though not as numerous as the cottontails, are also found here. The gray squirrel may be found in the higher elevations of the Huachuca Mountains. Coyotes, bobcats, and the occasional mountain lion may also be encountered.

Fishing The fishing on Fort Huachuca is quite good. There are several ponds spread out across the installation, all stocked with fish. The predominant species in all the ponds is largemouth bass, bluegill, redear sunfish, and channel catfish. During the winter months, the ponds are stocked with rainbow trout.

The post is open to public fishing. The fishing permit costs $6 for those fourteen and older. Youths nine to thirteen pay $2 for an annual permit. There is no charge for children eight or under. Visitors can purchase a nine-day permit for $3. All fishermen must have a valid Arizona fishing license and trout stamp prior to purchasing a Fort Huachuca permit.

The post regulations and bag limits generally follow those of the state. The only differences are the five-fish limits on largemouth bass, rainbow trout, and channel catfish. There is no limit on bluegill or other sunfish. Bass must be at least twelve inches long and catfish must be over ten inches.

Fishermen are not allowed to carry firearms while fishing on Fort Huachuca. Boating and swimming are not allowed at any of the fort's ponds. Live fish may not be used for bait on post, though live bait (worms and crickets) is allowed. Fly Pond and Garden Canyon Creek are open to fishing with artificial lures and flies only.

Most of the ponds on the post have set hours. All water except Golf Course Pond and Gravel Pit Pond are open daily from 5:00 A.M. until 9:00 P.M. Both Golf Course and Gravel Pit are open twenty-four hours a day. Garden Canyon Creek is closed between May 1 and October 31 each year.

Miscellaneous Hunting and fishing licenses are available at the Fort Huachuca Sportsman's Center on Garden Canyon Road. The Sportsman's Center is closed Tuesdays and Wednesdays. The phone number of the Sportsman's Center is (602) 538-8013.

Camping is not allowed at most ponds on Fort Huachuca. There are four authorized camping areas on the installation. Apache Flats is open to recreational vehicles only. Golf Course Pond, Lower Garden Canyon, and West Range II camping areas are for primitive camping or fully self-contained recreational vehicles. No potable water is available at any of these facilities. All the campgrounds except Apache Flats are subject to closure during the big game hunting seasons, range firing, maneuvers, or training.

The topographic maps covering Fort Huachuca are the Fort Huachuca, Pyeatt Ranch, Lewis Spring, Miller Peak, Huachuca City, Fairbank, and Huachuca Peak quadrangles.

The office with overall responsibility for hunting and fishing on Fort Huachuca is the game management office. Its hours are 7:30 A.M. to 4:00 P.M., Monday through Friday, and 1:00 P.M. to 4:00 P.M. on weekends and most holidays. The office can be reached at: Game Management Branch (ASQH/DEH/B), U.S. Army Garrison, Fort Huachuca, AZ 85613-6000, phone (602) 538-7339.

Air Force Installations

BARRY M. GOLDWATER AIR FORCE RANGE

- Near Yuma
- 2.7 million acres
- Includes Cabeza Prieta National Wildlife Refuge
- Installation permit required
- Big and small game

Hunting There is no military reservation per se on the Goldwater Air Force Range. There is a small Air Force station at Gila Bend where the people responsible for range maintenance are housed. The eastern half of the range is controlled by Luke Air

Force Base, the western half by Marine Corps Air Station Yuma, and the Cabeza Prieta National Wildlife Refuge by the refuge headquarters in Ajo.

While the range is open to the public, that doesn't mean it's easy to get access permission. Since the Goldwater Air Force Range covers such a vast area, there are several agencies one must contact before entering the range. The first step in getting there is to obtain a range information kit from any of the three offices listed below. The kit will tell you exactly who to contact and what forms to submit to use the range. The agencies are: 832 CSG/AOR, Luke AFB, AZ 85309-5000, phone (602) 856-7653; Fleet Liaison Office, S-3 Dept., MCAS Yuma, AZ 85369, phone (602) 726-3401; and USFWS, Box 418, Ajo, AZ 85321, phone (602) 387-6483.

After receiving the information kit, you'll learn that there are several forms you will have to complete and submit to one of the above offices, depending on which section of the range you'll be entering. Additionally, you'll have to either receive an entry permit by mail or pick one up in person at either Gila Bend AFS, MCAS Yuma, or the Cabeza Prieta NWR Headquarters in Ajo.

Is it worth all the trouble? If you like hunting monster desert bighorns, desert mule deer, javelina, cougars, coyote, bobcat, civet cat, badger, cottontail rabbits, quail (both Mearns and Gambel), three species of dove, jack rabbits, and fox in unspoiled desert habitat, it is! Hunters after big or small game on the Barry Goldwater Range need nothing more than a valid Arizona hunting license and an entry permit.

In addition to the game found on the range, this piece of real estate is home to the extremely rare and endangered Sonoran Desert pronghorn antelope and the federally protected desert tortoise. Both animals are protected, but photographic opportunities are abundant.

All big and small game seasons on the range follow those of the state. The same holds true for big game tags. You must submit an application to the state to receive one. Tags for the desert bighorn are extremely hard to come by. Only eighty are issued each year. Tags for other big game species are more abundant and easier to get.

Space prohibits listing all the topographic maps that cover the Goldwater Air Force Range, but it runs from the Yuma quadrangles in the west through the Antelope Peak and Vekol mountains sectionals in the east. There are seventy-six maps in all.

For more information about the Barry M. Goldwater Range, contact one of the agencies mentioned earlier in this section.

Other DOD Recreation Areas

In addition to the preceding installations, three others in Arizona have recreation areas on major lakes in the state. Luke Air Force Base runs the Fort Tuthill Recreation Area four miles south of Flagstaff. The recreation camp is up in the cool ponderosa pines in some of Arizona's beautiful high country.

Fort Tuthill is open to active duty military and retirees, their dependents, and DOD civilians.

For more information, contact: Fort Tuthill Air Force Recreation Area, Oak Creek Star Route, Box 5, Flagstaff, AZ 86001, phone (602) 774-8893.

Williams Air Force Base runs the Waterdog Recreation Area on Apache Lake. It is a recreation facility for hunting, fishing, water skiing, boating, picnicking, camping, and hiking. Waterdog is open to active duty military, retirees, and their dependents.

The facility is in the Tonto National Forest. While hunting is not allowed within the recreation area, the surrounding national forest land offers excellent chances at mule deer, javelinas, and upland game including rabbits and quail.

Fishing is excellent at Apache Lake, with striped bass and largemouth bass being the predominant species. Fishermen can also catch crappie, catfish, trout, and panfish.

For more information on the Waterdog Recreation Area, contact: 82 ABG/SSRO, Williams AFB, AZ 85224, phone (602) 467-2663.

On the western side of the state, Marine Corps Air Station Yuma operates the Lake Martinez Recreation Area. Located along the Colorado River, Lake Martinez is open to active duty military, retirees, and their dependents.

Camping and fishing are allowed at Lake Martinez. The facility is open year-round and offers recreational vehicle pads with and without hookups, cabins, tent camping, a marina, and a snack bar.

Fishing is generally good in the Colorado River and a valid Arizona or California fishing license is required to fish the Colorado.

For more information on Lake Martinez, contact: Special Services, Marine Corps Air Station, Yuma AZ 85634, phone (602) 988-6753.

ARKANSAS

Though Arkansas is mostly privately owned, there are sixty-seven state wildlife management areas in the state. There is one area managed by the U.S. Army.

FORT CHAFFEE

- Southeast of Fort Smith
- 50,000 acres open to hunting and fishing
- Installation permit required
- White-tailed deer, turkey, small game
- Fishing

Hunting   Up to 50,000 of Chaffee's 72,337 acres may be open at any given time during the hunting season. The reservation is open to the public and big game hunting with a gun is controlled by the Arkansas Game and Fish Commission. Permits are issued on a drawing basis. Hunters must have a valid Arkansas hunting license and, if born after January 1, 1969, must have proof of completing a state-certified hunter safety course.

The installation is divided into fifteen public-use areas. Most, but not all, areas are open to the public on any given day. Anyone hunting on the reservation must check in with one of the range information stations, located at the entrances to all the areas, prior to entering. Hunters may determine which areas are open daily by calling (501) 484-2472.

Twenty-two-caliber rimfire weapons are illegal on Fort Chaffee. They may not be carried afield in any of the hunting areas at any time. Areas 2 and 3, west of Vache

Grasse Creek, are restricted to shotgun, muzzleloader, and archery hunting. The rest of the installation is open to high-powered rifles. Crossbows are also legal on Fort Chaffee.

The deer hunting on Fort Chaffee is good. Hunter success on whitetails was 11.5 percent in 1989. Bowhunters and crossbow hunters also do well on the fort.

Fort Chaffee also offers excellent turkey hunting from October 1 through February 28 each year. Unfortunately, turkeys can only be hunted with a bow and arrow or crossbow. There is no spring turkey season.

Small game hunting is excellent in the bottomlands on Fort Chaffee. The hardwoods support a healthy, but wary, population of squirrels and waterfowl. The briar patches along the roads are home to tons of cottontails. The bobwhite quail is also present in fair numbers on Fort Chaffee.

Small game on Fort Chaffee can only be taken with shotguns or archery equipment. During the deer season, other weapons may be used in open areas. The varmints on the post—coyotes, fox, and bobcat—may be taken with a shotgun or with any legal hunting weapon during the deer season.

Fishing   The waters on Fort Chaffee offer fishermen a smorgasbord of fine southern fishing. Largemouth bass, crappie, bream, and three types of catfish can all be found on the installation. All that's needed is an Arkansas fishing license and fishing pole. Commercial fishing is not allowed on Fort Chaffee, so you won't find any gill nets or trotlines on the installation.

You can fish with multiple rods or poles and lines on the post, and just about anything you can get on a hook for bait is legal. Minnows and crawfish, as well as artificials, are good for bass. Minnows and small jigs should put crappie in your boat. The catfish will respond to cut bait, stink bait, nightcrawlers, and shiners. The bream are best caught on worms and crickets.

Miscellaneous   No camping or ORV use is allowed on Fort Chaffee.

The maps that cover Fort Chaffee are the Barling, Lavaca, Charleston, Barber, Burnville, and Greenwood quadrangles in the 7.5-minute series.

For more information on Fort Chaffee's outstanding hunting and fishing, contact: Environmental Branch, Natural Resources Section, Fort Chaffee, AR 72905-5000, phone (501) 484-2231 (7:30 A.M. to 4:30 P.M., weekdays).

PINE BLUFF ARSENAL

- 13,450 acres open to hunting
- Installation permit required
- Deer
- Fishing

Hunting   According to Department of the Army (DA) information, Pine Bluff Arsenal has 13,450 acres open to hunting for whitetails.

The cost of an arsenal hunting permit is $20 for military, arsenal employees, and the public. Last year, sportsmen spent a total of 3,689 days in the woods and fields of Pine Bluff Arsenal.

There were 141 deer taken from arsenal lands. Eighty-seven of those deer were bucks and fifty-four were does. The average field-dressed weight of the bucks taken was ninety-three pounds. That might not seem large to most people, but it is an indication of a healthy one- or two-year-old buck in this part of the South.

There is no information on small game hunting on the arsenal.

Fishing   There are a total of 333 acres of water with four and eight-tenths miles of shoreline available for fishermen on the installation.

There are no fees charged for fishing on Pine Bluff. It is apparently a popular place to go, though. Fishermen put in 4,897 days of fishing on the lake in 1990.

For more information on hunting and fishing on Pine Bluff Arsenal, contact: Wildlife Management Branch, U.S. Army Armament and Munitions Command, Pine Bluff Arsenal, Pine Bluff, AR 71602-9500.

Air Force Installations

LITTLE ROCK AIR FORCE BASE

- 11,548 acres
- Closed to the public
- Installation permit required
- White-tailed deer and small game
- Fishing
- Restricted camping

Hunting   Hunting is allowed on Little Rock Air Force Base. White-tailed deer may be taken on the installation with bow and arrow, shotguns, or black-powder weapons. The base is only open to active duty military, retirees, their dependents, and DOD civilians employed on Little Rock Air Force Base.

Deer seasons follow those set by the state. All hunters born after January 1, 1969, must complete a state-certified hunter safety course prior to getting either a state license or a base permit. The base is divided into separate hunting areas and hunters must reserve an area prior to going afield.

Hunters may change areas during the day, provided they check in with the base security police prior to changing areas. For safety reasons, only a certain number of hunters are allowed in any one area at a given time.

Small game hunters on Little Rock Air Force Base may hunt cottontails and squirrels with shotguns or archery equipment. Again, hunters must check in with the security police prior to going afield.

Fishing   Fishermen on Little Rock AFB will find catfish, bass, crappie, and bream in the base waters. A base permit and state license are required prior to going fishing. Fishing is restricted to base employees and military personnel.

Miscellaneous   Little Rock Air Force Base also runs a military recreation area on Lake Conway. The Lake Conway Air Force Landing is open year-round and offers camping, fishing, hiking, and a marina. Boat rentals, bait, fishing, and ski equipment are available at the recreation area.

Some camping is allowed on the base, both in the family camping area and at primitive sites in certain areas.

For more information on hunting and fishing on Little Rock Air Force Base, contact: Outdoor Recreation Section, 314th Combat Support Group, Little Rock Air Force Base, AR 72076.

CALIFORNIA

According to the latest figures, California is America's most populous state. Still, it has some relatively wild areas. Unfortunately, most of these areas are privately owned and not open to the public. The few national forests and refuges become more crowded each year. There are, however, 2,935,637 acres of land owned by the Department of Defense that are open to hunting or fishing.

Though there are some 105 military installations in California, only a handful are large enough to support hunting or fishing.

Army Installations

FORT HUNTER LIGGETT

- 20 miles west of King City
- 144,441 acres open to hunting and fishing
- Surrounded on three sides by Los Padres National Forest
- Installation permit required
- Deer, wild pig, turkey, and small game
- Fishing
- Camping

Hunting Fort Hunter Liggett is one of the best places in California to take a deer or wild pig on public land. Up to 144,441 acres may be open to hunting at any given time. During the deer and pig seasons, Fort Hunter Liggett is open to the public

31

on weekends and federal holidays. A limited amount of hunting is allowed after 5:00 P.M. on weekdays. Legal hunting hours on weekends and holidays are one-half hour before dawn until one hour after dark.

Both mule deer and coastal blacktails are found on the reservation. Their ranges overlap so some crossbreeding occurs. Most of the bucks taken on post are one to three years old. Yet, some older deer grow to impressive size as the accompanying photograph illustrates.

The minimum legal age to hunt big game on Hunter Liggett is twelve, in accordance with California law. Additionally, all hunters in California must complete a state-certified hunter safety course prior to obtaining a license. All hunters on Hunter Liggett must have a post hunting permit.

Hunter Liggett is managed in conjunction with Fort Ord, sixty-five miles up the coast. A hunting permit is good for both installations and is available at either. The cost of the permit is reasonable at $12 for one day, $18 for two days, $55 for an annual civilian permit, or $25 for an annual military permit. The permit is required for both large and small game hunting.

Hunter Liggett is an open military installation, meaning that you can hunt with the weapon of your choice as long as it meets California law. Handguns are authorized for hunting on post provided they have a barrel at least six inches long and are .38 Special caliber or larger. Rimfire handguns are not authorized. Anything smaller than .38 Special may not be used for hunting. Single-shot handguns must be .243 caliber or larger.

Pig hunting on Hunter Liggett is quite good, depending on the season. I took a large boar there in 1974 after two days of hunting. From what I understand, the pig population has grown considerably since those days.

There was no turkey hunting allowed on Hunter Liggett when I visited there in the 1970s. That has changed. Today, the installation has several flocks of wild turkeys and there is a spring hunting season.

Tule elk were transplanted to Hunter Liggett in the 1980s. Their numbers are still low. They cannot yet be legally hunted.

Small game hunting on this installation can be good or bad, depending on the species. If you're after valley quail, cottontails, or jack rabbits, the hunting is excellent. Tree squirrels, mountain quail, band-tailed pigeons, waterfowl, and doves can be tougher to come by, as the populations are spotty or seasonal.

There are thirty hunting areas on Fort Hunter Liggett ranging in size from three and one-half to over thirteen square miles. Reservations for a hunting area may be made beginning on Wednesday of each week during the hunting season. Reservations for military ID card holders and one guest may be made beginning at 9:00 A.M. Civilian reservations may be made beginning at noon. Up to four reservations may be made per phone call. The reservations number is (408) 385-1205.

When making reservations, you must specify the area and days preferred and provide your full name and your current California hunting license number. While it's a good idea to make reservations prior to hunting on this installation, you don't have to. All reservations not claimed at the game check station by 7:00 A.M. on the day of the hunt are put back in the pool and reissued on a first-come, first-served basis.

Hunters must check in and out of their hunting areas at the game check station daily. If a hunter wishes to change hunting areas, he must check out of that area with the check station and check into another area.

Fishing   There are several ponds and small reservoirs on Hunter Liggett. All the bodies of water are stocked with one species or another. The fish available are large-mouth bass, smallmouth bass, green sunfish, channel cats, suckers, Sacramento squaw-fish, carp, and rainbow trout.

During high-water years, Lake San Antonio backs up onto some of the installation's lands. When that happens, fishing for stripers, largemouths, and catfish can be excellent in the backwaters along the San Antonio River on the reservation.

Fishermen on Hunter Liggett must have a valid California license, the appropriate stamps, and a post permit. Fishing is authorized after the duty day ends (5:00 P.M.) and on weekends. Lakes and ponds in open hunting areas during the big game seasons are closed to fishing.

Miscellaneous   Camping is allowed in the small, primitive campground on the installation. The campground is just behind the game check station, so checking in and out is convenient. Camping is not authorized in any of the hunting areas. This is a very dry area so fires are not usually allowed.

The installation has an extensive road network. ORVs are neither authorized nor needed. Street-legal four-wheel drive vehicles are allowed on the reservation but they must remain on established roads and trails.

Fort Hunter Liggett has a well-rounded and well-managed wildlife and fisheries program. It is one of the best-kept secrets in California.

The topographic maps covering Hunter Liggett are the Junipero Serra Peak, Alder Peak, Cone Peak, Lockwood, and Burro Mountain in the 15-minute series. Maps of the Ventana Wilderness Area from the U.S. Forest Service cover much of the north and west sides of the post.

For more information on hunting and fishing on Hunter Liggett, contact: AFZW-HL-PACR (WCS), Box 896, Jolon, CA 93928, phone (408) 385-1205.

FORT IRWIN
NATIONAL TRAINING CENTER

- 35 miles northeast of Barstow
- 636,457 acres of desert
- Small game

Hunting   Currently, Fort Irwin is not open to big game hunting. There simply aren't that many big game animals to hunt. Small game hunting, on the other hand, can be excellent if you hunt around the few springs and waterholes on the installation. Cottontails and pygmy cottontails inhabit this part of California, along with valley quail, chukar, and jack rabbits.

Hunters on Fort Irwin must have a valid California hunting license. Prior to going afield, hunters must check in with range control to identify the area they want to hunt and to receive a range pass. Upon completion of hunting, the hunter must again check with range control and return the pass. Legal hunting hours are from one-half hour before sunrise until one hour *before* sunset. No night hunting is allowed. The range must be cleared by dark.

High-powered rifles, rimfire rifles or handguns, centerfire handguns, and muzzle-loading rifles and handguns are not allowed on Fort Irwin. In fact, the only weapons authorized for hunting on Fort Irwin are shotguns using shot and archery equipment. Shotguns must meet the same standards as those used for migratory waterfowl—capable of holding no more than three shells, shot size no larger than #2, and 10 gauge or smaller. Falconry is also allowed.

Speaking of waterfowl, duck hunting is allowed on Fort Irwin. There are two two-man blinds set up on the waste-water treatment pond. Hunters are allowed to hunt from 5:00 A.M. until 8:00 A.M. two days a week from these blinds. Waterfowlers, like everyone else, must check in and out with range control prior to hunting. A state and federal duck stamp is required for duck hunting.

There is no camping allowed on Fort Irwin and, since there is no water, there's no fishing.

Fort Irwin/National Training Center is covered by the following topographic maps in the 15-minute quadrangles: Quail Mountains, Goldstone Lake, Lane Mountain, Leach Lake, Tiefront Mountains, Alvord Mountain, Avawatz Pass, Red Pass Lake, and Cave Mountain.

For more information on outdoor activities at Fort Irwin, contact: Tom Clark, ATTN: AFZJ-EHE-EN, Fort Irwin & NTC, Fort Irwin, CA 92310, phone (619) 386-5291 (7:30 A.M. to 4:00 P.M., Monday through Friday).

FORT ORD

- North of Monterey
- 28,000 acres
- Installation permit required
- Deer and small game
- Freshwater and saltwater fishing

Hunting Wildlife management at Fort Ord is done in conjunction with that at Fort Hunter Liggett. Consequently, the rules are pretty much the same.

The terrain at Fort Ord differs considerably from Hunter Liggett. Where Hunter Liggett is covered in oaks and grassland, Ord is covered with scrub oak and brush. Temperatures at Hunter Liggett can reach well over 100 degrees in summer. Temperatures at Fort Ord, at least the western part of the installation, rarely exceed eighty-five.

Fort Ord is open to hunting for black-tailed deer. Presently, it is an archery-only proposition. There may be special-drawing permit hunts for black powder or shotguns in the future.

The permit requirements for Fort Ord are the same as those for Hunter Liggett. Hunters must sign in and out with outdoor recreation prior to going afield.

Small game hunting on Fort Ord is excellent. Pygmy cottontails, alias bush bunnies, can be found all over the post. It's possible to limit out just after sunrise as the rabbits come out of the brush to sit along the trails and roads to sun.

Valley quail are also abundant on Fort Ord. Here, they tend to hold tight for dogs, so the hunting can be quite good. It's also possible to flush them without a dog, and limits are not terribly difficult to reach.

Jack rabbits can be found all over this installation. In 1974, I was the range master for the Fort Ord Rod and Gun Club pistol range. More than once, I've seen jack rabbits wander out onto the fifty-yard range while people were firing.

Hunter success on Fort Ord and Fort Hunter Liggett combined is 30 percent for big game and 60 percent for small game.

Fishing   Freshwater fishing is limited at Fort Ord. The few ponds on post are stocked with bass, perch, crappie, and catfish. Saltwater fishing is another story. Monterey Bay contains salmon, sea bass, cod, perch, shark, eel, albacore, and tuna. You can fish from the beach on the fort or the fishing pier in Monterey.

Licensing requirements for Fort Ord fishermen are the same as for the state of California. A post fishing permit is also required.

Miscellaneous   There is a travel camp on Fort Ord, but it is open only to military identification card holders. No primitive camping is allowed.

Fort Ord has an excellent outdoor recreation program with archery, rifle, pistol, and skeet ranges. The Fort Ord Shooting Center offers a reloading room at a nominal fee and reloading classes. The shooting center has a junior rifle range, open five days a week. The shooting center can be contacted at: EGRA, Bldg. T-456, Fort Ord, CA 93941-5600, phone (408) 242-2466.

For information on all of Fort Ord's outdoor activities, contact: Outdoor Recreation, Bldg. 3109, 4th Avenue, Fort Ord, CA 93941-5600, phone (408) 242-7322.

Air Force Installations

BEALE AIR FORCE BASE

- In the Sacramento Valley
- 18,250 acres open to hunting and fishing
- Closed to the public
- Installation permit required
- Big game and small game
- Fishing

Hunting   Beale AFB is classified as a "Category 1" installation, meaning that it has suitable habitat for conserving and managing fish and wildlife, including threatened and endangered species and nongame species. The base does a pretty good job of it, too.

The base is not open to the public. Active duty military members and their dependents, retired military members and their dependents, federal civil service personnel employed on base, and dependents of federal civil service employees when accompanied by their sponsor are eligible to hunt on Beale. Guests of those eligible while accompanied by the sponsor may also participate. Hunters on Beale must hold a valid California hunting license prior to purchasing a base hunting permit from either the base exchange or the rod and gun club. Under California law, all hunters must have proof of having completed a hunter safety course prior to buying a license. Hunters under sixteen must be accompanied by an adult over eighteen when afield.

Beale is open to big game hunting. For the last two years, twenty buck-only permits have been issued in a lottery drawing to deer hunters on base. Hunter success has been running around 20 percent.

The deer found on Beale are California blacktails. They may be hunted with shotguns using slugs, muzzleloaders, and archery tackle. Bucks must be a forkhorn or better. The deer season on Beale coincides with local seasons.

Small game hunting is allowed and is excellent. The base even has its own resident pheasant farm.

Centerfire rifles, handguns of any type, and pneumatic weapons are not authorized for taking any game on the installation. The only weapons legal are 10-gauge shotguns or smaller using a shot size smaller than BB. Shotguns can hold no more than three shells.

Because of Beale's pheasant farm, pheasant are one of the premier game birds found on the installation. The rolling grassland and brush on Beale should make for some excellent hunting for these Chinese imports. That grass and brush is excellent habitat for valley quail and cottontails. Jack rabbits are also found on this installation.

The migratory birds on Beale are doves, mallards, wood ducks, and just about any other type of migratory waterfowl found in the Pacific Flyway. Duck hunting is authorized on the base lake. Hunters may construct blinds and set out decoys.

The blinds may be no closer than 100 yards to any other blinds or decoy spreads. Blinds must blend in with the natural surroundings and not be an eyesore. Floating blinds are not authorized but hunting from boats is. Additionally, natural vegetation may not be removed or dug up for the construction of blinds. Duck hunters are urged to be extremely cautious because people may be fishing during the duck season.

Grazing rights to most of the land on Beale are leased by local ranchers and farmers. The land is still open to hunting, but hunters must be sure to close all gates when passing through them. Additionally, cattle and horses should not be disturbed.

Fishing Beale has several ponds on base ranging in size from one-half acre up to ten or fifteen acres. They are all stocked with fish of one type or another including catfish, bass, sunfish, crappie, and carp.

Salmon and steelhead can be found on the installation. The creek that is dammed to form Beale Lake is a tributary of the Feather River. Salmon and steelhead use it for spawning.

Fishing regulations on Beale AFB follow those of the state of California. Fishermen must have a valid California freshwater license prior to purchasing a base fishing permit. Fishermen after steelhead or salmon must also have the appropriate state trout/ salmon stamps.

The eligibility requirements for fishing on Beale are the same as for hunting. Active duty military, their dependents, retired military, their dependents, and base employees are the only ones eligible.

Creel limits on Beale are liberal. A fisherman may take two salmon, five bass over twelve inches, ten crappie, ten channel catfish over twelve inches, any number of bullheads over six inches, up to fifteen sunfish, and no more than five trout per day. There is no daily limit on carp or goldfish.

Any method of fishing legal in the state is also legal on Beale. Carp and goldfish may be taken with bow and arrow as well as conventional fishing gear. Carp and goldfish must be removed from the lake area when taken. Anyone bowfishing on Beale must use a bow with a minimum draw weight of forty-five pounds. Arrows must be of the "harpoon" type, no longer than thirty-six inches. Arrows must be attached to the bow by a line, preferably of braided nylon, with a breaking strength of at least forty pounds. Bow-fishing lines can be no more than 100 feet long.

Miscellaneous   Camping is not allowed on Beale except by special permission of the base commander. ORVs may be used in the designated ORV area only. Vehicles must stay on existing roadways. Vehicle travel on jeep trails and fire breaks is not allowed. Vehicles should be parked in designated parking areas. When no parking area is available, vehicles may be parked no more than eight feet from the shoulder of the road. Vehicles may not be parked in any area marked by no-parking signs.

Beale hosts an active rod and gun club. The club is an excellent place to get tips on the best areas for hunting and fishing on the installation, as well as a place for sportsmen to meet.

Beale Air Force Base is covered by the Smartsville and Brown's Valley topographic quadrangles in the 7.5-minute series.

For more information on the outdoor opportunities on Beale Air Force Base, contact: 814 CES/DEEV, ATTN: John Thompson, Beale AFB, CA 95903-5000, phone (916) 634-4485/4486.

VANDENBERG AIR FORCE BASE

- Northwest of Santa Barbara
- 70,000 acres open to hunting
- 35 miles of coastline
- 5 freshwater fishing ponds
- Closed to the public but some fishing areas open to the public
- Big game and small game
- Freshwater and saltwater fishing
- Camping and boating

Hunting   Of the 100,000 acres that is Vandenberg, 70,000 are open to hunting. Hunters can take either big or small game with the appropriate base permits and access.

Vandenberg is open only to active duty military members, their dependents, retirees, and their dependents. It is not open to civilians.

All types of hunting on the base are excellent. Hunter success for deer runs over 50 percent. That is equal to or better than many private hunting preserves. The deer herds are exceptionally well managed for the habitat. Even areas normally closed are opened from time to time to take excess deer.

Feral pigs are also found on Vandenberg Air Force Base. When people think of feral pigs, they think of somebody's little pig that has wandered away. Nothing could be further from the truth. These are truly wild animals, born and bred in the wild. In many cases they have bred with descendants of European wild boars introduced here at the turn of the century. These pigs grow to impressive sizes and can be dangerous if not hunted properly.

Big game hunters on Vandenberg must have valid California licenses and tags for the species they wish to hunt. They must also have a current Vandenberg use-fee stamp affixed to their state licenses. The use-fee stamp is available from the main base exchange and costs $5 each for deer and pig, $3 for small game, or $10 for a stamp covering all three.

Most areas on Vandenberg are open to hunting with centerfire rifles during the general gun season. Hunters may use centerfire rifles of .25 caliber or larger. Handguns are not authorized in the field. Rimfire rifles are also prohibited as are pneumatic weapons and crossbows.

Archers may hunt deer and pig on Vandenberg using archery tackle that is legal in the state of California. Crossbows are not authorized. Arrows must meet California requirements and may not be fitted with poison pods or barbed heads.

Shotgunners after deer must use slugs. Muzzleloaders must be of .40 caliber or larger. Muzzleloading shotguns are also allowed. Buckshot of any size is prohibited.

Hunters after deer during the general season must sign in and out at the game check station daily and when they change hunting areas. As with most installations, Vandenberg is divided into several hunting areas and only a limited number of hunters is allowed into an area at one time.

Deer hunters must also have a general deer pass with them when afield. The passes are only good for one day and are issued at the game check stations. Archery deer hunters must also have a pass. The archery deer pass is good for the entire deer season. Feral pig passes are good for thirty days, as are small game passes.

Small game hunting on Vandenberg is excellent. This part of California is ideal habitat for cottontails, jack rabbits, squirrels, quail, dove, and waterfowl. Columbian ground squirrels, considered varmints, are also extremely abundant on this installation.

Small game may only be taken with shotguns shooting shot, or archery tackle. Shotguns may hold no more than three shells total, magazine and chamber. Bowhunters must use small-game heads when hunting outside the deer archery deer seasons.

The small game use-fee stamp is required when hunting small game. Additionally, small game hunters must have a pass from the base game warden prior to going afield. The pass is good for thirty days. All hunters must have a valid California hunting license.

Hunting is not allowed in certain areas on base. There are eleven special-use areas where hunting is specifically barred, except when allowed under special circumstances.

Fishing With thirty-five miles of shoreline, you would imagine the saltwater fishing at Vandenberg Air Force Base to be good. It is. Freshwater fishing on this installation is also good.

Like hunting, access to fishing is primarily limited to active duty military, retirees, and their dependents. A limited number of civilian permits are available for special-use areas. Additionally, military sponsors may take up to three guests fishing with them.

Saltwater fishing is permitted on Vandenberg year-round. The fishing area covered by Vandenberg stretches from Point Sal in the north to one-half mile north of the tip of Point Arguello. A special fishing region is designated in the Boathouse Area of South Vandenberg Air Force Base. It is open to only thirty fishermen per day from sunrise to sunset, by reservation only. All fishermen on Vandenberg must have the applicable state licenses and stamps prior to purchasing a freshwater use stamp, available from the main base exchange. Children under sixteen must be accompanied by an adult over eighteen.

There are special civilian-use areas for fishing on Vandenberg. The public may fish along the beach from the mouth of the Santa Ynez River southward to the first rock outcropping, approximately 2.5 miles south of the river mouth. Public fishing is also allowed from Jalama Park north 1.5 miles to the first rock outcropping. No driving is allowed on the beach.

The base maintains a permit system called the "civilian fishing list." It is valid for up to fifty civilians at a time. The area open to those on the civilian fishing list is from one-half mile north of the Santa Ynez River mouth northward along the coast to Purisima Point. People wanting to fish in this area must call the Fish and Wildlife Office at (805) 986-6804, between 8:00 A.M. and 5:00 P.M. Wednesday and Thursday, and between 8:00 A.M. and 4:00 P.M. on Friday to make a reservation. When making reservations, anglers must provide their name, vehicle description, vehicle license number, and California fishing license number. This information is passed to the 13th Street (Solvang) Gate. The gate guard will issue the angler a visiting anglers pass. Prospective anglers must sign a civilian anglers liability agreement before being allowed access to the base.

Freshwater fishing on Vandenberg is permitted in Mod III Lake, the Pine Canyon Lakes chain, Punchbowl Lake, Rawlinson Pond, and Mitchel Pond twenty-four hours a day. The ponds are stocked with largemouth bass, channel cats, redear sunfish, crappie, and Sacramento perch. The limits match those of the state.

Miscellaneous Boats are allowed on all the freshwater ponds on base. Electric motors are also allowed, but gasoline engines are not. If a gasoline engine is permanently mounted to a boat prior to the boat entering the water, the engine must be disabled so that it may not be started.

Camping is allowed on certain parts of Vandenberg Air Force Base. An ORV special-use area and dog and horse training areas are available. Vandenberg has established a wildlife viewing area where one may watch various types of big and upland game in their natural habitat.

For more information on hunting and fishing on Vandenberg Air Force Base, contact: Base Game Warden, 4392 SPS/SPOF, Vandenberg AFB, CA 93437-5000, phone (805) 866-6804 (7:30 A.M. to 4:00 P.M., Monday through Friday).

Naval Installations

NAVAL AIR STATION POINT MUGU

- South of Oxnard
- Closed to the public
- Saltwater fishing
- Camping

Fishing Fishing on Point Mugu is open only to those who routinely have access to the installation. It is not open to the public. For active duty and retired military, their dependents, installation civilian employees, and DOD contractors, there is a small fishing area with a pier.

Fishermen must have a California saltwater license and the appropriate stamps. There is no freshwater fishing on Point Mugu. Species available are halibut, surf perch, rock bass, assorted other sea basses, and perch, sand dabs (a flounder), turbot, and the occasional shark and salmon.

Camping is allowed on Point Mugu for active duty and retired military members. Cottages are available for retired and active duty military members E-7 and above.

For more information on Point Mugu, contact: Morale, Welfare and Recreation (Code 6030), NAS Point Mugu, Point Mugu, CA 93042-5000, phone (805) 989-8349 (9:30 A.M. to 5:00 P.M., weekdays, and 10:00 A.M. to 2:00 P.M., Saturdays).

NAVAL COMMUNICATIONS STATION STOCKTON

- On the San Joaquin River
- 1,433 acres open to freshwater fishing
- Closed to the public

Fishing NCS Stockton is a closed installation. The only people allowed to fish on it are military identification card holders and civilians with a valid U.S. government employee identification card. All fishermen must have a valid California freshwater fishing license with the appropriate stamps.

There are 1,433 acres open to freshwater fishing on NCS Stockton. Species available are catfish, crappie, Sacramento perch, largemouth bass, and the occasional sturgeon. Fishermen may use either live bait or artificials. Seasons and bag limits match those of the state.

For more information on fishing NCS Stockton, contact: Director, Recreation Services, NCS Stockton, Stockton, CA 95203-5000, phone (209) 944-0582.

NAVAL WEAPONS CENTER CHINA LAKE

- 96 miles northwest of Barstow in the desert
- 100,000 acres open to hunting
- Installation permit required
- Small game

Hunting   Naval Weapons Center China Lake owns 1,127,266 acres of land, and 100,000 of these acres are open to hunting. Since there aren't a lot of big game animals to hunt in this barren land, there is no big game hunting. The only game animals that can be hunted on the China Lake reservation are cottontail rabbits, valley quail, jack rabbits, and, in the hills, chukar partridge.

Hunting on NAVWPNCEN China Lake is open to the public, but there is one drawback. The reservation is open only two weekends during the entire season. Hunters apply for a permit prior to the season, and a drawing is held to select a specific number of hunters for each weekend.

Once selected, hunters must purchase a reservation permit from the installation game warden. The day of the hunt, hunters must check in with the main gate for access and attend a morning briefing prior to going afield. All hunters must have the required California hunting licenses and stamps.

If you are selected to hunt on NAVWPNCEN China Lake, expect to find some of the best chukar hunting available anywhere. While the chukar hunting is still tough because of the country, getting a limit is fairly common—provided you can shoot straight.

Miscellaneous   Due to the nature of the military activities on this installation, camping, ORV use, and other outdoor activities are not allowed or are severely restricted. This is an area of stark beauty with a very active wildlife management program.

For more information on hunting at Naval Weapons Center China Lake, contact: Environmental Resources Branch (Code 2662), NAVWPNCEN, China Lake, CA 93555, phone (619) 939-3411, ext. 382/300 (8:00 A.M. to 4:30 P.M., Monday through Friday).

NAVAL WEAPONS STATION SEAL BEACH

- Closed to the public
- Installation permit required
- Saltwater fishing

Fishing   Seal Beach offers 350 yards of Pacific coastline for saltwater fishermen. There is no freshwater fishing. All fishermen must have an installation permit and a valid California saltwater license.

This is a closed installation. The only people allowed access are those with a valid identification card. Fishing is from a beach, so surf gear is required.

Fishing is good here, with close to thirty saltwater species available.

For more information on Seal Beach, contact: Code 101, Pass and I.D., NAVWPNSTA, Seal Beach, CA 90740-5000, phone (714) 594-7230.

Marine Corps Installations

CAMP PENDLETON

- Near San Clemente
- 60,000 acres open to hunting and fishing
- 17 miles of coastline
- Installation permit required
- Deer and small game
- Freshwater fishing closed to the public
- Limited public access to saltwater fishing
- Camping

Hunting   Sixty-thousand acres of Camp Pendleton's 186,139 acres are open to hunting. The installation offers both big and small game hunting and limited waterfowl hunting. The installation's hunting areas are open to the public.

Big game hunting on Camp Pendleton is strictly for black-tailed deer, a subspecies of the mule deer. The hunts are controlled by the California Department of Fish and Game. The department considers Camp Pendleton a special-use area with its own season. Unlike the surrounding areas in the state, Camp Pendleton's deer season is in November rather than September.

Access to the Camp Pendleton deer hunt is by drawing permits through the state of California. Hunters drawn for the Camp Pendleton hunt must have all the required California licenses and tags as well as the required Camp Pendleton permits. All hunters must register their firearms with the duty game warden prior to bringing them on Camp Pendleton.

The firearms authorized for big game on Camp Pendleton are centerfire rifles, muzzleloading rifles, and shotguns. Muzzleloaders have special restrictions, depending on fire danger conditions during the season. Shotgunners must use slugs for big game. Handgun hunting of any sort is banned on the installation.

Bowhunters have their own special-use areas on the installation. Archery equipment for deer must meet the minimums set by the state of California. Crossbows are illegal in the archery-only areas and during the archery-only season but may be used in certain areas during the general gun season.

How good are the seasons on Camp Pendleton? According to the figures for the 1989–90 season, hunter success for bucks was 25 percent. Fifty-three percent of the hunters were successful on antlerless hunts.

Deer hunters must check in personally with the duty warden at Building 25155 immediately before checking into any hunting area. Check-in during the general deer season may be done up to one and one-half hours before legal shooting time. When changing areas, hunters must check in with the duty warden again, but they may check by phone. After the hunt, hunters must sign out with the duty warden. Check-out must be done within two hours after the close of legal shooting time. Failure to comply with the check-in and check-out procedures will result in an automatic suspension of hunting privileges for a minimum of thirty days. A second offense results in a loss of hunting privileges for at least a year.

Small game hunting is also good on Camp Pendleton. Hunters may seek cotton-tails, California quail, mourning dove, band-tailed pigeons, and jack rabbits. Waterfowl may also be hunted on the installation, but is open only to military members and retirees. All other species of small game may be hunted by the general public.

Hunters must have all the necessary state licenses and a Camp Pendleton permit before hunting. Public small game permits for the installation are issued on a lottery basis. The lottery is controlled by the Camp Pendleton Natural Resources Office. Applications are accepted during May of each year; they must have May postmarks. The lottery is held on the third Wednesday in June. Successful applicants are notified by mail and have until August to claim their permits.

To apply for a permit, send a self-addressed stamped postcard in an envelope. On the back of the postcard, print the applicants' names, status (active duty, retired, civilian, etc.), and work and home phone numbers. Up to three people may apply per card. Send the card in an envelope to: Director, Natural Resources Office, Marine Corps Base, Camp Pendleton, CA 92055-5010. Print "Small Game Lottery" on the bottom-left corner of the envelope's front.

Fishing Camp Pendleton offers both freshwater and saltwater fishing. There are ten freshwater impoundments and close to seventeen miles of surf fishing available along the beach. Freshwater fishing is open to military ID card holders only. Limited public access is allowed along the beach.

All fishermen on Camp Pendleton must have the appropriate state licenses and tags. Fishermen must also have an installation license. Public access to the beach is by a lottery similar to that held for small game hunters. Applications are accepted during November with the drawing in January. The permits are good from February 1 through January 31 the following year. Public permits cost $30.

Freshwater species available on Camp Pendleton are largemouth, bluegill, catfish, carp, and put-and-take rainbow trout. Fishing methods are the same as those for the state.

Miscellaneous   With a beach-access permit, the holder is allowed to camp along certain areas of the beach. ORV use is not authorized on the installation.

Camp Pendleton is covered by the Morro Hill, Fallbrook, San Clemente, Las Pulgas Canyon, San Onofre Bluff, Oceanside, and Margarita Peak quadrangles.

For more information on the outdoor opportunities available on Camp Pendleton, contact: Commanding General, AC/S Facilities (Natural Resources Office), Marine Corps Base, Camp Pendleton, CA 92055, phone (619) 725-3528/4512.

COLORADO

Hunters and fishermen in Colorado are lucky. They have millions of acres of national forests and U.S. Bureau of Land Management lands on which to hunt and fish. Unfortunately, Colorado becomes more popular every year, and the state is becoming more urbanized. Ski resorts are replacing elk habitat. Condominiums are flourishing where mule deer once fed.

There are thirteen Army and Air Force installations in Colorado. Not all are open to hunting and fishing. Those that are, are in prime territory.

Army Installations

FORT CARSON

- South of Colorado Springs
- 340,000 acres
- Includes Pinon Canyon Maneuver Site
- Installation permit required
- Big game and small game
- Fishing
- Camping and boating

Hunting Fort Carson holds excellent populations of both big and small game. The fort itself holds whitetails, mule deer, antelope, and elk. Nearby Pinon Canyon Maneuver Site (PCMS) is home to mule deer, antelope, and whitetails. Both have huntable populations of cottontails, squirrels, quail, jack rabbits, waterfowl, and prairie dogs. You may even find a few bobcats and coyotes.

Fort Carson lands are open to hunting on a land-use priority system. People in Category I are active duty military personnel and their dependents either assigned to or directly supported by Fort Carson.

Category II individuals are active duty military personnel not assigned to Fort Carson, military retirees, dependents of active duty and retirees, and Fort Carson civilian employees and their dependents.

Category III is the public.

The categories make a difference when signing up for a hunting area during the big game season. Category I individuals may obtain their passes at 8:00 A.M. the day before their use. Category II individuals may obtain their passes beginning at 10:30 A.M. the day prior to their uses. Category III individuals must wait until 1:00 P.M. to obtain their passes.

Prior to getting passes, all individuals must have a valid Colorado hunting license. If you were born after January 1, 1949, then, according to Colorado law, you must provide proof of having completed a hunter safety course when purchasing a Colorado license. In addition to having the appropriate Colorado license, all hunters on Fort Carson must have a Fort Carson permit prior to obtaining a pass.

Permit fees are reasonable at $10 for either a hunting or fishing permit. A combined hunting and fishing permit may be purchased for $15. Permits may be purchased at the outdoor recreation branch, as can Colorado licenses.

Individuals under the age of eighteen may not hunt alone. They must be accompanied at all times in the field by an adult eighteen or over.

Hunting areas are assigned on a quota basis. Only a certain number of big game hunters are allowed into any hunting area. There are fifty-six hunting areas on Fort Carson and five large hunting areas on the PCMS. Of the fifty-six areas on Fort Carson, seven are open to bowhunting or shotguns only. Fort Carson is not open to hunting with centerfire or rimfire rifles, but muzzleloaders, shotguns with slugs, and archery tackle may be used to take big game on Fort Carson.

PCMS is open to hunting with centerfire and rimfire rifles. In fact, any weapon legal for hunting in Colorado is legal on PCMS.

Hunters must sign in and out with sportsmen's control when going afield. They may sign in and pick up their passes the day before hunting but must check back in with sportsmen's control when finished. When checking in with range control, hunters exchange their Fort Carson permit for a pass. The pass, with the results of the hunt annotated, is then exchanged for the permit after the hunt.

How good is hunting on Fort Carson? The big game success rate for all species is 25 percent. That's exceptional for an area close to a large city. With the chance of taking Rocky Mountain elk, mule deer, whitetails, and antelope all in one spot, Fort Carson definitely holds promise.

The procedures for obtaining a permit and range pass are the same for small game hunters. If you like hunting small game, the minor inconveniences of getting a pass are well worth it. With terrain ranging from grasslands to mountains, the habitat on Fort Carson and PCMS for many species of small game is good.

Fishing There are thirteen impoundments on Fort Carson, all stocked with rainbow trout, Snake River cutthroats, channel cats, crappie, bluegill, bullheads, and brookies. The fishing is good.

Neither corn nor live fish may be used as bait on Fort Carson waters. Additionally, fishermen may use only one rod unless they have the appropriate state of Colorado stamps. While the limits on Fort Carson waters are the same as those of Colorado, only two trout *over* fourteen inches in length may be kept on Fort Carson.

Gale Reservoir is a designated catch-and-release fishery. Here anglers must use artificials with barbless hooks, and all fish caught must be immediately released.

Anglers fifteen and over must have both a Colorado fishing license and a Fort Carson permit prior to going fishing. Those under fifteen do not require a license but are allowed only one-half the daily creel limit.

The waters of Fort Carson are open twenty-four hours a day in season. Ice-fishing is not allowed. Fishermen headed for Teller, Spring Branch, or any other reservoirs designated by the environmental engineering branch need to obtain passes from the sportsmen's control office. The other waters on the fort have no such requirement.

Miscellaneous Boats are allowed on Fort Carson waters. Electric trolling motors are allowed, and everyone on the boat must have his or her own USCG-approved life preserver readily available.

There is camping on Fort Carson in designated areas. During the big game seasons, camping is also allowed on the Pinon Canyon Maneuver Site. ORVs are prohibited on this installation.

The topographic maps covering Fort Carson are as follows: Colorado Springs; Fountain; Timber Mountain; Pierce Gulch; Steele Hollow; Cheyenne Mountain; Mt. Pittsburg; Buttes; and Stone City. The following are Pinon Canyon Maneuver Site topographic maps: Sheep Canyon; Riley Canyon; Thatcher; Stage Canyon; Beaty; Brown Sheep Camp; Doss Canyon North; Lambing Spring; Doss Canyon South; Packer's Gap; Bates; Lockwood Arroyo; OV Mesa; Tyrone; Rock Crossing; Johnson Canyon; and Painted Canyon.

For more information on hunting and fishing at Fort Carson and Pinon Canyon Maneuver Site, contact: HQ Fort Carson & 4 ID(MECH), AFZC-FE-ENR, Fort Carson, CO 80913-5023, phone (719) 579-2752 (7:00 A.M. to 3:30 P.M., weekdays).

PUEBLO ARMY DEPOT ACTIVITY

- Closed to the public
- Installation permit required
- Fishing

Fishing Pueblo Army Depot Activity is not open to hunting. It is, however, open to fishing. The installation has a small reservoir covering seventeen surface acres. The reservoir is stocked with channel catfish and Snake River cutthroat trout.

Pueblo Army Depot is not open to the public. Military members, depot civilian employees, and their guests are the only people authorized to fish there. Fishermen must have a Colorado fishing license and the appropriate stamps prior to obtaining a Pueblo Depot Activity fishing permit.

The limit on Pueblo Depot Activity is eight fish per rod. Fishermen may use any method legal in Colorado to take fish. The use of live minnows as bait is prohibited.

Fishermen may use the reservoir year-round, except when it is ice-covered. No ice-fishing is allowed.

For more information on fishing the Pueblo Army Depot Activity, contact: Commander, Pueblo Depot Activity, ATTN: SDSTE-CFR, Pueblo, CO 81001-5000, phone (719) 549-4716 (7:30 A.M. to 6:00 P.M., weekdays).

ROCKY MOUNTAIN ARSENAL

- Near Denver
- Installation permit required
- Fishing

Fishing   Fishermen on Rocky Mountain Arsenal must have a Colorado license prior to obtaining a Rocky Mountain Arsenal fishing permit. The lakes on the installation are open for only six months of the year.

The waters and surrounding woodlands on Rocky Mountain Arsenal are used extensively by bald eagles. Access to the lakes is controlled so as not to interfere with the eagles' use of the lakes.

There are three lakes on the installation that range in size from about nine acres to ninety-four acres and that contain fish. The species of fish available are northern pike, largemouth bass, bluegill, bullhead, carp, green sunfish, yellow perch, and channel catfish. The bag limits and size limits are the same as for the state of Colorado.

For more information on fishing opportunities available at the Rocky Mountain Arsenal, contact: U.S. Fish and Wildlife Service, Rocky Mountain Arsenal, Bldg. 1111, Commerce City, CO 80022, phone (303) 289-0232.

Air Force Installations

PETERSON AIR FORCE BASE
BUCKLEY AIR GUARD BASE

- Near Colorado Springs
- Closed to the public
- Installation permit required
- Fishing

Fishing Both of these installations offer fishing only. Both are open only to military personnel and base civilian employees. A Colorado fishing license with the appropriate stamps is required by both installations prior to obtaining installation fishing permits.

Both installations have small ponds and streams stocked with brook trout, rainbows, cutthroats, and channel catfish. Creel limits and other regulations are the same as those for the state.

For more information on Peterson Air Force Base fishing opportunities, contact: 3SSW/SSRO/MWR, Stop 11, Peterson AFB, CO 80914-5000, phone (719) 7751/53.

For information on Buckley Air Guard Base, contact: Natural Resources Branch, Buckley Air Guard Base, CO 80011.

UNITED STATES AIR FORCE ACADEMY

> * Near Colorado Springs
> * 19,268 acres
> * Part of the National Park and Preserve System
> * Installation permit required
> * White-tailed deer
> * Fishing limited to Air Force Academy personnel
> * Camping

Hunting Big game hunting (there is no small game hunting) on the Air Force Academy grounds is a unique experience. It is open to the public, but getting a permit for the hunt is by lottery.

All hunters must have a valid Colorado hunting license prior to obtaining an academy permit. Additionally, hunters must attend a prehunt orientation. All hunters are required to check in and out at the hunter check station when going to and returning from hunting areas.

The only big game animal hunted on academy grounds is the white-tailed deer. Though other animals may be seen, they can't be hunted. Hunter success for whitetails on the academy is a whopping 50 percent. That's excellent by anyone's standards.

Any weapon legal for hunting deer in Colorado is legal on the Air Force Academy. Some areas have weapons restrictions due to their proximity to buildings and other activities.

Fishing Fishing is allowed on the Air Force Academy. The information I have available indicates access to fishing may be limited to Air Force Academy personnel.

There are several streams and impoundments on the academy stocked with rainbows, cutthroats, and brook trout. A Colorado fishing license is required prior to purchasing an academy permit.

Most Colorado fishing regulations apply to the academy. The only major difference is that the multiple-rod stamp legal in the state is not recognized on academy waters. Additionally, the creel limit on academy waters is six fish.

Miscellaneous There is camping on academy grounds in designated camping areas. Hiking is also a popular activity, as are nature photography and biking.

The topographic maps covering the United States Air Force Academy are the Pikeview and Palmer Lake quadrangles.

For more information on hunting and fishing at the Air Force Academy, contact: HQ USAFA/DEPN (Natural Resources Branch), USAF Academy, CO 80840-5546, phone (719) 472-3336.

FLORIDA

The state of Florida is seeking to protect its wildlife by purchasing land and thereby preserving valuable wildlife habitat against encroaching development. Wildlife is also protected in the several forests and parks spread across the state. The best news for hunters and fishermen, though, is the fact that the Department of Defense manages close to a million acres of land in the state. Most of that land is open to the public for hunting and fishing.

Air Force Installations

AVON PARK AIR FORCE RANGE

- 95 miles east of Tampa, bordered by Lake Arbuckle
- 106,210 acres
- Installation permit required
- Big game and small game
- Fishing
- Camping

Hunting This part of central Florida provides excellent habitat for several small game species, as well as deer and feral hogs. The land is a mixture of swamp, palmetto and oak bottoms, and pine-covered ridges. Big game hunting on this installation for eastern white-tailed deer and wild hogs is good.

Avon Park Range, like most installations, is divided into several hunting areas.

Some of these areas are open to the public, while others are open to military personnel only. There are fourteen separate hunting areas on the installation. Due to military operations, some of the areas may be closed from time to time.

All hunters must have the appropriate state and federal licenses before purchasing an Avon Park hunting permit. Avon Park hunting permits are available from the Natural Resources Office. There are several different types of permits available. A full hunt permit allows the holder to hunt every weekend during each hunting season, including archery, muzzleloading, general gun, small game, and spring turkey season. A limited hunt permit covers the same basic time periods, except the holder may not hunt the opening weekend of each of the deer seasons.

Centerfire and rimfire rifles are not allowed on the reservation. Hunters may take big game with shotguns, muzzleloading rifles, handguns with barrels less than nine inches, and archery tackle. The installation has designated areas where only bowhunting is allowed, even during the general gun season.

Though the seasons vary from year to year, the archery deer season generally runs from September 23 through October 22, muzzleloader deer season from October 28 through November 5, and the general gun deer season from November 18 through January 7. A small game season is held from January 8 through March 4. Spring turkey season is from March 17 through April 22.

Small game on Avon Park Air Force Range is bountiful. Hunters may hunt with shotguns, muzzleloading rifles, handguns with barrels less than nine inches, and archery tackle for cottontails, squirrels, quail, snipe, dove, and raccoons. The only varmints found on the installation are opossum and bobcat.

All hunters, whether after big or small game, must check in and out at the check stations located at either Morgan Hole Campground or Willingham Campground. When checking in, hunters may sign up for as many as three hunting areas. Authorized hunters are permitted to bring guests, but the guest must have a guest permit before going afield.

Fishing Fishing at Avon Park Air Force Range is excellent. Aside from Lake Arbuckle on the range's northwestern corner, Avon Park also has several other lakes, streams, and swamps. Before sampling the fishing, though, one must have a valid Florida freshwater fishing license and an Avon Park fishing permit.

The species available to anglers on Avon Park are largemouth bass, catfish, warmouth bass, redear sunfish, bluegill, and chain pickerel. Fishermen may also stumble across both longnose and alligator gar and the lowly carp. Fishing methods and bag limits match those of the state of Florida.

The bass found on Avon Park are the Florida strain, so be prepared for some heavyweights. Additionally, alligator gar grow to impressive proportions in Florida.

Miscellaneous Camping is permitted on the reservation. There are two public campgrounds on the range at Morgan Hole and Willingham. There is a group campground at Austin Hammock in the cantonment area.

Avon Park Air Force Range also offers miles of hiking trails, including a nature hike through the Sandy Point Wildlife Refuge. All the trails offer the beautiful central Florida flora and fauna. Yes, even including some king-sized alligators.

The topographic maps covering the Avon Park Air Force Range are all in the Florida 1:50,000 series. They are Lake Arbuckle, Lake Arbuckle—NE, Lake Arbuckle—SE, Fort Kissimmee, and Fort Kissimmee—NW.

For more information about the hunting and fishing on Avon Park Air Force Range, contact: Game and Fish Management, 56CSS/DEN, Avon Park AF Range, FL 33825, phone (813) 452-4119 (7:30 A.M. to 3:30 P.M., weekdays).

EGLIN AIR FORCE BASE

- 40 miles east of Pensacola
- 250,000 acres open to hunting and fishing
- Installation permit required
- Big game and small game
- Freshwater and saltwater fishing
- Camping

Hunting   Eglin is one of those installations where I've had the pleasure of being stationed. While I was there, it had one of the best game management programs in the United States. It is open to the public and offers some outstanding deer hunting.

The only two big game species legal to hunt on Eglin are the white-tailed deer and feral hog. Bag limits and seasons pretty well match those of the state, with a few exceptions. Huntable feral hogs must be at least fifteen inches at the shoulder. During the general gun and muzzleloading seasons, hunters may take only buck deer with one or more antlers at least one inch in length visible above the hairline.

Unlike most installations, at Eglin there is no need to sign in and out when going afield. The installation is divided into several hunting areas according to the type of weapon and hunting the hunter is doing. Some areas are archery only; others are open to still-hunting only. A few are open to hunting with dogs during the general gun season.

Centerfire rifles and pistols are not allowed for hunting on Eglin. Hunters may use rimfire rifles and pistols, excluding the .22 magnum, to take small game and varmints. Deer and hogs may be taken with muzzleloaders .40 caliber or larger with metallic sights only, shotguns shooting either slugs or buckshot, and archery tackle. Crossbows are legal during the general gun season only. All big game taken must be checked at one of the several hunter check stations on the reservation.

While hunter success on big game is rather low at 15 percent, that isn't a good indication of the amount of game available. I've sat on deer stands on Eglin and counted upwards of fifty deer during a single day. The trick to being successful at Eglin is finding the bottoms and thickets and hunting them hard.

Small game hunting on Eglin is also excellent. Hunters may take cottontails, squirrels, waterfowl, bobwhite quail, beaver, mink, otter, dove, and turkeys. Varmints can also be taken on the installation. You'll find raccoons, opossum, lots of armadillos, skunks, and coyotes on the reservation. Though you can't hunt them, fox also abound here, and you may even stumble upon a black bear or two.

Unfortunately, it is rather expensive to hunt this reservation. In addition to all the normal state and federal licenses, permits, and stamps, Eglin permits are also required. Prices are as follows: hunting permit, $35; dove permit, $5; small game permit, $10; archery stamp, $5; muzzleloading gun stamp, $10; trapping permit, $10; varmint/predator permit, $35. Dove and small game permits are not required if you hold a general hunting permit.

Hunters on Eglin must have proof of having completed a state-certified hunter safety course if born after January 1, 1970. In October 1991 the rule will change to include only those born after June 1, 1975. During the general gun season, muzzleloading guns season, and the small game season, hunters must wear a blaze orange coat or vest as an outer garment at all times when afield. Archers must also wear a blaze orange vest or coat when hunting during any of the above seasons if hunting outside an archery-only area.

Youngsters are allowed to hunt on Eglin, but those under sixteen must be under the direct supervision of an adult at all times. Hunters under sixteen do not need a permit for varmints or predators but must have one for other types of hunting.

Fishing With several lakes and ponds, over fifty miles of riverbank, and thousands of acres of beach shoreline, Eglin is a fisherman's paradise. Almost all the lakes and ponds on Eglin are stocked with one species or another, and the Yellow and Shoal rivers along Eglin's northern boundary contain all the indigenous freshwater fish found in this part of Florida. The waters of Choctawhatchee Bay and the Gulf of Mexico form Eglin's southern boundary.

Freshwater species found in the lakes and rivers of Eglin Air Force Base are bluegill, shellcracker, largemouth bass, catfish, carp, warmouth bass, pickerel, crappie, alligator gar, longnose gar, and several types of rough fish. The fishing is good and the regulations all match those of the state except for bag limits. All lakes on Eglin have a five-bass and ten-catfish limit.

Freshwater fishermen on Eglin must have a valid Florida freshwater license and an Eglin permit. The Eglin fishing permit is $12 a year and well worth the cost. Fishermen under sixteen do not need a permit on Eglin. I've never returned empty-handed from a fishing trip on this installation.

A permit is not required to fish the many miles of saltwater beach on Eglin. Here, the saltwater angler can find speckled trout, flounder, redfish, pompano, cobia, white trout, redfish, sheepshead, black drum, mullet, mackerel, snapper, and the occasional shark. Fishermen can use a boat or wade the warm waters of Choctawhatchee Bay.

Miscellaneous Camping on Eglin is permitted at any of several campgrounds. All the campgrounds are primitive and campers must obtain a $5 Eglin camping permit.

ATVs are not allowed on this installation, but that's not a problem. The reservation is crisscrossed with dirt roads and trails. Four-wheel drive is a good idea if you plan on taking off on any of the backwoods trails.

The Harold, Holt, Niceville, DeFuniak Springs, Holley, Fort Walton Beach, Villa Tasso, and Point Washington topographic maps in the 1:50,000 series quadrangles cover Eglin Air Force Base. They are a must if you plan to hunt on this installation. With them, your chances of success are increased by 100 percent!

Permits for all activities may be purchased either in person or by mail from Jackson Guard. Make money orders or cashier's check payable to the AFO Eglin AFB.

For more information on Eglin Air Force Base outdoor opportunities or to purchase a permit, contact: Jackson Guard, 107 Crestview Avenue, Niceville, FL 32578, or: Natural Resources Branch, 3200 SPTW/DEMN, Eglin AFB, FL 32542-5000, phone (904) 882-4164 (7:00 A.M. to 3:15 P.M., weekdays).

TYNDALL AIR FORCE BASE

- On the Gulf of Mexico near Panama City
- 18,000 acres open to hunting and fishing
- Installation permit required
- White-tailed deer and small game
- Freshwater and saltwater fishing
- Restricted camping

Hunting Tyndall Air Force Base is on an island in the Gulf of Mexico. It has a well-established and well-managed hunting program. The only big game animal on the installation is the white-tailed deer, and the deer hunting areas are generally very brushy, so hunting them is a real challenge.

Tyndall is divided into different hunting areas. Some are open to the public, while others are restricted to military personnel, retirees, their dependents, and other DOD personnel. The hunting areas are subdivided into special-hunt units, archery-only units, general-hunting units, and primitive-weapons units.

Anyone hunting big game on Tyndall must have the appropriate state license and stamps prior to purchasing the required Tyndall Air Force Base permits. Persons under sixteen or over sixty-five may acquire a free hunting and fishing permit, except for special hunts and early dove permits. The cost of Tyndall's permits are quite reasonable. Based on an individual's pay grade, they are as follows:

	E-4 and Below	All Others
Archery	$ 6	$10
Annual Hunting	12	20
Combination Hunt/Fish	15	25
Dove Hunting	6	10
Fishing	6	10
Special Hunt (DOD Only)	$6 per weekend	

Hunters under sixteen must have proof of completing a state-certified hunter safety course before obtaining a permit. Additionally, they must be accompanied in the field at all times by an adult.

Centerfire and rimfire rifles and handguns are not allowed on Tyndall for hunting. The only legal weapons for deer are muzzleloading rifles of .40 caliber or larger, shotguns shooting slugs or buckshot, and archery tackle. Crossbows are not allowed.

Hunters participating in the general gun, primitive weapons, and special hunts must wear a minimum of 500 square inches of blaze orange. Archers do not have to wear blaze orange if they are hunting during the archery-only season or in one of the archery-only areas.

Hunters are required to check in at a hunter checkpoint prior to going afield and upon returning. All deer taken must be checked in when taken during the archery season or one of the other seasons.

Most of the hunting areas on Tyndall, such as the archery-only and primitive-weapons areas, are open to DOD and military personnel only. During the general gun season, however, the East Range is open to the public. As usual, all hunters must have a Tyndall permit.

During the archery season, hunting is permitted daily from about October through the second week in November every year. The general gun deer season is from the day before Thanksgiving through the following weekend and from the second week in December through the middle of February. A special either-sex deer season is open each year only to DOD personnel the second weekend in December, the first weekend in January, and the last weekend in January. Except for archery season, hunting is permitted on Saturdays, Sundays, Wednesdays, federal holidays, Thanksgiving and the day after, and daily from the third weekend in December through the end of the month.

Small game except dove and waterfowl may be taken during the deer seasons. Dove and waterfowl may only be taken during the state seasons. The small game available on Tyndall are squirrels, waterfowl, quail, and dove. There are ten dove fields on the installation. Together they can accommodate up to 350 hunters. The regulations and bag limits match those of the state. Firearms regulations are the same for small game hunting.

Fishing Fishing is excellent at Tyndall. Not only can one take all the species found in the northern Gulf of Mexico but also bream, bass, crappie, and catfish from freshwater lakes on this installation surrounded by saltwater.

Many of the lakes on Tyndall are restricted to DOD personnel. A few are open to the public. All fishermen on the installation over sixteen must have a valid state license prior to obtaining a Tyndall fishing permit. Anglers sixty-five and older can get a free permit. No license or permit is required for saltwater fishing along the shores of the installation.

The legal methods of taking fish on Tyndall differ only slightly from state regulations. Trotlines or bush hooks are not legal on the installation. All other methods legal in the state are legal on Tyndall. Likewise, bag limits also pretty well match state guidelines, except for catfish. The limit for catfish on Tyndall is ten fish or ten pounds of catfish.

Miscellaneous Camping is not allowed on Tyndall, except military members using the base FAMCAMP. All-terrain vehicles are also illegal on the reservation. All vehicles must stay on known roads. No beach or cross-country driving is permitted.

For more information on the outdoor opportunities available at Tyndall Air Force Base, contact: 325 CSG/DEN, Natural Resources Office, Tyndall AFB, FL 32403-5000, phone (904) 283-2641 (7:30 A.M. to 3:30 P.M., weekdays).

Naval Installations

NAVAL AIR STATION CECIL FIELD

- Southwest of Jacksonville
- 17,000 acres open to hunting and fishing
- Closed to the public
- Installation permit required
- White-tailed deer, turkey, and small game
- Fishing
- Restricted camping

Hunting Seventeen thousand acres at Cecil Field and nearby Weapons Department (Yellow Water), Outlying Landing Field Whitehouse, and the Rodman Target Area are open to hunting and fishing. The excellent hunting and fishing programs on NAS Cecil Field are not open to the public but they are open to active duty military, their dependents, and retirees and their dependents.

The only big game found on any of the Cecil Field areas is the whitetail. The seasons match those of the state and all hunter safety requirements must be met.

All hunters on Cecil Field must have valid Florida hunting licenses and the appropriate tags prior to picking up their Cecil Field permits at the rod and gun club. Hunters over sixteen must have a state license and tags. All hunters must be at least twelve years of age. Hunters between twelve and sixteen must be accompanied by their military sponsor at all times.

Cecil Field itself is open to big game hunting with shotguns, muzzleloaders, or bow and arrow. The other areas—Whitehouse, Yellow Water, and Rodman—are all restricted to big game hunting by shotgun or bow and arrow. Cecil Field is divided into four hunting areas, A through D. Areas B and C also contain cattle, so hunters are urged to identify their targets carefully.

Hunters in Areas A and D of Cecil Field may take deer of either sex, except spotted fawns, when the appropriate state permits are obtained. All game taken must be checked at the main gate. Areas A, B, and C are open every day. Area D is open only on weekends. Hunters wishing to hunt in any areas of Cecil Field, except D, must check in at the main gate and sign out for the area.

Area D is a special-use area for bowhunting only. Hunters wishing to pursue deer in this area must gather at the rod and gun club for a safety briefing. No smoking is allowed in Area D. All hunters must surrender any flame- or spark-producing device prior to going afield.

At OLF Whitehouse, the regulations are much the same. No more than ten hunters are allowed in any area. There are three areas open on the facility. Area A is open seven days a week. Areas B and C may be closed at any time due to military necessity.

All hunters on OLF Whitehouse must meet the same requirements as those on Cecil Field. Shotguns are the only weapons authorized on this installation, and all hunters must check in and out at the crash shack before going and upon returning from the field.

The Yellow Water area is an ordnance-storage facility. Consequently, access is more controlled. It is a shotgun- and bow-and-arrow-only area. Hunters wishing to take deer on Yellow Water must go to the main gate at Cecil Field to exchange their Cecil Field permits for special passes.

At Yellow Water, hunters must surrender their passes to the Marine sentry at Post #1. The special pass and another issued by the sentry must be placed on the dashboard of the hunter's vehicle and displayed at all times. Hunters must surrender their passes upon leaving Yellow Water. All game taken must be reported at the main gate on Cecil Field.

The Rodman Target Area regulations are a little different. Here hunters must check in and out by phone with the range duty officer at (904) 778-5456/5457 or 759-2111. Check-ins may be done the day prior to hunting. Only twenty-five hunters are allowed in the Rodman Area at a time. Here, shotguns and bow and arrow aren't the only legal weapons. Hunters may also use rifles, except during the organized rod and gun club hunts.

Hunters with permission may stay overnight at Rodman. All the seasons legal in the state of Florida are legal on Rodman.

Small game hunters must meet all the same requirements as those for big game. Small game available on the Cecil Field complex are turkeys, cottontails, squirrel, and waterfowl.

Fishing There are several freshwater lakes and streams on the Cecil Field complex. All contain rough fish, largemouth bass, bluegill, and catfish. Florida regulations are enforced on Cecil Field. No special permit is required for fishing on Cecil Field or the outlying areas. However, certain areas require that a fisherman check in before going fishing.

Miscellaneous Camping is not allowed in most areas of Cecil Field. The only exception is the Rodman reservation, but prior approval is needed. Cecil Field does offer a recreation area with camping at Lake Fretwell. Again, it is only open to authorized personnel.

For more information on hunting and fishing at NAS Cecil Field, contact: Department of the Navy, Box 181, Naval Air Station, Cecil Field, FL 32215-5000, or MWR,

Naval Air Station, Cecil Field, FL 32215-5000, phone (904) 778-6112/13 (7:30 A.M. to 4:00 P.M., weekdays).

NAVAL AIR STATION PENSACOLA

- 16,500 acres
- Closed to the public
- Freshwater fishing
- Camping and boating

Fishing NAS Pensacola has four acres of freshwater fishing available to military members and retirees and their dependents as well as Department of Defense civilians. A state fishing license is all that's required to take the bream, bass, and catfish found in the station's freshwater pond. All fishing regulations are the same as those of the state; any method legal in the state is allowed on the installation.

Although the freshwater fishing at NAS Pensacola may be limited, saltwater angling opportunities more than make up for it. The station operates a recreation area, Oak Grove Park on the Gulf of Mexico, which offers fishing and camping right on the beach. A marina located at Sherman Cove provides eligible personnel with rental boats and motors, fishing tackle, and bait.

For more information, contact: Recreation Services, FMD Code 18222, Bldg. 1754, NAS Pensacola, FL 32508-5000, phone (904) 452-4515.

NAVAL AIR STATION WHITING FIELD

- Florida panhandle near the Florida-Alabama border
- 3,973 acres
- Closed to the public
- Freshwater fishing
- Recreation area on the Blackwater River

Hunting Hunting is not allowed at Whiting Field, but it is permitted at nearby Eglin Air Force Base.

Fishing Naval Air Station Whiting Field covers 3,973 acres, which includes the main part of the station and fifteen outlying landing fields. The station offers three acres of ponds for freshwater fishing. Species stocked in the ponds are bass, shell-cracker, bream, bluegill, and catfish. Angling is open only to military members and retirees and their dependents.

Aside from the ponds found on the station, the installation also has a recreation area along the Blackwater River that offers a small marina and fishing supplies. Fishing in the river can be excellent.

Miscellaneous Whiting Field offers a camping area, skeet range, and archery range.

For more information, contact: MWR Office, Bldg. 1464, NAS Whiting Field, Milton, FL 32570-5000, phone (904) 623-7502/03.

GEORGIA

Hunting in Georgia is like that across much of the South, on overcrowded wildlife management areas or by lease on private land. The picture is not all that gloomy, though. The Department of Defense has control of over 556,000 acres in the Peach State. Most of that is open to the public for hunting and fishing.

FORT BENNING

- South of Columbus on the Chattahoochee River
- 180,000 acres
- Closed to the public
- Installation permit required
- White-tailed deer, turkey, and small game
- Fishing
- Camping and boating

Hunting The only big game animal found on Fort Benning is the white-tailed deer. Fortunately they are found in excellent numbers. The hunter success rate on whitetails here is over 45 percent. That is one of the highest hunter success rates in the United States.

Fort Benning isn't open to the public for hunting and fishing. The only people authorized to hunt on Fort Benning are active duty military, retirees, their dependents, and Department of the Army civilians. Active duty members and retirees are allowed two civilian guests with them at a time.

All hunters over sixteen on Fort Benning must have a valid Alabama or Georgia state license. Alabama residents must have the Alabama license and Georgia residents must have a Georgia license. Both licenses are valid in all parts of Fort Benning open to hunting. All hunters born after January 1, 1961, must have a state-certified hunter safety course prior to receiving either a Georgia license or a Fort Benning permit.

Hunters between the ages of twelve and sixteen are allowed to hunt on the installation if they are under the direct supervision of their sponsor. Kids ten to twelve years old may go afield but cannot carry a weapon.

All weapons legal in Alabama or Georgia are legal on Fort Benning. Hunters may use centerfire rifles and handguns, muzzleloading rifles over .44 caliber, shotguns 20 gauge or larger with slugs, or archery tackle to take deer on the installation. Crossbows are prohibited on this reservation as are certain handgun calibers. All handguns must have a barrel length over five inches.

The seasons and bag limits generally follow Alabama and Georgia regulations. The only exception is that the season limit on deer is five, rather than the one per day in Alabama. Additionally, hunters may take no more than two bucks annually and no more than three deer can be taken with a firearm. The remaining two must be taken during the archery season.

Though technically not a big game animal, the eastern wild turkey is also found on Fort Benning in respectable numbers. The seasons match the state seasons and the permit requirements are the same. For both firearms deer and the general turkey season, hunter orange is required.

Upland game and varmints/furbearers are numerous on Fort Benning. Rabbit and squirrel seasons run from mid-November through the end of February with a limit of ten each per day. Quail, woodcock, and snipe have the same seasons but the limit is lower. Opossum and raccoon are found on this installation in huntable numbers. There is no limit on possum and the season is from mid-October to mid-February. Raccoon season is divided into two parts—mid-October through the end of November and December 1 through mid-February. The bag limits are one per day and no limit, respectively.

The license requirements for small game hunting are the same as for big game, with the exception of big game tags. Hunters may take small game with rimfire rifles and pistols, shotguns, archery tackle, and muzzleloaders smaller than .44 caliber. Please note, however, that small-bore muzzleloaders and rimfire rifles are not allowed during the general deer season.

Fishing Since Fort Benning is such a large installation in the southeastern United States, is encompasses literally hundreds of surface acres of water. All the waters contain fish of one type or another. The primary game fish found here are largemouth bass, bream, and catfish. The creel limits for these species are ten bass over twelve inches, fifty bream with no size limit, and eight catfish over twelve inches.

Fishermen must follow the regulations of Georgia and Alabama. In addition, Fort Benning regulations stipulate that trotlines can only be used in the Chattahoochee River, Upatoi Creek, Uchee Creek, Pine Knot Creek, and their tributaries. All trotlines in these waters must be marked with the owner's name, address, and telephone number. The lines must be checked once every twenty-four hours.

All fishermen on Fort Benning over sixteen must have the appropriate state license and an installation permit. Children under sixteen do not need either. Certain waters on the post are open to fishing by young fishermen only.

Miscellaneous Camping is allowed in the family camping (FAMCAMP) area of the post. Other campgrounds are available in the surrounding area. ATVs are not allowed on this installation. There are special regulations governing the use of boats with gasoline engines.

For more information on hunting and fishing at Fort Benning, contact: Outdoor Recreation Office, ATTN: ATZB-PAR, Fort Benning, GA 31905, phone (404) 545-4155.

FORT GORDON

* Southwest of Augusta
* 30,000 acres open to hunting and fishing
* Closed to the public
* Installation permit required
* Big game, turkey, and small game
* Fishing
* Camping

Hunting Fort Gordon offers the southeastern hunter an excellent opportunity to take either white-tailed deer or bear. The post has a large deer herd and hunter success is over 60 percent. The bag limits on deer are the same as those for the state of Georgia—generous.

Fort Gordon has 30,000 acres open to hunting. It is divided into numerous hunting areas. Hunters must sign in and out of hunting areas.

This installation is not open to the public. It is only open to active duty military personnel, their dependents, retirees, their dependents, Department of Defense civilians entitled to base support and their dependents, and DOD contractors and their dependents. All authorized hunters may have two bona fide guests hunting with them at a time.

Fort Gordon is another installation where rifles and handguns—both centerfire and rimfire—are not allowed for hunting. Hunters may take deer using muzzleloaders, shotguns 20 gauge or over, and archery tackle. The muzzleloaders cannot be scope-equipped. Shotgun hunters must use slugs for deer. Archery tackle must conform to state rules.

Small game hunting is allowed on the post. The eligibility requirements and firearms allowed are the same as those for big game, except that small game hunters must use shot smaller than #2.

The small game hunting should be good for cottontails, squirrels, quail, raccoon, and waterfowl. Hunters can also find excellent numbers of wild turkey on this installation. The seasons for all the game animals match those of the state.

All hunters on Fort Gordon must have the appropriate state and federal licenses and tags before purchasing a Fort Gordon permit. The costs of the hunting permits are as follows: hunting and fishing permit, $12; hunting permit (small game only), $7; big game tag, $10; and bona fide guest permit (daily), $5. Hunters must have a post hunting permit prior to purchasing a big game tag, and a guest permit is good for both big and small game.

Hunters must have proof of having completed a hunter safety course in accordance with Georgia regulations. All hunters sixteen and over must have the required state licenses. Hunters between twelve and sixteen may hunt on post if they have completed a hunter safety course. Twelve- to sixteen-year-olds must hunt within 300 yards of their sponsors.

Fishing The fishing and fisheries-management programs at Fort Gordon are excellent. The fort has no less than twenty-six lakes, and Brier Creek borders the southwest corner of the reservation. All the lakes are open to fishing at one time or another.

The fishing regulations generally follow those of the state, with a few exceptions. Some of the lakes are designated as catfish lakes. On these lakes, the creel and size limits differ from those of the state. Some of the other lakes have slot limits on bass.

In all of the lakes, anglers are limited to no more than two rods and lines. Bush hooks, trotlines, and jug-fishing are not allowed. Bait restrictions are also in effect on most of the lakes. Minnows are allowed on half of the lakes.

Access to fishing on Fort Gordon is the same as it is for hunting. All fishermen over age sixteen must have a valid state license prior to purchasing a post permit. Costs of the post fishing permits are $7 for a general fishing permit. A special catfish permit is required for certain lakes and costs $10 in addition to the basic post permit. Guest permits are $5 per day, good for all lakes and species.

Miscellaneous Primitive camping in designated areas is allowed on Fort Gordon. Some of the lakes are open to boating. The post is not open to ATV use and fire breaks are open to limited access only.

Fort Gordon is covered by the Augusta West, Grovetown, Blythe, Harlem, Avondale, and Bodens Pond topographic maps.

For more information on Fort Gordon, contact: Stephen C. Willard, Environmental/Natural Resources Management Office, Directorate of Installation Support, ATTN: ATZH-DIE, Fort Gordon, GA 30905-5040, phone (404) 791-2403/2459 (7:30 A.M. to 4:00 P.M., weekdays).

FORT McPHERSON/FORT GILLEM

- Near Atlanta
- Installation permit required
- Limited dove hunt
- Fishing

Hunting The only hunting authorized on forts McPherson and Gillem is a limited dove hunt conducted on Gillem every September and October. A special permit and a state license are required.

Fishing There are several small lakes on McPherson and Gillem containing catfish, bass, and bream. The licensing requirements are the same as for the state. All fishermen over sixteen must have a state license before purchasing an installation permit.

For more information on Fort Gillem and Fort McPherson, contact: ATTN: Mr. Henry Jameson, Equipment Center, Bldg. 366, Fort McPherson, GA 30330-5000, phone (404) 752-3535 (9:00 A.M. to 5:30 P.M., weekdays).

FORT STEWART

- 41 miles southwest of Savannah
- 290,000 acres
- Installation permit required
- Big game and small game
- Fishing
- Camping and boating

Hunting Fort Stewart offers the eastern big game hunter a variety of game. The installation has an excellent whitetail population and an ever-expanding population of feral hogs. The seasons are long and the bag limits are generous.

Fort Stewart is open to the public. While the fees for public hunting may seem a bit steep at first, they are considerably cheaper than fees for hunting on private land. The hunting-permit fees on Fort Stewart are as follows: hunting and fishing (military), $6 yearly; hunting and fishing (civilian), $84 yearly; hunting and fishing (DOD employee), $24 yearly; hunting and fishing (National Guard/Reserve), $44 yearly; hunting (civilian), $60 yearly; and one-day hunting (civilian), $15.

The big game regulations generally follow those of Georgia with one exception; feral hogs are considered big game animals on Fort Stewart.

All weapons legal for hunting in Georgia are legal on Fort Stewart. Some areas of the post are archery-only, while others may be restricted to shotgun-only. One minor difference between Fort Stewart and the state is the use of buckshot. Shotgun hunters on Fort Stewart must use slugs.

Fort Stewart and nearby Hunter Army Airfield are divided into 120 hunting areas. Some of those areas are restricted to archery hunting or shotguns. All the areas have a limited number of access permits available at any given time. Some areas may have only one permit while others may have dozens. All hunters are required to check in at the MSA Outdoor Recreation Pass and Permit Office prior to going to and upon returning from the field.

Prior to getting the Fort Stewart permits and passes, though, all hunters over sixteen must have a valid state license and the applicable state and federal tags, stamps and/or permits. Kids between twelve and sixteen are allowed to hunt on the reservation when accompanied by their sponsor/parent.

Hunter safety is a great concern on this installation, as it is on all DOD lands. Hunters must wear 500 square inches of hunter orange above the waist during the firearms and muzzleloader deer seasons. Additionally, alcoholic beverages are strictly forbidden afield. All big game hunters must check out with the pass and permit office no later than one and one-half hours after the end of legal shooting time.

All big game animals taken—deer, hogs, and turkey—must be checked at the outdoor recreation office. All game must be tagged immediately upon retrieval in the field. Immediately upon retrieval means tag it before you clean it.

The small game seasons on Fort Stewart coincide with the Georgia small game seasons. Waterfowl seasons are the same as those set by the state and federal governments. The small game on Fort Stewart are cottontails, squirrels, quail, dove, raccoon, possum, fox, and bobcat.

The licensing requirements for small game hunting are the same as those for big game hunting. The permits cover both types of hunting. Small game hunters must follow the same check-in and check-out procedures as big game hunters. Small game hunters are not required to wear hunter orange except during the general and muzzle-loader deer seasons.

Fishing There are dozens of ponds, lakes, and streams on Fort Stewart. All are stocked with fish of one type or another. The species found on this installation are largemouth bass, bluegill, redear, sunfish, black crappie, hybrid striped/white bass, catfish, and redbreast sunfish.

Fishing rules on Fort Stewart and Hunter Army Airfield generally follow those of the state of Georgia, with a few exceptions. All fishermen on Fort Stewart must have a Fort Stewart fishing permit in addition to a Georgia license if they are over sixteen. Additionally, most of the waters on Fort Stewart are considered "managed waters." That means they have special regulations for taking fish and the types of watercraft permitted. Generally, all managed waters are off limits to gasoline-powered boats. Boats with electric motors are okay.

Most fishing areas on Fort Stewart require fishermen to check in, just as the hunters do. Twenty-two of the areas do not require fishermen to check in, but all anglers must follow a specified route to and from the fishing area.

An annual civilian fishing license for the post costs $24; a one-day permit, $10. Military members pay $6 for an annual permit. Fishing licenses are available from the same place as the hunting licenses: the pass and permit office.

Bag limits generally follow those of the state. Fort Stewart anglers are allowed five largemouth bass over fifteen inches from managed waters and ten from unmanaged waters. Anglers may also take fifty bream or crappie, fifteen pickerel, five hybrids over fifteen inches, and ten catfish over ten inches.

Miscellaneous Camping is allowed on Fort Stewart. There are both a primitive campground and an improved campground at Holbrook Pond. The campground is open only to authorized individuals.

There are special rules governing the use of ATVs and horses on this installation. Special areas and trails are set aside specifically for each of their uses.

Topographic maps covering Fort Stewart are available from the Department of the Army. The map's title is: Edition 2-DMA, Series V7455, Sheet Fort Stewart.

For more information on the outdoor opportunities available at Fort Stewart and Hunter Army Airfield, contact: Directorate of Personnel and Communities, AFZP-PA, Outdoor Recreation, Pass and Permit Office, Fort Stewart, GA 31314-5000, phone (912) 767-5032 (10:30 A.M. to 6:00 P.M., Wednesday through Monday, or 5:30 A.M. to 9:00 P.M., Monday through Sunday, October through January).

Air Force Installations

MOODY AIR FORCE BASE

- 10 miles northeast of Valdosta
- 6,000 acres
- Closed to the public
- Installation permit required
- White-tailed deer and small game
- Fishing
- Camping and boating

Hunting The only big game animal found on Moody Air Force Base is the whitetail. The herd on the base is in excellent shape. The hunter success rate on Moody for whitetails is low at 10 percent, but that doesn't accurately reflect the chances available to the hunter.

Moody is not open to the public. The only people authorized to hunt on Moody are active duty military members and their dependents, retirees and their dependents, and DOD employees of Moody Air Force Base. Authorized hunters may have guests upon approval from the base commander.

All hunting on Moody is done from assigned stands. Stalking, except for the archery area, is not allowed. The hunting regulations match those of the state, including legal weapons, bag limits, hunter orange, and hunter safety course requirements.

Hunters after big game on Moody must register on the hunting roster no later than the last duty day preceding the hunt. No reservations are allowed. Access is strictly on a first-come, first-served basis. All hunters must check in at the Mission Lake Pavillion no later than one hour before sunrise. Hunters must also check in with the security police gate guard upon entering the installation with a weapon.

Stands are assigned on a draw system and hunters must print their name next to the applicable stand number on the sign-in board. Hunters leaving for the day sign out by erasing their names from the board.

Hunters going to their assigned stands must use approved trails that do not cross wildlife food plots. While on the stand, hunters must remain within 100 yards of their assigned stand until the morning or afternoon hunt has ended. They must not wander through the woods.

All hunters on Moody must have the appropriate state and federal license, tags, and stamps before purchasing a Moody Air Force Base hunting permit for $10. A combined hunting and fishing permit is $15. Hunters under sixteen or over sixty-five are not charged for a permit.

The success rate on small game is much higher than it is for big game. At 50 percent, Moody seems to be a pretty good place to take rabbits, squirrel, quail, mourning dove, raccoon, and waterfowl. Legal weapons for small game are the same as those allowed by the state.

The use of dogs is allowed for hunting all small game animals except raccoon. Dogs on a leash may also be used to track and recover wounded game.

Fishing   Fishing on Moody Air Force Base and the Grassy Pond Recreation Area is excellent. All the waters are stocked and well managed. In fact, Grassy Pond is a former U.S. Fish and Wildlife Service experimental station.

Access to fishing on Moody is the same as for hunting. All fishermen on the installation must have the applicable state licenses before purchasing a Moody Air Force Base fishing permit. The permits are inexpensive: $10, or $15 for a combined hunting/fishing permit. People under sixteen or over sixty-five can get a free permit.

The waters on Moody Air Force Base contain largemouth bass, channel catfish, bluegill, and crappie in addition to several species of rough fish. The creel limits on Moody are the same as those of the state, as are the legal methods of fishing.

Miscellaneous   Camping is allowed in the FAMCAMP on Moody and at the Grassy Pond Recreation Area. Access to camping is limited to those individuals specified in the hunting section.

There are some special regulations governing boating on Moody, so check the rules. ATVs are allowed on this installation, but they must be street-legal.

Topographic maps covering Moody Air Force Base are the Bemiss, Lakeland, Nalor, and Ray City quadrangles in the USGS 7.5-minute series.

For more information on hunting and fishing at Moody Air Force Base, contact: Randall D. Rowland, 347 CSG/DEEV, Moody AFB, GA 31699-5000, phone (912) 333-3070 (7:30 A.M. to 4:30 P.M., weekdays).

Naval Installations

KINGS BAY
NAVAL SUBMARINE BASE

- 40 miles south of Brunswick
- 1,000 acres open to hunting
- Closed to the public
- Installation permit required
- Deer, feral hog, and waterfowl
- Freshwater and saltwater fishing

Hunting Kings Bay has 1,000 acres open to both big game and small game hunting. The only two big game species found here are deer and wild hog. Both populations are in excellent shape, which makes big game hunting on Kings Bay exceptional, with a hunter success rate of over 40 percent. Small game hunting is limited to waterfowl.

Kings Bay is open only to military personnel, retirees, their dependents, and DOD civilians. All hunters on the installation must have a valid Georgia license and a Kings Bay permit. Hunters must be over sixteen, and must have completed a hunter safety course if born after January 1, 1961.

Kings Bay hunting regulations follow those of the state. The only major difference is in the weapons allowed. Big game and small game hunters on Kings Bay must use shotguns or archery tackle. Other firearms, including black-powder weapons, are not allowed.

Fishing Fishing is allowed on this installation. Again, access is limited to DOD civilians, military personnel, their dependents, retirees, and their dependents. All fishermen must have the applicable Georgia fishing licenses and an installation permit.

Kings Bay Naval Submarine Base offers both freshwater and saltwater fishing. Freshwater species available in the Saint Mary's River and other waters on base are largemouth bass, channel catfish, sunfish, bream, bluegill, and crappie. Saltwater species are those found in this part of the Atlantic.

Miscellaneous ATVs are not allowed on this installation. Neither is camping.

For more information on hunting and fishing at Kings Bay Naval Submarine Base, contact: Outdoor Recreation, N-83, Kings Bay Naval Submarine Base, GA 31547, phone (912) 673-2000 (Family Services).

Marine Corps Installations

MARINE CORPS LOGISTICS BASE ALBANY

- On the Flint River
- Installation permit required
- White-tailed deer and small game
- Fishing

Hunting Marine Corps Logistics Base Albany is open to the public for both big and small game hunting. The only big game available is America's most popular, the white-tailed deer. The hunter success rate is fair at 20 percent. There are 1,422 acres open to hunting.

All hunters on this installation must have a valid Georgia or Florida state license and the applicable tags prior to purchasing a base permit. Hunters under the age of sixteen must be accompanied by an adult at all times. The hunter safety requirements are the same as those for either Florida or Georgia, depending on which license you have. This installation allows the use of shotguns and archery tackle. No other firearms, or crossbows, are allowed.

With cottontails, squirrels, quail, and dove available, small game hunting is excellent by anyone's standards. Small game hunters must meet the same licensing requirements as big game hunters. Both big game and small game seasons and bag limits match those of the state. The only exception is that the fox squirrel is protected on this installation.

Fishing Marine Corps Logistics Base Albany also offers a well-managed fishing program. The waters of the installation contain catfish, bass, crappie, bream, and chain pickerel.

Licensing requirements for fishermen are basically the same as those for hunters—state licenses and an installation fishing permit are required. Fishing methods and creel limits are the same as those of the state with the exception of live bait, which is banned in all installation waters except Indian Lake.

Miscellaneous Camping and ATVs are not allowed on Marine Corps Logistics Base Albany.

The East Albany topographic map in the 7.5-minute series covers this installation.

For more information, contact: Natural Resources and Environmental Affairs Office, (Code 506), F&S Division, Natural Resources Manager, Marine Corps Logistics Base, Albany, GA 31704-5000, phone (912) 439-6261 (8:00 A.M. to 4:00 P.M., weekdays).

HAWAII

There are fifteen Army installations in the fiftieth state, ranging in size from the 29-acre Fort Ruger National Guard Headquarters in Honolulu to the 109,893-acre Pohakuloa Training Area on the island of Hilo.

Army Installations

POHAKULOA TRAINING AREA

* In the mountains of Hilo
* Bowhunting for pigs, goats, and sheep
* Shotgun hunting for quail, doves, and turkey

Hunting Pohakuloa Training Area (PTA), on the island of Hilo, is open for bowhunting only every weekend throughout the year. It is open to the public, and all hunters must have a standard Hawaii license. Game available includes pigs, goats, and sheep.

In December, January, and February, the PTA is open for bird hunting. Bird hunters may use shotguns, and they can expect to find quail, doves, and turkey, among many other varieties of birds.

Hunters must check in with the military police at PTA to show their license and weapons and to obtain a kill card. The area is patrolled by the military police to ensure cooperation with the rules.

Some weekends, certain areas of the PTA are used for training exercises and are unavailable for hunting.

Miscellaneous Occasionally, there are overnight stays for hunting parties at the PTA, but these are only open to military personnel or DOD employees. A state park adjacent to PTA has hunting lodges for civilians.

There is no fishing at the Pohakuloa Training Area.

For more information, contact: Commander, Headquarters, Pohakuloa Training Area, ATTN: Range Scheduling, APO San Francisco, 96559-5100, phone (808) 969-2410.

SCHOFIELD BARRACKS

- 25 miles north of Honolulu
- Closed to the public
- Limited hunting
- Wild boar
- Freshwater and saltwater fishing

Hunting Schofield Barracks is located twenty-five miles north of Honolulu on the island of Oahu. Wild boar hunting is permitted on the installation, but the only weapons allowed are knives and spears. Dogs may also be used when hunting boar. An attempt is underway to have Schofield Barracks reopened for hunting with traditional weapons, so check with them before you go.

Hunters need a hunting safety card and a Hawaii state hunting license. Nonmilitary personnel must be accompanied by a military sponsor.

Fishing Freshwater and saltwater fishing are available for those holding a Hawaii fishing license. Nonmilitary personnel must be accompanied by a military sponsor. Fishing is allowed at the East Range.

Freshwater fish varieties available include snakehead, largemouth and smallmouth bass, catfish, oscar, tucunare, and bluegill.

Marine life is abundant in the ocean. Some of the species you can expect to find in saltwater include kala, kumu, uku, ama'ama, sailfish, octopus, crabs, and lobster.

For more information, contact: Schofield Barracks Military Peace Company, U.S. Army Law Enforcement Command, Western Command, Schofield Barracks, HI 96857-5500, phone (808) 655-9510.

IDAHO

From the Snake River Plains in the south to the Cabinet Mountains in the north, Idaho is an outdoorsman's paradise. Much of the land is already in the public domain. There is only one major military installation in the state, Mountain Home Air Force Base.

Air Force Installations

MOUNTAIN HOME AIR FORCE BASE

- 118,579 acres
- Limited hunting at Saylor Creek Range

Hunting Mountain Home Air Force Base is a large installation, covering 118,579 acres. It has control over another 109,466 acres on the Saylor Creek Range. There is no hunting or fishing at Mountain Home, and hunting at Saylor Creek is by special arrangement only. Arrangements can be made through the range officer at Mountain Home.

The Bureau of Land Management controls millions of acres that surround Mountain Home AFB where public hunting is allowed.

For more information, contact: Mountain Home Rod and Gun Club, Mountain Home Air Force Base, ID 83648, phone (208) 828-6800.

ILLINOIS

There are six Army installations in Illinois. Two of them, Joliet Army Ammunition Plant and Joliet Army Training Area, are open to the public. Chanute Air Force Base offers fishing, but it is not open to the public.

Army Installations

JOLIET ARMY AMMUNITION PLANT

- 16,900 managed acres
- White-tailed deer
- Small game

Hunting There are 16,900 managed acres on the Joliet Army Ammunition Plant complex. Hunting on Joliet AAP for white-tailed deer is outstanding. Hunter success rate on Joliet AAP is a whopping 60 percent. That's good by anyone's standards but especially so in a heavily populated state like Illinois.

Hunters must have an Illinois license. The regulations were being revised as of this writing, so there may also be a fee. Check before you go. A limited number of civilians are allowed to hunt each day, but that also may be changed.

The main game hunted at Joliet AAP is white-tailed deer, but some upland game, including pheasant and rabbit, may also be hunted. The recommended annual take of white-tailed deer is 237. In 1988, the total take was 109 with shotguns and 41 with bow and arrow.

There is no fishing at Joliet AAP.

For more information, contact: Joliet Army Ammunition Plant, ATTN: Commander's Representative, Joliet, IL 60436-5000, phone (815) 424-2001.

JOLIET ARMY TRAINING AREA

- 4,200 acres open to hunting and fishing
- Adjacent to Joliet Army Ammunition Plant
- Installation permits required
- Deer and small game
- Fishing

Hunting   There are 4,200 acres open to hunting and fishing at Joliet Army Training Area, which is adjacent to Joliet Army Ammunition Plant but managed separately. In addition to having a state hunting license, hunters at Joliet Army Training Area must have an installation hunting permit for the game they wish to hunt. Permits are issued and controlled by the Fort Sheridan Department of Outdoor Recreation. Three types of permits are available: shotgun deer, archery, and sportsmen (for small game and fishing). Permits cost $8 each for active, reserve, and retired military members and $25 each for civilians.

One hundred permits for hunting deer with shotguns are issued by lottery in April or May of each year—seventy to military members and thirty to civilians. The number of archery and sportsmen's permits is not limited. Applications for permits may be obtained by writing to the address below and specifying which permit you want and whether you are a military member or a civilian. Military personnel should enclose a copy of their military ID card. Everyone should enclose a self-addressed, stamped envelope.

All hunters must sign in and out at the range control building. Rifles are not permitted at Joliet Army Training Area. Seasons and other regulations follow that of the state.

Rabbit hunting is especially good at the training area. Other small game available include pheasant, quail, fox, gray squirrel, waterfowl (ducks, geese, and coots), woodcock, snipe, rail, and crows. Premade duck blinds are available on a first-come, first-served basis and must be signed for at the range control building.

Fishing   Fishing is available in the Des Plaines River, which runs through the training area, but is usually not very good because of contaminants in the water. Species of fish in the river include smallmouth bass, bluegill, sunfish, bullhead, carp, and channel catfish. A sportsmen's permit is required to fish on the training area.

For more information and permit applications, contact: Outdoor Recreation, ATTN: Gene Jones, Fort Sheridan, IL 60037, phone (708) 926-6331.

Air Force Installations

CHANUTE AIR FORCE BASE

- 125 miles south of Chicago
- 2,000 acres
- Closed to the public
- Fishing
- Camping and boating

Fishing Fishing is allowed at the Rantoul Recreation Area, which is south of the base. The seventeen-acre lake is stocked with bluegill, channel catfish, redear sunfish, largemouth bass, and both black and white crappie.

The fishing is not open to the public. Active duty military personnel, their dependents, retirees, their dependents, and DOD civilians are the only people authorized access to the Rantoul area. All anglers over ten years old must have a base permit prior to going fishing. A state license is *not* required on this installation. Creel limits are three catfish over fourteen inches and three bass over fifteen inches on the lake. Creel limits for other species match those of the state.

Miscellaneous The base operates a camping area at Rantoul. Boats are allowed on the lake, but no gasoline engines may be used. Ice-fishing is not allowed in the winter.

For more information on this installation, contact: 3345 ABG/SSRO, Outdoor Recreation Office, Chanute AFB, IL 61868, phone (217) 495-3444 (7:30 A.M. to 4:30 P.M., weekdays).

INDIANA

While there are only a few military installations in Indiana, there are three major installations open to hunting and fishing. Altogether, they cover nearly 130,000 acres of prime hunting and fishing territory.

Army Installations

INDIANA
ARMY AMMUNITION PLANT

- Near Charlestown
- 6,300 acres
- White-tailed deer and small game
- Fishing not open to the public

Hunting   There are only 6,300 acres open to hunting big game and small game at INAAP. What it lacks in size, though, is more than made up for in quality and quantity of game.

The white-tailed deer is the only big game animal found on the installation. Deer hunting is well managed and only a specified number of deer are taken each year.

During the 1988–89 season, 200 whitetails were harvested on the reservation. There were 104 bucks taken and 96 does for a hunter success rate approaching 15 percent. The average field-dressed weight of *yearling* bucks was 117 pounds! That is an extraordinarily heavy weight for yearling bucks, indicating an extremely well-managed program.

Small game available on the reservation includes quail, squirrel, and the ubiquitous cottontail. Hunter success on small game is 100 percent. This reservation is an excellent place to introduce a young person to hunting.

Because it is an ammunition plant, there are some rather stringent rules associated with hunting on this installation. The installation is open to the public, but not on the same access level as for military and civilian employees. Military, civilian employees of the plant, retirees, and their dependents have access to hunting areas on the plant throughout the season for a $4 annual fee for small game and a $10 annual fee for big game. The public is authorized access on a daily basis for a $10 daily fee.

All hunters must check in and out at the assigned registration points, normally at Gates 2, 26, and 5. When checking in, hunters will be given maps of the plant and assigned a hunting area. The hunting areas are normally limited to ten or twenty hunters during the gun season, and more during the archery-only season. Hunters wanting to change areas must check through the registration point prior to moving.

While the hunting regulations on Indiana Army Ammunition Plant generally follow those of the state, there are some major differences. The only weapons allowed on the installation are shotguns, muzzleloaders, and archery tackle. Hunters may not bring any flame-producing device such as matches, cigarette lighters, or fire starters on the installation, which makes sense since the place makes explosives. Additionally, hunters must be extremely careful about where they are shooting. Shooting toward a bunker door can cost you your hunting privileges and maybe your life!

Young hunters eight and over are allowed to hunt on the INAAP as long as they are accompanied by an adult. A hunter safety course is not required by the installation or the state. Hunters over sixteen must have a state license and the appropriate tags before purchasing an INAAP small game or big game permit. The public is allowed to participate only in specified big game hunts on a daily basis.

Fishing Fishing is allowed on the installation but is only open to active duty military personnel, their dependents, retirees, their dependents, and civilian employees and their dependents. An INAAP fishing permit is $2 a year.

The plant has 3.5 miles of stream with 4.5 miles of shoreline, including seventy-five surface acres of water. The waters contain bass, catfish, redear sunfish, bluegill, and crappie. The creel limits and general regulations follow those of the state.

Miscellaneous Access to the Indiana Army Ammunition Plant is strictly controlled. Vehicles are subject to search at all times. The people in the security section at the plant are very serious about their jobs. *Do not* joke with them about starting fires or having matches. It can get you into serious trouble.

The topographic maps covering the Indiana Army Ammunition Plant are the Charlestown and Jeffersonville quadrangles in the 7.5-minute series.

For more information on hunting and fishing at the Indiana Army Ammunition Plant, contact: Capt. Joseph P. Eddy, SMCIN-XO, Indiana Army Ammunition Plant, Charlestown, IN 47111-9667, phone (812) 284-7814 (7:30 A.M. to 4:00 P.M., weekdays).

JEFFERSON PROVING GROUND

- 55,264 acres
- Closed to the public except for white-tailed deer hunting
- Installation permit required
- White-tailed deer, turkey, and small game
- Fishing
- Camping
- Restricted boating

Hunting Jefferson Proving Ground is open to hunting for both big and small game. The only big game found here is the white-tailed deer. Small game animals found on the post are squirrels, cottontails, quail, dove, turkey, raccoon, and waterfowl.

Hunter success for deer on Jefferson Proving Ground is pretty high at 30 percent. Small game hunters bat .500 on this installation.

This installation is not generally open to the public. However, the state of Indiana has a cooperative agreement with Jefferson Proving Ground for a drawing-permit hunt for deer on the installation each year. Anyone holding a state license and submitting an application is authorized to participate in this hunt. Otherwise, public access to JPG is not allowed.

JPG is open during the entire season to eligible personnel. Active duty military personnel, retirees, civilian employees, and veterans with a 100 percent disability are allowed access with their dependents to hunt and fish. Additionally, those eligible may have up to three guests at a time.

All hunters on the installation must check in and out when going afield. During the general deer season, the hunter checkpoint is located at the Old Timbers Lodge. During the archery and small game seasons, hunters check in at the security office in Building 149. All hunters must stay in their assigned areas when afield. If a hunting party wishes to change areas, they must check back in with the hunter checkpoint prior to switching.

For safety considerations, all hunters must hunt in groups of at least two. Sponsors must stay with their hunting parties at all times. A hunter safety course is required to hunt on this installation. Additionally, all hunters must not touch any metal object they may find in the field. This is a weapons proving ground. They test things here that are designed to kill people. If you don't know what it is, don't touch it!

In the event of an emergency or short-notice closure of an area, a vehicle will drive around the hunting unit sounding the alarm with a horn or siren. Upon hearing the warning notice, all hunters must exit the area and go to the hunt checkpoint.

During the general deer season, hunters must wear a blaze orange vest or jacket. An orange cap is also advised. Bowhunters may wear camouflage clothing during the archery season.

Hunting regulations generally follow those of the state. Small game animals may be taken with rimfire rifles, shotguns, archery tackle, and muzzleloading rifles. Deer may only be taken with archery tackle, muzzleloaders over .44 caliber, and shotguns of 20 gauge or larger. Crossbows are only authorized for handicapped hunters.

All hunters on JPG must have the appropriate state licenses prior to purchasing a JPG permit. Up to two deer may be taken on the installation, providing the hunter has the appropriate two-deer license.

There are albino deer that are protected on the Jefferson Proving Grounds. Do not shoot or in any way harass them. Piebald (partial albino) deer may be taken.

No alcohol is permitted in the field on Jefferson Proving Grounds. Even non-hunters in a party are prohibited from consuming or possessing alcoholic beverages in the field.

Loaded guns in a vehicle, including detachable clips containing cartridges, are prohibited at all times. Handguns are not authorized for hunting on this installation and they may not be carried in the field.

Fishing Fishing is authorized at Jefferson Proving Ground. It is open only to those specified in the hunting section. It is not open to the public. Anglers are required to have the appropriate state licenses to qualify for a JPG fishing permit.

There are numerous ponds, lakes, and streams on the installation. Almost all are open to fishing year-round. Fishermen, like small game hunters and bowhunters after deer, must check in with the security office prior to going fishing.

The waters of Jefferson Proving Ground contain a variety of freshwater species, with everything from largemouth bass to crappie and walleye. The creel limits are generous and match those of the state. Methods of fishing also match state regulations.

Miscellaneous   There are special regulations governing boating on JPG. Generally, outboards or gasoline engines of any type are not permitted. All boats used on the installation must contain at least two adults when afloat, and the rated capacity of the boat must not be exceeded. Each boat must have a personal flotation device for every person on board.

Camping is allowed on the installation with both primitive and modern camping sites available. ATVs are not authorized, but horses are.

The topographic maps covering Jefferson Proving Ground are the San Jacinto, Clifty Falls, Versailles, Rexville, and Holton quadrangles. The maps are available from: Division of Public Information, 612 State Office Building, Indianapolis, IN 46204.

For more information and complete rules on hunting and fishing at Jefferson Proving Grounds, contact: Kenneth G. Knouf, Supervisory Natural Resource Manager, STEJP-EH-R, U.S. Army Jefferson Proving Ground, Madison, IN 47250, phone (812) 273-7436 (8:00 A.M. to 4:00 P.M., weekdays).

Naval Installations

NAVAL WEAPONS SUPPORT CENTER CRANE

- 70 miles south of Indianapolis
- 50,395 acres open for hunting and fishing
- Small game hunting closed to the public
- Installation permit required
- White-tailed deer and small game
- Fishing
- Camping closed to the public

Hunting   Big game hunting on Naval Weapons Support Center Crane is strictly for white-tailed deer. Fortunately, all big game hunting on the installation is managed by the state through a lottery-style drawing. That means that everyone, military and civilian alike, has the same chance of being drawn for an installation permit.

Small game hunting is open only to the center's military and civilian employees and their dependents. Military and DOD retirees are also allowed to hunt small game on the installation. Small game hunters should have a smorgasbord of animals to pursue. Species available are cottontails, squirrels, quail, grouse, turkey, dove, and waterfowl.

All hunters on the installation must have a valid state license and the appropriate tags. Small game hunters must have a Weapons Support Center permit.

The center is divided into thirty-five hunting areas covering 50,395 acres. Only a certain number of hunters are allowed into any area at a given time. Consequently, all hunters must check in at the hunt headquarters prior to going afield.

Hunters after big game on the reservation may use black-powder weapons, shotguns in 20 gauge or larger, and archery tackle to take their deer. Hunters must abide by all state safety regulations, including bag limits and wear hunter orange.

Small game hunters must follow the same rules as those after big game. Hunter orange is not required.

Fishing The center is open to the public for fishing and other water sports. Fishermen must have the appropriate state licenses prior to purchasing either a yearly installation permit for $15 or a weekly permit for $5.

The permits are well worth the cost. Lake Greenwood, the installation waterway open to the public, is a large body of water with excellent fishing for largemouth bass, bluegill, crappie, channel catfish, redear sunfish, white bass, and other species.

All state regulations apply to the center. Creel limits, fishing methods, and boating regulations all follow those of the state.

Miscellaneous Travel to and from Lake Greenwood is by specified route only. Smoking is prohibited while on the installation because of the stored munitions.

Camping and waterskiing are allowed on this installation. Camping is open only to center personnel. ATVs are not permitted, except by special permission for handicapped hunters and fishermen.

Naval Weapons Support Center Crane is a heavily forested installation. It's easy to get lost here, so good maps are a must. The topographic quadrangles covering the installation are Kolsen, Owensburg, Williams, Indian Springs, Shoals, Odon, and Scotland.

For more information on this installation, contact: Mr. Lynn Andrews, Natural Resources Manager, Naval Weapons Support Center, Crane, IN 47522-5009, phone (812) 854-1165 (8:00 A.M. to 4:00 P.M., weekdays).

IOWA

IOWA ARMY AMMUNITION PLANT

- Near Middleton
- 13,000 acres open to hunting and fishing
- Installation permit required
- White-tailed deer, turkey, and small game
- Fishing

Hunting   The Iowa Army Ammunition Plant is open to the public for both big and small game hunting. All hunters on the installation must have a valid Iowa license and the appropriate tags in addition to Iowa Army Ammunition Plant permits. The permits cost $5 for military members and retirees and $8 for civilian employees and the public.

Big game hunting for white-tailed deer on the reservation is excellent, with a hunter success rate of 60 percent. The deer herd is so large, in fact, that the Iowa Department of Natural Resources allowed hunters to take two deer each during the 1988–89 hunting season. The deer are large, as well. The average field-dressed weight of yearling bucks is about 115 pounds. That means a large, mature whitetail from this reservation could exceed 200 pounds.

Small game hunting is also good here, with the species normally found in this part of the country being the preferred game. Turkey hunting on the installation is especially good, with sixty gobblers taken in 1988.

All hunters must abide by Iowa hunting regulations as well as the installation's check-in and check-out procedures. Deer hunters must use 20-gauge or larger shotguns with slugs, black-powder rifles over .45 caliber, or archery tackle on this installation. Rifles and handguns are not allowed.

Fishing Fishing is allowed on the installation. Public permits for fishing at Iowa Army Ammunition Plant are $5.50 and military permits are $2.50. All fishermen must have the applicable state license before purchasing an installation permit.

The Iowa Army Ammunition Plant has over twenty-one miles of stream and 110 surface acres of water in ponds with a total shoreline of nine miles. All the waters contain game fish of some sort, from bass to bream.

For more information, contact: Iowa Conservation Commission, Wallace State Office Building, Des Moines, IA 50319.

KANSAS

Kansas is known throughout the hunting world for its excellent upland game hunting. Recently, it has been featured in the outdoor media as a place to take monster white-tailed deer and for its outstanding fishing.

Most of Kansas is privately owned. Still, the Kansas Department of Wildlife and Parks does an excellent job of maintaining public hunting areas around the state. The KDWP manages sixty-nine public hunting areas ranging in size from the 80-acre Barber Wildlife Area to the 15,714-acre Milford Wildlife Area. The federal government administers another eight areas totaling 150,660 acres.

That may sound like a lot of land, but it isn't when it's compared to the number of people who hunt and fish in the state. Fortunately, the Department of Defense is able to add another 110,000 acres or so to that total.

Army Installations

FORT RILEY

- Near Junction City
- 68,000 acres open to hunting and fishing
- Installation permit required
- Limited big game hunting
- Small game
- Fishing
- Camping
- Restricted boating

Hunting There are roughly 68,000 acres of wildlife habitat open to hunting on Fort Riley. Those 68,000 acres are open to the public on a limited basis. All Kansas residents and active duty military personnel and their dependents stationed in Kansas are allowed to hunt big and small game on Fort Riley. Nonresidents may hunt only small game and migratory waterfowl.

The big game on Fort Riley are white-tailed deer, mule deer, and elk. Whitetails on Fort Riley grow to truly impressive proportions. Since 1980, three have placed well in the Boone and Crockett record book. With an excellent management program, the mule deer also grow large. Though not as numerous as whitetails, some of the mulies may soon place high in the records. Elk were introduced in the mid-1980s and the herd is healthy and growing at a good rate. No exact figures are available on elk harvest as yet. Overall hunter success for all species of big game is 40 percent.

Small game hunters will find a paradise on Fort Riley. The 68,000 open acres contain exceptional populations of squirrels, pheasant, quail, cottontails, dove, and waterfowl. The eastern wild turkey was introduced on the installation in 1984 and 1985, and its population should reach a huntable level by the time this book is in print.

One note on the turkeys—in Kansas and on the post the wild turkey is considered a big game species. Consequently, nonresident hunters may not hunt them.

All Kansas Wildlife and Parks regulations apply on Fort Riley. All hunters must have the appropriate Kansas licenses and tags before purchasing the special Fort Riley permits. In accordance with state regulations, hunters born after July 1, 1957, must have a hunter safety course certificate prior to purchasing a license. Hunters under sixteen are not required to purchase a hunting license but must carry with them in the field proof of having completed a hunter safety course. Children under sixteen are not allowed to hunt big game on Fort Riley.

The hunting seasons on Fort Riley generally follow those of the state. The only exceptions are the deer and elk seasons, which are scheduled around troop training activities. All state bag limits and tagging requirements are enforced on the post.

All hunters on the installation must check in and out at the self-service hunter checkpoint. While there, hunters must fill out cards indicating where they are hunting prior to going afield. Upon returning, hunters must complete a harvest survey indicating the type of game taken.

Post permits are inexpensive at $10 for hunting, $15 for a combination, $25 for a conservation permit, and $10 each for deer and turkey permits. Deer and turkey permits are currently issued through a state lottery. Hunters must apply for the permits during the state application period.

Fishing Fort Riley offers extensive and well-managed fishing. The post's waters are stocked or naturally contain every species of fish from largemouth bass to rainbow trout and pike. The post is open to public fishing and all regulations generally follow those of the state.

Creel limits on Fort Riley match those set by the state, but minimum size requirements vary slightly. On Fort Riley, all largemouths under fifteen inches must be returned to the water. In Funston Lake and Moon Lake, all pike under thirty inches must be released. All white amurs caught on the installation must be released.

All anglers between sixteen and sixty-four years of age must have a valid Kansas fishing license and a post permit before going fishing. Fishermen of all ages after rainbow trout in Cameron Springs must have a post trout permit.

The post fishing permits are $10. A combination permit for hunting and fishing is $15. A conservation permit is $25 and the post trout permit is $10.

Fishing is permitted twenty-four hours a day at Fort Riley, except at Cameron Springs, which is open only from sunrise to sunset. All anglers should check with the natural resources branch before going fishing to be sure an area isn't temporarily closed for military activities.

Trotlines are legal in the free-flowing waters on Fort Riley but may not be used in ponds. Bowfishing for nongame species only is allowed in Marshall, Whitside, and Funston lakes and in all free-flowing streams. Spearguns and scuba gear may not be used for fishing on Fort Riley.

Miscellaneous There are certain boating restrictions in effect on Fort Riley. ATVs are not authorized for use on the post. Camping is allowed, but there are no designated campgrounds. All camping is primitive, with no hookups or facilities.

For more information on hunting and fishing on Fort Riley and maps of the post, contact: Natural Resources Branch, AFZN-DE-N, Bldg. 1020, Fort Riley, KS 66442, phone (913) 239-6211/6669 (7:30 A.M. to 4:00 P.M., weekdays).

KANSAS
ARMY AMMUNITION PLANT

- Near Parsons
- 13,000 acres
- Closed to the public
- Big game and small game
- Fishing

Hunting Both big and small game animals are hunted on the Kansas Army Ammunition Plant. During the 1988 season, small game hunters harvested 864 quail, 316 doves, 39 ducks, 73 squirrels, and 40 rabbits. Big game hunters took 11 deer with archery tackle.

The plant is not open to the public. The only people allowed to hunt here are employees, active duty military personnel, their dependents, and guests. Deer hunting is closed to everyone except plant employees. All hunters on the plant must have a valid Kansas hunting license and the appropriate tags and a plant permit.

All state bag limits and season dates apply to the plant. The plant is not open to big game hunting with any type of firearm. Deer hunters must use archery tackle. Small game hunters may use shotguns with shot smaller than #4.

All hunters must check in and out through the Security Office at Gate 1 prior to going afield and upon returning.

Deer hunters had a 35 percent hunter success rate during the 1988 season. The average weight for a field-dressed yearling buck was 115 pounds.

Fishing Fishing on the Kansas Army Ammunition Plant is restricted to person-nel normally allowed access to the plant. There are fifty-one ponds on the plant stocked with fish. Fishermen must have a valid Kansas fishing license and a plant permit and must check through the security office before going fishing.

In 1988 anglers took 3,500 keeper-sized fish and 139 bullfrogs from the plant's waters. Fishing success was 100 percent.

For more information, contact: Day & Zimmerman, Inc., Kansas Division, Kansas Army Ammunition Plant, Parsons, KS 67357.

SUNFLOWER ARMY AMMUNITION PLANT

- Near De Soto
- Fishing

Fishing The Sunflower Army Ammunition Plant covers less than 10,000 acres. The plant does not offer any hunting. Fishing is limited to a three-and-one-half-acre impoundment stocked with bass, catfish, and bluegills.

All Kansas fishing regulations apply on the plant. Fishermen must have both a Kansas license and an installation permit. Fishing is only allowed during the daytime.

For more information, contact: Sunflower Army Ammunition Plant, ATTN: SMCSU-OR (M. J. Cornella), P.O. Box 640, De Soto, KS 66018-0640, phone (913) 791-6733 (8:00 A.M. to 4:00 P.M., weekdays).

Air Force Installations

McCONNELL AIR FORCE BASE

- Near Wichita
- 41,555 acres
- Closed to the public
- Installation permit required
- Fishing

Fishing Fishing is allowed at McConnell Air Force Base and is open only to active duty military personnel, military retirees, active duty dependents, retiree dependents, and base civil service employees and their dependents.

McConnell has two small fishing ponds next to the base golf course. The ponds are stocked with largemouth bass, catfish, and bluegill. The fishing regulations follow those of the state. All anglers on McConnell must have the applicable state licenses and a base fishing permit.

No boating is allowed on the ponds. Trotlines and bush hooks are also not allowed.

For more information on fishing at McConnell, contact: 384 CSG/SSRR, McConnell AFB, KS 67221, phone (316) 652-4003 (7:30 A.M. to 4:30 P.M., weekdays).

SMOKY HILL AIR FORCE RANGE

- South of Salina
- 22,000 acres open to hunting and fishing
- Closed to the public
- Big game, turkey, and small game
- Fishing
- Camping

Hunting Smoky Hill is open to hunting for both big and small game. Because it is an active range, access is open only to National Guard, reserve, active duty, and retired military personnel, their dependents, and guests. Each person authorized unescorted access is allowed to have up to three guests at a time. All hunters born after July 1, 1959, must have proof of having completed a hunter safety course. Hunters under eighteen must be accompanied at all times by their sponsors.

Big game found on the Smoky Hill Range are mule deer and whitetails. The deer herds are in good shape, as indicated by a 30 percent annual hunter success rate. Unlike most installations, deer hunters on Smoky Hill are allowed to use the weapons of their choice, provided they meet Kansas state law.

There are 22,000 acres open to hunting on Smoky Hill Range. Aside from the mule deer and whitetails found on the range, there are thirteen species of small and upland game here. Hunters may also take cottontails, squirrels, pheasant, quails, varying hare, prairie chickens, turkeys, coyotes, bobcats, raccoons, badger, beaver, and skunk. The only catch is that small game is not allowed to be taken during the deer season.

All hunters on Smoky Hill must have a valid Kansas hunting license and the appropriate tags and stamps before obtaining a trespass permit for the range. Hunter safety is a prime concern on the range. Consequently, all deer hunters during the gun season must wear a blaze orange vest. Camouflage orange garments are not allowed. All small game hunters must wear a blaze orange hat when going afield. Deer permit holders (both firearms and bow) must attend a briefing prior to deer season. The place and time of the briefing are announced no less than two weeks before the briefing.

Trespass permits are good for only two consecutive days. Only a certain number of hunters are allowed in an area at a time. All hunters must check in and out daily at the range headquarters, and hunters must hunt in the areas they have chosen or check back through range headquarters prior to changing areas. Successful hunters must immediately tag their kill and check it with range headquarters.

The use of alcohol while hunting or handling firearms on the range is strictly forbidden. It makes sense. Booze and guns mix just about as well as booze and gasoline.

Fishing There are numerous lakes, ponds, and streams on the Smoky Hill Range. All of them contain fish of some sort. The premier species are largemouth bass, catfish, bluegill, and white amur. The white amur was stocked in a few of the ponds to help control vegetation.

Fishing on Smoky Hill is closed to the public. Fishermen must meet the same eligibility requirements as hunters and meet the licensing requirements set by the state. No fishing permit for the range is required, but fishermen, like hunters, must obtain a trespass permit from the range headquarters prior to fishing.

All Kansas fishing regulations apply to Smoky Hill Range except one. Trotlines are not allowed on the installation.

Miscellaneous Since Smoky Hill Air Force Range is an active range, certain restrictions apply as to where and when one may go afield. There is a clearly marked weapons drop zone in the center of the range. The drop zone is assumed to be active daily from 8:00 A.M. to 4:30 P.M. Just because you don't see aircraft flying, don't assume the drop zone is safe.

Camping is allowed on the reservation. There are no established camp sites and all camping is primitive. Campers must meet the same eligibility requirements as hunters and anglers.

The topographic maps a hunter or angler may need on Smoky Hill Air Force Range are in the USGS 1:27,500 series. They are: Marquette, Series V778, Sheet 6461 III; Ellsworth, Series V778, Sheet 6361 II; and Brookville, Series V778, Sheet 6461 IV.

For more information on hunting and fishing at Smoky Hill Air Force Range, contact: M. Sgt. Steven C. Shinn, Resource Management, Smoky Hill Air Force Range, 8429 W. Farrlley Rd., Salina, KS 67401-9407.

KENTUCKY

Most of the military installations in the Bluegrass State are too small to offer hunting and fishing. Fortunately, two Army installations are open to sportsmen. Together, they cover almost 250,000 acres of Kentucky countryside.

Army Installations

FORT CAMPBELL

- Between Hopkinsville, Kentucky, and Clarksville, Tennessee
- 75,000 acres open to hunting and fishing
- Installation permit required
- White-tailed deer, turkey, and small game
- Fishing
- Camping

Hunting   Of the 105,397 acres that make up Fort Campbell, up to 75,000 may be open at any time to hunting. Fort Campbell is open to the public. Hunters on Fort Campbell may take white-tailed deer, eastern wild turkey, squirrels, rabbits, waterfowl, and quail.

All hunters on Fort Campbell must have the appropriate state licenses. Kentucky residents may use their Kentucky resident licenses to hunt on the post, and Tennessee residents may use their Tennessee resident licenses. Nonresidents of either state may use a nonresident license issued by either Kentucky or Tennessee.

All hunters must have a post permit in addition to a state license. The post permits are inexpensive at $2 for military members and retirees or $13 for the public.

Hunters under sixteen are required to have a junior license issued by Kentucky or Tennessee. All hunters born after January 1, 1969, must have proof of a hunter safety course. Those under sixteen may hunt small game but not big game, except during youth hunts held early in the season every year.

Before going afield, all hunters must have a copy of the post's area assignment form, available from the hunting and fishing unit of the outdoor recreation branch. Hunters may reserve an area by picking up the area assignment form the day prior to going hunting. The form must be picked up in person. Phone reservations are not accepted.

The hunting areas are divided into weekday and weekend assignments. Weekday hunts are authorized on Monday, Thursday, and Friday on a first-come, first-served basis. Weekend hunts are based on a drawing from all applicants.

All types of legal firearms except handguns are authorized for hunting on Fort Campbell. Rifles are allowed only in certain areas during certain periods of the general deer season. Bows are allowed during the archery-only season and in certain areas during the gun season.

Bag limits and general hunting regulations vary by the type of state license a hunter holds. If the hunter has a Kentucky license, Kentucky's rules and bag limits apply. If a Tennessee license is held, then Tennessee rules apply.

Hunter success at Fort Campbell is not outstanding but pretty good. Small game hunters average 20 percent on the post, while big game hunters are successful about 5 percent of the time.

Fishing Fishing is good on Fort Campbell. Anglers may take any species normally found in this part of the country, including bass, bluegill, crappie, and catfish. The installation has miles of open water for fishing, so overcrowding should not be a problem.

All anglers on the post must have a valid state license, the same as hunters, and a post permit. The fishing permit is $2 for military and civilians. The same rules apply to fishing as to hunting. Anglers must follow the fishing regulations of the state that issued their licenses—Kentucky or Tennessee.

Kids under sixteen and senior citizens over sixty-five do not need a state fishing license, but they must have a post fishing permit.

Miscellaneous Camping is allowed only in the FAMCAMP areas of Fort Campbell. It is not authorized around the reservation. ATVs are authorized only for hunting by the handicapped. ATVs may be used to retrieve downed game.

Maps for the installation and more information on hunting and fishing at Fort Campbell may be obtained by contacting Outdoor Recreation, Virginia Salyer, Hunting and Fishing Unit, AFZB-PA-CR-O, Fort Campbell, KY 42223-5000, phone (502) 798-2175 (7:30 A.M. to 4:00 P.M., weekdays).

FORT KNOX

- North-central Kentucky on the Indiana-Kentucky border
- 109,000 acres
- Installation permit required
- Big game, turkey, and small game
- Fishing
- Camping closed to the public
- Restricted boating

Hunting Fort Knox is open to the public on a priority basis. This means that military members, retirees, military dependents, retiree dependents, and Department of the Army civilians all have priority over the public during the deer season. But don't despair; few civilian hunters are turned away every year. Access to small game hunting is not a problem.

Deer hunting on Fort Knox is good, with a hunter success rate of 30 percent. Mature whitetails here average 150 to 200 pounds live weight, and good bucks are entirely possible.

The eastern wild turkey is the only other big game animal found on Fort Knox. While turkeys are by no means "big," most states treat them as big game, with a season. Kentucky and Fort Knox are no different. Turkey hunting regulations on the installation match those of the state, though the exact season dates may vary.

Fort Knox is divided into 112 hunting areas. Like most installations, only a limited number of hunters are allowed into any area a time. The areas are in effect during the bow season, the general gun season, and the small game season. All hunters must go to the outdoor recreation hunt control office in Building 9333 no more than two days prior to the day they desire to hunt and obtain area clearance. All hunters are required to check in at control points prior to going afield. Hunters must also call the hunter checkpoint when returning from the field, unless big game is taken. If a hunter takes a big game animal, he or she must go to the check station in person.

All hunters on Fort Knox must have a valid Kentucky license prior to purchasing a Fort Knox permit. There are three different types of permits. One is for small game, the other two are for deer—one for bowhunting, the other for firearms hunting. The cost of the permits is $15 each for military members and $25 for civilians.

While most of the Kentucky regulations apply to the fort, all of them do not. The limit on deer at Fort Knox is one per season, either with a gun or a bow. Firearms are also restricted at Fort Knox. Weapons allowed are shotguns over 20-gauge shooting slugs and black-powder rifles over .38 caliber. Bows and arrows must meet state rules.

Civilian deer hunters, both bow and gun, are selected by a drawing. Hunters must apply for a tag in August each year. For more information on application procedures, please contact the hunt control office at Fort Knox.

Small game abounds on Fort Knox. Hunters may take cottontails, squirrels, waterfowl, quail, and raccoons. Small game hunters may use .22 rimfire rifles for most species. Small game hunters must check in at the hunt control office.

Youngsters under sixteen may hunt both big and small game on Fort Knox. There is a special big game hunt for youths only early in the season. Young hunters must have a junior hunting license if they are residents of Kentucky. Otherwise, they must have proof of having completed a state-certified hunter safety course.

All hunters on Fort Knox must have proof of completing a hunter safety course. Proof of completion must be presented when purchasing a permit.

Fishing   Fort Knox has the finest trout fishing in the Commonwealth of Kentucky. Other species found on the installation are catfish, largemouth bass, bluegill, rock bass, and crappie. There are numerous lakes, ponds, and streams on the post. All are open to fishing.

Fishermen on Fort Knox must have a valid Kentucky fishing license and a post permit if they are between sixteen and sixty-five. Anglers under sixteen and over sixty-five may fish without a state license but must have a valid post permit, issued free.

All Kentucky fishing regulations apply to Fort Knox. Several of the lakes on Fort Knox have special restrictions that go beyond those of the state. On the managed lakes, live bait fish are prohibited, trotlines are illegal, and anglers may not use more than two fishing rods. On the remaining unmanaged lakes, all state rules apply.

Miscellaneous   There are special boating restrictions in effect on all the managed lakes on Fort Knox. On these lakes, electric trolling motors and paddles are the only means of propulsion allowed. The motors cannot exceed four horsepower or forty-one pounds of thrust. On the unmanaged waters, motors can be no more than ten horsepower.

Camping on this installation is limited to military personnel and retirees only. There are three campgrounds available, one modern and two primitive.

ATVs are allowed in certain areas of the installation. A permit is required, and riders must complete an approved safety course. Hunting areas 8 through 14 are open to ATV use.

For more information on hunting and fishing at Fort Knox and a comprehensive pamphlet and map of the installation, contact: Community Recreation Division, Outdoor Recreation Hunt Control Office, ATZK-CFR, Bldg. 9333, French Range, Fort Knox, KY 40121-5000, phone (502) 624-7311 (7:30 A.M. to 4:30 P.M., weekdays).

LOUISIANA

Louisiana is rightfully known as the "sportsman's paradise." I know, I grew up there. Like most states, though, things are changing down on the bayou. The area where I used to hunt has been developed for housing tracts. Millions of acres of hardwood bottom lands have been plowed under to plant soybeans.

The Louisiana Wildlife and Fisheries Commission, in an incredible show of foresight, has purchased prime tracts of wildlife habitat throughout the state. Additionally, the Department of Defense owns almost 300,000 acres of land in the state.

Army Installations

FORT POLK

- Near Leesville
- 198,325 acres
- Installation permit required
- Big game and small game
- Fishing

Hunting Hunting on Fort Polk is managed by the state. All state rules and regulations apply. Fort Polk is open to the public and is managed like all the other wildlife management areas in the state.

All hunters on Fort Polk must have a valid Louisiana hunting license, the appropriate tags, federal stamps, and a Fort Polk hunting permit prior to going afield. The regulations on the fort match those of the state, except for the season dates, which, due to training requirements, differ from those of the state.

Hunters are required to get daily clearance to hunt. All hunting, except for the either-sex deer permits, is by a self-clearing permit system. Hunters may register for the self-clearing permit once a year. The either-sex deer permits are issued daily at the hunter check stations.

Besides the whitetails available here, hunters may also take feral hogs during the deer season. These hogs grow to impressive proportions in Louisiana and make a worthy trophy. No special tag is required.

The small game seasons and regulations match those of the state, except that the small game season is closed during the deer season. Small game hunters use the self-clearing permit system. Small game hunters must have a post permit.

Fishing   The post is open to the public for fishing. All state licensing rules apply. Each body of water on the post is managed differently. Rules are posted at each entrance.

Anglers on the post must have a post permit and a state license. The permits are available from the same office as the hunting permits.

Louisiana has a variety of fish available to the angler. Though some of the species are typically not thought of as sport fish, try one on the end of your line and you'll change your mind.

Miscellaneous   Camping is not allowed on Fort Polk except for military personnel. ATVs may be authorized in certain areas. Any area may be closed at any time for military activities.

For more information on hunting and fishing at Fort Polk, contact: Outdoor Recreation Branch, Bldg. 7803, North Fort Polk, LA 71459, phone (318) 535-5715/5255 (7:30 A.M. to 4:30 P.M., weekdays).

Air Force Installations

BARKSDALE AIR FORCE BASE

- Near Shreveport–Bossier City
- 18,000 acres open to hunting and fishing
- Installation permit required
- Big game and small game
- Fishing
- Restricted camping

Hunting   Barksdale is open to the public for hunting both big and small game. Hunters on the base must abide by Louisiana licensing requirements and have a Barksdale Air Force Base permit.

Most of the base's seasons match those of the state. The exception is the deer season. During the general deer season, the base sets a separate fifteen-day hunt within the dates of the general season. Hunters may use firearms to take deer on base during that fifteen-day period only. Hunters may take up to three deer, but no more than one a day.

Hunter success for deer and turkey is pretty good on the 18,000 acres of Barksdale that are open. Small game hunter success rates are even higher. Small game seasons match those of the state, and the bag limits are the same.

Hunters born after January 1, 1969, must have proof of completing a hunter safety course before purchasing a base license. All hunters allowed unescorted access to the base must complete the base hunter safety course.

There is no minimum age limit to hunt on Barksdale, but hunters under sixteen must be accompanied by an adult at all times when afield.

Hunters are not required to sign in and out on Barksdale except when they are hunting during the general deer season. Deer hunters must sign in and out of areas daily. This procedure is DOD-wide to ensure hunter safety.

Fishing Barksdale is open to public fishing. All the state licensing requirements must be met before purchasing a base permit. All state rules apply on base as to fishing methods and creel limits.

The species available on Barksdale are largemouth bass, spotted bass, channel catfish, white bass, black crappie, bluegill, bream, redear sunfish, yellow catfish, alligator gar, spotted gar, smallmouth buffalo, largemouth buffalo, carp, and bowfin. Bowfishing is allowed in accordance with Louisiana fishing regulations, as is frog hunting.

Miscellaneous Camping is allowed on this installation in both primitive and modern campsites. Camping privileges are extended only to military members, retirees, DOD civilians, and their dependents.

ATVs are restricted to a 900-acre section of the base. ATVs must be registered and the rider must have proof of completing a training course.

For more information on hunting and fishing at Barksdale Air Force Base, contact: 2 CSG/DEMN, Base Conservation Office, Barksdale AFB, LA 71110, phone (318) 456-2231/3353 (7:30 A.M. to 4:30 P.M., weekdays).

MAINE

Much of Maine is still pristine wilderness dotted with small towns and villages. The state offers vast tracts of wilderness. Spruce, fir, and northern hardwood forests cover much of the northern and western sections of this 31,885-square-mile state. Many of these forests are privately owned but open to the public for hunting and fishing. In the more populous southern and eastern areas of the state, most of the privately owned land is posted and hunting and fishing are not allowed.

Both the Navy and the Air Force have major installations in Maine. Only two of the eight installations are open for hunting and fishing.

Air Force Installations

LORING AIR FORCE BASE

* 8 miles east of Caribou, near the Canadian border
* 5,000 acres open to hunting and fishing
* Installation permit required
* Big game and small game
* Fishing
* Camping

Hunting Loring Air Force Base is open to the public for hunting. It offers over 5,000 acres of prime wildlife habitat containing white-tailed deer, moose, black bear, squirrels, waterfowl, pheasant, grouse, snowshoe hare, and woodcock. Those 5,000 acres are divided into eight hunting areas with controlled access.

All hunters on Loring AFB must have a valid Maine hunting license and a Loring AFB land-use permit, available for $2. No hunter safety course is required to get a Loring AFB land-use permit as of this writing, but that may change. Hunters on Loring Air Force Base must use either shotguns or archery tackle. Rifles, handguns, muzzle-loaders, and crossbows are not allowed. Hunters must be at least ten years old to go afield on Loring. Those between ten and seventeen must be accompanied by an adult at all times while hunting.

During the big game seasons, only four hunters are allowed in any hunting area at a time. Reservations are not allowed for the hunting areas and access is strictly on a first-come, first-served basis. The big game seasons follow those of the state but are subject to emergency closure when the desired number of animals has been taken.

During the hunting season, the law enforcement desk in the security police building runs the hunter sign-in process. Hunters must sign in to a hunting area in person at the desk. No more than four hunters are allowed in a hunting party in one area and all members of the group must sign in.

Upon completion of hunting, hunters must check back in with the law enforcement desk. Successful big game hunters must do so in person. Unsuccessful hunters may phone in.

Small game hunters face the same restrictions as big game hunters. All hunters must sign in for specific areas at the law enforcement desk and check out upon returning. Small game seasons match those of the state.

Due to the size of the hunting area, the big game hunter success rate at Loring is low. Still, hunters willing to put in the hours scouting and hunting should be success-ful. Small game hunting is good at Loring. Most small game hunters return with game.

Fishing Fishing, like hunting, is open to the public at Loring Air Force Base. Fishermen must have a valid Maine license and a Loring Air Force Base land-use permit prior to wetting a line.

The base has some ponds and streams stocked with eastern brook trout. Catfish and rough fish may also be taken here. The creel limit on trout is five per day. Creel limits on the other species match those of the state.

Fishermen on Loring may use either artificial or live bait. Multiple lines, trotlines, or bush hooks are not allowed.

The fishing seasons and general regulations are the same for Loring AFB as they are for the rest of Maine, with one exception. Trout fishing on Loring is closed for one week after trout are stocked.

Miscellaneous ATVs are allowed on Loring Air Force Base. In fact, snow-mobiles and three- and four-wheelers may be the best way to get around on this installation in the winter and spring. All ATVs and snow machines must be registered with the state of Maine and have insurance as required by state law. The areas author-ized for snowmobile and ATV use change from year to year, so a prospective user should get a copy of the current regulations. Snowmobile and ATV riders must use the same safety equipment as motorcycle riders.

Camping, both primitive and RV, is allowed on the reservation. Overnight camp-ing is not allowed in the hunting areas during the hunting seasons. The different types of camping have various fees. Campers must register with the outdoor recreation branch.

Loring is covered in the Limestone and Caribou quadrangles of the USGS topographic maps.

For more information on hunting and fishing at Loring AFB, contact: Mr. Dave Hopkins, 42 CES/DEEV, Loring Air Force Base, ME 04751, phone (207) 999-2257 (8:00 A.M. to 4:00 P.M., weekdays); or Base Game Warden, 42 SPS/SPB, Loring AFB, ME 04751, phone (207) 999-6214/2412 (8:00 A.M. to 4:00 P.M., weekdays).

Naval Installations

NAVAL COMMUNICATION UNIT CUTLER

- East of Machias
- 2,999 acres
- Closed to the public
- Installation permit required
- White-tailed deer and small game
- Freshwater and saltwater fishing
- Camping

Hunting NAVCOMMU Cutler is not open to the public. The only people authorized to hunt and fish on this installation are active duty and retired military members, civilians employed at NAVCOMMU Cutler, and their dependents.

Hunters at NAVCOMMU Cutler are allowed to take white-tailed deer and small game. All hunters must have a valid Maine hunting license and proof of completing a hunter safety course recognized by the state of Maine. Hunters under eighteen must be accompanied by an adult at all times. All hunters at NAVCOMMU Cutler must have an installation permit.

Both deer and small game may be hunted with shotguns and archery tackle only. Hunters may not use rifles, handguns, muzzleloading firearms, or pneumatic weapons at NAVCOMMU Cutler. Hunters using shotguns for deer must use 00 buckshot only. Slugs are not allowed. Archery tackle must meet the requirements set by the state of Maine. Crossbows are not allowed.

There is no season hunting permit at NAVCOMMU Cutler. Permits are issued daily by Guard Post 1. Hunters must pick up a permit at Guard Post 1 prior to going afield and turn in the permit when they are finished for the day. All kills must be reported and logged at Guard Post 1.

Hunter access is well controlled here. No more than fifteen small game permits and ten deer permits are issued at a time. There are never more than fifteen hunters in the field.

The hunting areas on NAVCOMMU Cutler are set up according to species and weapons. For example, in certain areas only small game may be taken either with a shotgun or bow and arrow. In others, only archery hunting is allowed. No hunting is allowed in the high-frequency (HF) antenna area. The HF area may be used for access to the wooded area behind it when permission is obtained from the check-in/check-out station.

Hunter orange is required on this installation. All hunters must wear it, including bowhunters and duck hunters. Bowhunters and duck hunters, however, may remove their hunter orange garments when they reach their stands or blinds.

Deer hunting is good at NAVCOMMU Cutler. The hunter success rate is right at 10 percent. That's high when you consider that the hunting area covers only 2,500 acres.

Small game hunters at NAVCOMMU Cutler have excellent success on rabbits, squirrels, and partridge. Predator hunters occasionally take coyote and fox. Waterfowl hunting is outstanding since the installation lies in the middle of the Eastern Flyway and the base maintains duck blinds around the shores of the peninsula.

Fishing Fishing, like hunting at NAVCOMMU Cutler, is restricted to those authorized. There are two freshwater fishing areas and one saltwater area.

The freshwater areas, Huntley Creek and the station reservoir, are stocked with eastern brook trout. Saltwater species available are all those found in this part of Maine.

All fishermen on NAVCOMMU Cutler must have a valid Maine fishing license. A station permit is not required for fishing.

Miscellaneous ATVs are not allowed on this installation. Camping is allowed, but only four unimproved campsites are available.

Naval Communications Unit Cutler is covered by the 909362 through 909367 series of general development maps.

For more information on NAVCOMMU Cutler hunting and fishing opportunities, contact: J. W. Robinson, Guard Supervisor, Naval Communications Unit Cutler, East Machias, ME 04630-1000, phone (207) 259-8265, Code 13 (7:30 A.M. to 4:00 P.M., weekdays).

MARYLAND

Maryland has a rich hunting and fishing history. Commercial waterfowl hunting has flourished here. Visitors still come to shooting resorts along Chesapeake Bay to sample the fabulous waterfowling.

While most of the state has been developed and is in private hands, there are still places to fish and hunt. The Department of Defense has control over 110,000 acres of land in Maryland. Much of that land is open to hunting and fishing.

Army Installations

ABERDEEN PROVING GROUND

- 50 miles northeast of Baltimore
- 55,000 acres open to hunting and fishing
- Closed to the public
- Installation permit required
- Big game and small game
- Freshwater and saltwater fishing
- Camping

Hunting The 55,000 acres open to hunting on Aberdeen Proving Ground provide a unique opportunity for the East Coast hunter. The installation is open to both big and small game hunting, with certain restrictions. It is not open to the public, but members of the public may hunt on Aberdeen Proving Grounds as guests of authorized hunters.

According to Aberdeen Proving Ground regulations, authorized hunters are active duty military members, dependents entitled to an Armed Forces identification card, military retirees, Department of the Army APG civilians and their immediate families, retired Department of the Army APG civilians, and contractor employees under a multiyear contract with APG. Only active duty military personnel assigned to Aberdeen Proving Ground, retired military personnel, APG Army civilians, and retired APG civilian employees may bring guests to hunt. Each sponsor can have up to three guests. A guest hunter may have no more than two sponsors during the hunting seasons.

All hunters on Aberdeen Proving Ground must have the applicable state and federal licenses, tags, and stamps. All hunters must also have a STEAP-SS Form 54 (Hunting/Trapping) issued by outdoor recreation in Building 3507. The permits cost $5 per season for juniors under sixteen, seniors over sixty-five, and the handicapped. A multiple-season permit is available for $7. All other hunters pay $10 for a season permit and $15 for a multiple-season permit. The price of the permit is the same for both civilian and military hunters.

By 1:00 P.M. on the last work day prior to the desired hunting day, all hunters must submit an application for a hunting area. This rule applies to both big and small game hunters. All hunters must also have proof of successfully completing a state-certified hunter safety course prior to purchasing a permit.

At Aberdeen Proving Ground hunters after deer and wild turkey must show proof of competency with their weapons prior to having their permits validated. Both archers and gun hunters must pass shooting competency tests.

The bowhunting competency test is given by the Aberdeen Proving Ground Bowmen's Club board of directors. Before taking the test, bowhunters must have a hunting permit. Upon successful completion of the test, the STEAP-SS Form 54 is validated for bowhunting.

Bowhunters must use compound bows with a minimum peak draw of thirty-five pounds, or longbows and recurves with a minimum draw weight of thirty-five pounds. Broadheads must have at least a seven-eighths-inch cutting diameter. Arrow shafts must be marked with the hunter's first initial and last name. Crossbows are not allowed. Bowhunters may stalk deer in certain areas.

The gun hunter competency test is conducted at all deer checkpoints. To qualify, gun hunters must shoot five shots at a deer silhouette from forty yards. Three of those five shots must be in the twelve-inch kill zone marked on the silhouette. Two of the three kill-zone hits must be consecutive. Hunters must fire their own weapons and ammunition for the test. Once a hunter qualifies, gun hunters' STEAP-SS Form 54 is validated for deer hunting.

Gun hunters are allowed to use only shotguns in 10, 12, and 20 gauge with slugs or black-powder rifles over .44 caliber. Rifles, either centerfire or rimfire, handguns, and shotguns with buckshot, are not allowed.

Deer hunters on APG are allowed up to three deer. One of those deer must be antlerless. The other two can be whatever the hunter chooses. Deer taken on APG do not count against a hunter's total limit in the state.

Gun hunters after deer must hunt from assigned stands or shooting positions. Stalking is not allowed. Each hunter is assigned a stand and a clearly identified field of fire. Hunters must stay on their stands and only shoot within their field of fire.

All deer taken must be field dressed in the woods. The APG tag must be attached immediately and the deer taken to the nearest deer checkpoint. Entrails must be either covered with leaves or buried.

The seasons for deer and turkey generally follow those of the state. Extensions on the season may be granted to reach the required harvest. Hunter success on deer at APG is almost 20 percent. Not bad for a heavily populated state like Maryland.

Small game hunting on Aberdeen Proving Ground is excellent, but, again, there are some restrictions. Small game hunters must apply for a hunting area, just like deer hunters. While small game hunters are not required to pass a shooting competency test, they must have a hunter safety course under their belts.

Small game on Aberdeen Proving Ground are cottontails, squirrels, pheasant, quail, and waterfowl. Fox, raccoon, opossum, and groundhogs are also hunted here under varmint regulations.

Fishing Aberdeen Proving Ground is open to fishing but has severe restrictions on fishing access. Fishing is limited to authorized personnel and is divided into two types of access. Fishing is allowed in industrial areas and in security areas. The only people allowed in security areas, however, are those with the required security clearance.

Aberdeen Proving Ground provides both freshwater and saltwater fishing. The lakes and streams on the installation contain largemouth bass, crappie, yellow perch, and catfish. The bay areas on APG contain stripers, speckled trout, bluefish, and the other species found in northern Chesapeake Bay.

All fishermen must have an Aberdeen Proving Ground license and appropriate state licenses prior to wetting a line. All state rules and regulations apply. Creel limits are the same as for the state.

Miscellaneous A limited amount of camping is permitted on Aberdeen Proving Ground for authorized individuals. No ATVs are allowed and access to the installation is strictly controlled.

United States Geological Survey 7.5-degree quadrangles of Edgewood, Perryman, Spesutie, Gunpowder, and Hanesville cover Aberdeen Proving Ground.

For more information on the hunting and fishing at Aberdeen Proving Ground, contact: Community Recreation Branch, STEAP-PA-FR-P, Bldg. 3507, Aberdeen Proving Ground, MD 21005-5001, phone (301) 278-4124 (10:00 A.M. to 5:00 P.M., Monday through Thursday; 10:00 A.M. to 7:00 P.M., Friday; 7:00 A.M. to 3:00 P.M., weekends).

FORT GEORGE G. MEADE

- Midway between Washington, D.C., and Baltimore
- 13,745 acres
- Installation permit required
- White-tailed deer and small game
- Fishing

Hunting Fort Meade is open to the public for all hunting activities. All hunters after big and small game must have a valid Maryland hunting license and a post permit. Waterfowl hunters must have the mandatory federal duck stamps, as well. Big game hunters on Fort Meade must have valid Maryland big game tags in addition to the other requirements.

The only big game found on Fort Meade is the white-tailed deer. While the hunter success rate is low, between 3 percent and 8 percent, don't let that fool you. I've hunted Fort Meade and know that if you are willing to put forth the effort, you can be successful there. In fact, I saw one of the prettiest white-tailed bucks there that I have ever seen.

All hunters must check through the hunter control point before going afield and upon returning. The hunting areas on the post are strictly controlled to improve both the quality of hunting and its safety. A limited number of hunters, whether after big or small game, are allowed into any area at a time.

Modern rifles and handguns are not allowed in the hunting fields on Fort Meade. Hunters after both big game and small game must use shotguns or muzzleloaders. Crossbows are also not allowed on this installation, but normal archery gear is legal. In addition to the normal licensing requirements on Fort Meade, however, archery deer hunters must also pass a shooting competency test. The test is administered by personnel at the hunter control point.

These tests are becoming fairly common at controlled hunting areas throughout the nation. The tests usually consist of shooting at an animal silhouette at an unknown distance. Archers must be able to put their arrows into an unmarked kill zone on the target to qualify.

Small game hunters on this installation are in for a surprise. The small game hunting here can be excellent for cottontails, waterfowl, quail, and dove. It's only moderate for the eastern gray squirrel.

Varmint hunters should do well. Crows are abundant at Fort Meade. Hunters may also take foxes, bobcats, coyotes, and raccoons. Some night hunting is allowed for raccoons and foxes. When night hunting, hunters must check through the military police station before going afield.

All state hunting rules apply. Hunters under eighteen must have written permission from a parent or legal guardian prior to getting a post permit. All hunters must be at least fourteen years old.

Hunting permits for all hunters are available at the hunting control point in Building T-04. The control point is open from September 1 through the third Saturday in December. Its hours are from one hour before to one hour after legal daylight. From the fourth Saturday in December through the second week of January, the hunting control point is open from 7:00 A.M. to 3:30 P.M. daily.

Fishing You wouldn't expect good fishing in a heavily populated area like this part of the East Coast, but good it is! There are several lakes, ponds, and streams on the installation. The primary game fish found on the fort are largemouth and smallmouth bass, crappie, chain pickerel, bluegill, and channel catfish. Fishermen may also take carp and suckers on the installation.

All the rules applicable in the state are enforced on Fort Meade. Fishermen must have state licenses and a post permit prior to fishing. State creel limits apply to all species.

Some lakes are within the boundaries of active firing ranges, so fishermen must check with range control before going out. The ranges are normally quiet on weekends, so getting access is no problem.

Fishing permits are available from the outdoor recreation equipment issue center in Building 940. The hours are 7:30 A.M. to 5:00 P.M., Monday through Friday.

Miscellaneous Camping and ATVs are not allowed on the installation.

Fort Meade has an extremely active and well-run rod and gun club. The club sponsors special pheasant hunts for club members. It also has a retail store and rifle, skeet, and trap ranges.

Hunting and fishing maps of Fort Meade are available free from the hunting control point or outdoor equipment issue branch.

For more information on hunting and fishing at Fort Meade, contact: Natural Resources Management Office, DEH, Fort George G. Meade, MD 20755, phone (301) 677-3966 (7:30 A.M. to 4:00 P.M., weekdays).

Naval Installations

NAVAL AIR TEST CENTER PATUXENT RIVER

- 50 miles southeast of Washington, D.C., on the Chesapeake Bay
- 7,127 acres
- Closed to the public
- Installation permit required
- Big game and small game
- Freshwater and saltwater fishing
- Camping and boating

Hunting Naval Air Test Center Patuxent River, more commonly referred to as Pax River, is not open to the public. The public may hunt there as guests of authorized individuals and must be escorted at all times. Authorized individuals include active duty and retired military members, their dependents, federal civilian employees of the installation, and federal civilian retirees of the installation and their dependents.

All hunters on Pax River must hold valid Maryland licenses and stamps in addition to the installation permits. Hunters must also have proof of completing a hunter safety course recognized by the state of Maryland. Authorized hunters can receive a yearly permit. Guests of authorized hunters must have permits issued daily. House guests of authorized hunters may receive weekly permits. Permits are available from the morale, welfare, and recreation athletic director's office in Building 458, Room 8, Monday through Friday.

As is the case with almost all military installations, Patuxent River is divided into hunting areas. There are eighteen, each with a cap on the number of hunters allowed at one time. The hunting areas are strictly controlled and hunters must sign up for an area by species to be hunted.

On the opening days of firearms deer and dove seasons, hunting areas are filled by a lottery drawing. Applicants submit a pass request, and the successful applicants are notified prior to opening day. After opening weekend, hunters may sign up daily for areas.

Upland game hunting on Pax River is a little different. Hunters may reserve an area for upland game (rabbit, quail, and woodcock) up to a week in advance. Upland game hunting is only allowed on Monday, Thursday, and Saturday. On those days, hunters may use an area for half a day solely for upland game hunting. The area is closed to all other hunters until the hunting party with the reservation clears the field. Morning hunts for upland game must be completed by noon, and afternoon hunters must be out of the field one-half hour after sunset.

Raccoon and opossum may be hunted on the reservation on Friday and Saturday nights only. Legal hunting hours are from sunset to sunrise.

Waterfowl hunting on the installation is also available on a reservation basis. Hunters must reserve an area and sign for it prior to going afield. They also must sign out at the hunting checkpoint after returning from the field. Hunter success for waterfowl and upland game on Pax River is excellent at 80 percent.

Deer hunting is also excellent at Pax River. The installation is almost overrun with whitetails, and the hunter success rate is very high at 50 percent. Both archery and firearms hunting are allowed for whitetails, but there are some special rules.

In addition to signing in and out, bowhunters must also pass a shooting competency test prior to receiving an archery deer hunting permit. The test consists of shooting at a deer silhouette at ranges between ten and thirty yards. Hunters must be able to put three out of five broadhead-tipped arrows into the kill zone of the silhouette.

There are also certain archery equipment restrictions on Pax River not normally found elsewhere. Archers on Pax River must use a bow with draw weight no less than thirty pounds. Arrows must be full length and have a broadhead no less than seven-eighths inch wide. The bow must be held, drawn, and released without release aids or mechanical releases. Crossbows are not allowed.

Bowhunters have an early opportunity to harvest a whitetail during the archery-only season. Deer taken during the archery season must be tagged with an archery tag. Deer of either sex may be taken. Archers hunting during the general firearms season must use the firearms/muzzleloader tag for their deer rather than the archery tag.

Firearms hunters on Pax River may use only shotguns with slugs and muzzleloaders over .40 caliber. Like bowhunters, firearms hunters must also pass a shooting competency test prior to going afield. They must be able to put two out of three shots in the black at fifty yards. All weapons brought on the installation must be registered with the security department pass office when the hunter is entering the reservation.

Deer hunters afield during the firearms and muzzleloader deer seasons must wear blaze orange vests and caps. Bowhunters do not need to wear blaze orange garments during the archery season but must do so during the firearms and muzzleloader seasons. Small game and dove hunters must wear a blaze orange cap.

There is no minimum age to hunt on Pax River. Hunters under the age of sixteen must be accompanied afield at all times by an adult over twenty-one holding a valid installation hunting permit.

The hunter check station is set up on a self-help basis for all hunting except the firearms and muzzleloader deer seasons. The check station is at the rod and gun club, Building 3104 on Tate Road.

Fishing Fishing access on Naval Air Station Patuxent River is limited to the same individuals authorized access for hunting. It is not open to the public, but members of the public may be brought aboard as guests of authorized fishermen.

All anglers on Pax River must meet Maryland licensing requirements before purchasing an installation fishing license. Generally, all state regulations are enforced on the installation. Fishermen may take freshwater and saltwater game fish, crabs, and seashells in accordance with state regulations.

The fresh water on Pax River contains a wide assortment of game fish. Largemouth bass, bluegill, pumpkinseed, redear sunfish, channel catfish, brown bullheads, and black crappie can all be taken from the station's freshwater streams, lakes, and ponds. Creel and size limits for freshwater species vary slightly from state regulations. Pax River anglers may take two largemouth bass between nine and eleven inches per day and one bass per day over fifteen inches. No bass between eleven and fifteen inches may be kept. Anglers after catfish may keep no more than ten per day. All catfish must be at least ten inches long. Carp may be taken on Pax River by bowfishing.

Freshwater fish may not be taken by set lines or trotlines. Live bait, but not live fish as bait, may be used.

Pax River lies on the shores of the Chesapeake Bay. Consequently, saltwater fishing and crabbing on the installation are pretty good. Saltwater anglers on this installation may take bluefish, weakfish, flounder, croaker, spot, drum, and sea-run striped bass. Anglers may also take horseshoe and blue crab from installation waters.

Miscellaneous Camping is authorized on Patuxent River. There are three campgrounds with both improved and primitive campsites. Camping is only open to those individuals authorized access.

ATVs are not allowed on the installation. Certain boating restrictions also exist for the freshwater ponds on the installation.

Patuxent River is covered by the Solomon's Island quadrangle topographic map.

The hunting and fishing seasons on Pax River may change from year to year due to mission requirements. For more information, contact: Natural Resources Manager, Public Works Dept., Code 862, Naval Air Station, Patuxent River, MD 20670-5409, phone (301) 863-3670 (8:00 A.M. to 4:00 P.M., weekdays).

NAVAL ELECTRONIC SYSTEM ENGINEERING ACTIVITY

- 13 miles south of Lexington Park
- 300 acres open to hunting and fishing
- Closed to the public
- White-tailed deer and small game
- Fishing

Hunting Hunting is allowed on the installation, but only 300 acres are open and access is limited to employees with the proper security clearances. All hunters must have a current Maryland license.

White-tailed deer are hunted at the Naval Electronics System Engineering Activity on a limited basis, but hunter success is quite high. Hunters are allowed to use only primitive weapons, either archery tackle or muzzleloaders.

Small game may also be hunted here. Cottontails, waterfowl, pheasant, and quail inhabit the installation and hunter success is quite high. Hunters after big and small game must have the proper security clearance to enter the installation and must check out through the access gate.

Fishing Access to fishing on the installation is the same as hunting. The only species found on the installation is the largemouth bass. Maryland fishing laws apply.

For further information, contact: Facilities Management, Naval Electronics System Engineering Activity, Saint Inigoes, MD 20684.

NAVAL ORDNANCE STATION INDIAN HEAD

- 20 miles south of Washington, D.C., on the Potomac River
- Closed to the public
- 3,000 acres open to hunting
- Station hunting and fishing permits required
- White-tailed deer and small game
- Fishing
- Limited camping

Hunting   There are two main hunting areas on the station: The main hunting area is on the station itself; another area is available on the station annex. A little over 3,000 acres are open to hunting on the complex.

Only military personnel stationed in the local area and civilian employees are allowed to hunt on the installation. Hunters on the station must be at least eighteen and hold a valid Maryland hunting license and a station hunting permit, which costs $20 per year.

Big game hunting is limited to white-tailed deer, but deer hunting at Indian Head is excellent. Deer hunting is restricted to bowhunting only, and prospective hunters must pass an archery competency test administered by station wildlife personnel. Crossbows are not allowed.

Station wildlife biologists and field personnel maintain numerous hunting-stand sites throughout the installation and the annex. Hunters are assigned to a particular stand on a lottery basis and must remain within fifty yards of that stand for the entire day afield.

Small game may be taken on both the main station and the annex. Small game hunters on the annex and waterfowlers hunting from the main station's blinds may use shotguns. Small game hunters on Indian Head proper must use archery tackle. Handguns, rimfire and centerfire rifles, and crossbows are prohibited.

Small game available on the installation includes squirrel, waterfowl, quail, and cottontail rabbits. Waterfowl and squirrels are the most popular small game animals at Indian Head.

Deer hunters on the installation averaged a hunter success rate of over 65 percent during the 1989–90 season. Small game hunters hit 90 percent.

Fishing   Fishing at Indian Head is available in the brackish waters of the lower Potomac. Largemouth bass, some speckled trout, and an assortment of panfish can be taken from the installation's waters.

The restrictions on fishing at Indian Head are not as severe as those on hunting. Anyone holding a valid military identification card may fish in the installation's waters. Civilian anglers must be either employed on the station or guests of authorized individuals. All anglers must have a valid Maryland fishing license and a station fishing permit, which costs $5 for anglers over sixteen and is free for children under sixteen.

Miscellaneous   Limited camping is available on Indian Head but is only accessible to military ID card holders. ATVs are not allowed on the station or the annex.

For more information, contact: Wildlife Management Office, Naval Ordnance Station Indian Head, Indian Head, MD 20640, phone (301) 743-4133 (8:00 A.M. to 4:00 P.M., weekdays).

MASSACHUSETTS

For a small state, Massachusetts has a large military presence. There are twenty-two small military installations in a state that covers only 8,000 square miles. Most of the installations are in heavily populated areas where wildlife habitat is at a premium. Only one is large enough to harbor huntable numbers of game and is open for hunting and fishing.

FORT DEVENS

- 40 miles northwest of Boston
- 3,500 acres open to hunting and fishing
- Installation permit required
- White-tailed deer, turkey, and small game
- Fishing
- Camping closed to the public

Hunting Both small game and big game may be taken on Fort Devens. The installation offers approximately 3,500 acres of hunting area with fair populations of white-tailed deer and excellent populations of small game. Hunting on the installation is open to the public.

Hunters after either on Fort Devens must have a valid Massachusetts hunting license and proof of having completed a hunter safety course prior to purchasing an installation hunting permit. Hunters must also sign a waiver of liability relieving the U.S. Army of any responsibility should the hunter be killed or injured on the installation.

Firearms are restricted on Fort Devens. The only weapons authorized for taking either big or small game are muzzleloaders, shotguns, and archery tackle. Rifles, handguns, and crossbows are not allowed.

Deer hunting success on Fort Devens is only fair at 2 percent. Still, it's better than no deer hunting at all. Small game hunting on Fort Devens is much better at 45 percent. Small game hunters may take cottontails, squirrels, pheasant, waterfowl, grouse, varying hare, and woodcock. There is also a spring turkey season on Fort Devens. Predator hunters may take red fox or coyote on the installation, but night hunting is not allowed.

All state hunting laws apply on the fort. A hunter must be at least twelve years old to go afield. In addition to the state hunting laws, the fort also has some unique rules of its own. There is a daily quota for hunters on the fort. The quota may change from day to day based on training activities in the hunting areas. All hunters check in and out with the range control office before going afield.

Fishing Fort Devens is also open to the public for fishing. The fort has several ponds, reservoirs, and creeks stocked with eastern brook trout, largemouth bass, chain pickerel, bluegill, yellow perch, bullheads, rainbow trout, and brown trout.

All Massachusetts fishing laws apply on the fort. A fisherman must have a valid state license before purchasing a post permit. Fishermen may use either artificial lures or live bait and are limited to two hooks or lines. Trotlines are not allowed. Massachusetts law allows twelve trout a day, but on Fort Devens anglers may take only six.

Miscellaneous Camping is allowed on Fort Devens but is open only to active duty and retired military personnel and their dependents. ATVs are not allowed on the fort's lands.

The 1:25,000-scale maps covering Fort Devens are Ayer, Clinton, Bolton, and Fitchburg/Leominster quadrangles.

For more information on hunting and fishing at Fort Devens, contact: Forestry, Fish, and Wildlife Section Chief, Directorate of Engineering and Housing, HQ, Fort Devens, ATTN: AFZD-DEO (WILDLIFE), Fort Devens, MA 01433-5000, phone (508) 796-3021/2747 (7:30 A.M. to 4:00 P.M., weekdays).

MICHIGAN

There are several military installations in Michigan, but only K. I. Sawyer Air Force Base offered information on outdoor activities.

Air Force Installations

K. I. SAWYER AIR FORCE BASE

* 23 miles south of Marquette
* 5,300 acres
* Closed to the public
* Fishing

Fishing   K. I. Sawyer Air Force Base covers a little over 5,300 acres and is not open to the public for hunting and fishing. In fact, no hunting is allowed on K. I. Sawyer and fishing is limited to fifteen surface acres of water.

The species of fish available on K. I. Sawyer are small pike, sunfish, bass, and bluegill. Fishing regulations and bag limits match those of the state. Fishing is open only to people who have unlimited access to the base. In other words, only active duty military personnel, retirees, their dependents, and base civilians may fish there.

For more information on fishing on K. I. Sawyer, contact: Outdoor Adventure Program Office, 410 CSG/SSRO, K. I. Sawyer AFB, MI 49843-5000, phone (906) 346-2068 (8:00 A.M. to 5:00 P.M., weekdays).

MISSISSIPPI

Mississippi has a reputation for producing massive numbers of deer and quail every year, but many of the best hunting areas in the state are in private hands and are posted. There are farms and plantations that offer day hunts, but the fee is usually high, so hunting in Mississippi can be expensive.

The Mississippi Department of Wildlife Conservation does an admirable job of managing the few public hunting areas around the state. These areas, while well managed, receive intense hunting pressure for both big and small game.

There are only twelve Department of Defense installations in Mississippi. Only four of the installations are large enough to host a hunting or fishing program. Together, those four offer 29,000 acres of first-class hunting and fishing.

Army Installations

CAMP McCAIN

- 10 miles south of Grenada
- 7,500 acres
- White-tailed deer and small game
- Fishing
- No civilian vehicles allowed

Hunting Both big and small game hunting is open to the public on Camp McCain. Hunters on the installation need only a Mississippi hunting license. No post permit is required.

Because Camp McCain is a National Guard installation where weekend training is the rule not the exception, it is usually not open to hunting on the weekends. Consequently, most hunting is done during the week.

There are five hunting areas on Camp McCain. All are accessible from public roads bordering the installation. That's good because nonmilitary vehicles are not allowed on the reservation. Hunters must park their vehicles at an access gate and walk to their hunting areas. Gates and public roadways must not be blocked.

Since the reservation is not always open, hunters must check with the security office in Building S-200 prior to going afield to determine which areas are open. There is no requirement to check with the security office upon returning from the field.

All hunting regulations on Camp McCain, including seasons and bag limits, follow those of the state. Any weapon legal in the state of Mississippi for deer or small game is legal on the reservation. Hunter age limits and the requirement to complete a hunter safety course are also the same.

The only big game found on Camp McCain is the white-tailed deer. Deer hunting on the installation should be good, as it is generally throughout Mississippi. Small game hunters may take cottontails, squirrels, quail, waterfowl, and swamp rabbits.

Fishing Public fishing is allowed at Camp McCain. Fishermen must meet Mississippi licensing requirements. Creel limits, slot limits, and general fishing regulations all apply on the reservation. Like hunters, fishermen must park their cars at the installation boundaries and walk to their favorite fishing holes. Fishermen must also check with the security office before going on the installation.

According to my sources, there should be some monster largemouth bass lurking in the waters of Camp McCain. Since all fishermen must walk in, fishing pressure is light.

Miscellaneous Camp McCain is not open to any vehicle use or camping.

For more information on hunting and fishing at this installation, contact: Security Office, Bldg. S-200, Camp McCain Training Site, Box 686, Elliot, MS 38926-0686, phone (601) 227-3630 (7:30 A.M. to 4:00 P.M., weekdays).

MISSISSIPPI ARMY AMMUNITION PLANT

- In the Stennis Space Center, outside Picayune
- 3,200 acres open for hunting
- Big game and small game

Hunting The Mississippi Army Ammunition Plant has a small but growing deer herd. During the 1988 season, hunter success on the installation was only 7 percent. But, according to studies done at the plant, the deer herd is at its best health level since records of the installation have been kept.

The plant is open to the public for hunting. All Mississippi laws apply. Hunters on the installation must meet state prerequisites before purchasing a plant permit for $25.

The desired 1988 deer harvest at the plant was thirty-five. Only eighteen were taken, nine of each sex. The average field-dressed weight of yearling bucks taken from the plant was ninety pounds.

There are special restrictions for hunting on the plant. Hunters must check in with the security office prior to going afield. Additionally, only certain weapons are authorized on the installation.

Miscellaneous No camping, ATVs, or fishing are allowed on the installation.

For more information on hunting at the Mississippi Army Ammunition Plant, contact: Public Affairs Office, Mississippi Army Ammunition Plant, Stennis Space Center, MS 39466.

Air Force Installations

COLUMBUS AIR FORCE BASE

- In northeast Mississippi
- Administers hunting and fishing programs at Shuqualak Auxiliary Airfield
- 1,100 acres open to hunting and fishing
- Installation permit required
- White-tailed deer, turkey, and small game
- Fishing
- Camping at Shuqualak AAF
- Restricted boating

Hunting Columbus Air Force Base is open to the public for hunting both big and small game. The only big game found on the base is white-tailed deer. Small game hunted at Columbus AFB are cottontails, squirrels, quail, dove, duck, turkey, raccoon, and opossum.

Hunters on Columbus must have a valid Mississippi hunting license and a base permit. To receive base permits, hunters must first get a cash collection voucher from the environmental coordinator (14 ABG/DEEV) and then pay for the permit at the accounting and finance office. The license is then stamped, indicating the fee has been paid. Before going afield for the first time, all hunters must receive a safety briefing from the base game warden.

The Environmental Office at Columbus actually controls two installations. In addition to Columbus AFB proper, base officials also control the hunting at the auxiliary airfield at Shuqualak. The rules are slightly different for each. On Columbus

AFB, hunters can use only shotguns, including black-powder shotguns with shot or slugs, and bows of at least forty-five-pound draw weights. Rifles, handguns, crossbows, and poison pods are not allowed. Poison-pod arrows are allowed in the state, but not on the base. At Shuqualak, hunters may use the above-listed legal weapons and muzzle-loading rifles in .45, .50, or .54 caliber.

Columbus AFB and Shuqualak AAF are organized into five hunting areas, each with a specific quota of hunters. The number of hunters allowed on both installations at any time is capped at sixty-one: fifty-five on Columbus and six on Shuqualak. Hunters must have an area tag before hunting. Area tags are issued at the security police desk in Building 208. Each hunter must have his own area tag, and each hunter's license is checked by the security police before a tag is issued.

Area tags are color coded and valid for only one area on the installation. Prior to changing hunting areas, a hunter must return to the SP desk and exchange one area tag for another. Hunters must also return their tags to the security police desk after hunting.

All hunters on Columbus AFB and Shuqualak AAF must wear a minimum of 500 square inches of international orange when afield during the general gun deer season. Bowhunters hunting during the archery season and small game hunters hunting other than during the general gun deer season do not have to wear orange.

Aside from the gun restrictions and limitation on the use of arrow pods, most of the rules on Columbus Air Force Base and Shuqualak Auxiliary Airfield follow those of the state of Mississippi. There are some special restrictions on raccoon hunting on the installation, and all hunters under the age of seventeen must have a state-certified hunter safety course.

Hunter success on Columbus AFB and Shuqualak AAF is 20 percent for big game and 80 percent for small game.

Fishing Fishing is good on Columbus Air Force Base and Shuqualak AAF and is open to the public. Anglers on Columbus waters must have a valid Mississippi fishing license and a base fishing permit.

Several ponds and lakes on Columbus AFB and Shuqualak AAF are stocked with bass, bream, crappie, carp, and catfish. All state fishing regulations apply in addition to a couple of base restrictions. The use of trotlines, jugs, or bush hooks is not allowed on the installation. Additionally, the creel limit on catfish is five per person per day on the installation.

Miscellaneous Camping is not allowed on Columbus Air Force Base, but hunters may camp for up to forty-eight hours at Shuqualak AAF. Boats over fourteen feet are not allowed on SAC Lake at Columbus AFB.

The only ATVs allowed on Columbus Air Force Base are off-road dirt bikes and four-wheelers. Three-wheelers are not allowed. ATVs may only be used on nonhunting days. The only area open for ATV use is Area B.

The USGS Caledonia, Mississippi–Alabama quadrangle is the topographic map covering these installations.

For more information on hunting and fishing at these two installations, contact: 14 ABG/DEEV, Columbus AFB, MS 39701-5000, phone (601) 434-7301 (7:30 A.M. to 4:30 P.M., weekdays).

Naval Installations

NAVAL AIR STATION MERIDIAN

- 6,540 acres open to hunting and fishing
- Installation permit required
- White-tailed deer, turkey, and small game
- Fishing
- Restricted boating

Hunting   There are 6,540 acres open to public hunting on Naval Air Station Meridian. Hunters with a valid Mississippi hunting license, proof of having completed a hunter safety course, and an installation hunting permit may take white-tailed deer, wild turkey, cottontails, squirrels, quail, dove, waterfowl, coyote, and fox on this installation.

The installation's permits are available from the NAS gymnasium weekdays from 8:00 A.M. to 4:00 P.M. The costs for the installation permits are reasonable at $12 for a combination hunting and fishing license for adults; $6 for youths under sixteen. A hunting license costs $10 per year for adults and $5 per year for those sixteen and under. Trapping licenses are also available at $75 per year. NAS Meridian also offers a daily fee schedule where adults can purchase a daily hunting permit at $5 for the first day and $2 for each additional day. Youth hunting permits are also available at the same price.

In addition to the licensing requirements listed above, all hunters on the installation must attend an installation hunting safety and rules briefing at least annually. The briefing covers station wildlife management practices and conservation, in addition to station rules and safety.

All hunters after either big game or small game must sign in at the sportsmen's association lodge, indicating in which area they will be hunting. Hunters are allowed to sign for up to two areas. When changing to another area not listed on their sign-in sheet, hunters must return to the lodge and sign for the new area. Hunters on Joe Williams Field must sign in at the field operations section before going hunting.

The Naval Air Station Meridian Sportsmen's Association also offers organized deer hunts during the general deer season. For these hunts, hunters must check in with the appointed hunt master for assignment to a hunting area. The areas used by the sportsmen's association for its organized hunts are not open to the public for hunting. Organized hunts can only be held from 6:00 A.M. to 3:30 P.M. on weekends, holidays, and Wednesdays. The areas used for organized hunts reopen to the public at 3:30 P.M. on those days.

Gun hunters on NAS Meridian must wear international orange when afield during the gun seasons. Hunters after small game during the small game season must wear an

international orange garment visible from all sides. Normally, an orange hat will do. During the big game gun season, hunters must wear a vest in addition to the hat.

NAS Meridian hunters are subject to certain weapons restrictions. Hunters cannot use centerfire rifles, rimfire rifles, or handguns on the installation. The only weapons authorized are shotguns with slugs or buckshot for deer (standard shot for small game), muzzleloading rifles in .45 caliber or larger for deer or small game, and archery tackle. Crossbows are not allowed on the installation.

There are four hunting areas on the base. Most of the areas are subdivided for better hunter control. During the deer season, two of the areas are open to deer hunting, one is open to small game hunting, and one is closed. The areas are rotated on a daily basis to effectively manage game populations and hunting pressure.

Hunting on NAS Meridian is extremely well managed. Of 125 permits issued for whitetails in 1989, 104 hunters took deer. That equates to a hunter success rate of 83 percent!

Fishing The fishing program on NAS Meridian is also well managed. There are over 200 surface acres of water open to fishing, including thirteen lakes. Anglers on NAS Meridian can expect to catch largemouth bass, bluegill, redear sunfish, green sunfish, warmouth bass, white crappie, and channel catfish.

All Mississippi fishing license requirements and rules apply on NAS Meridian. In addition to state licenses, fishermen on the station must also have a station permit. Annual station permits are available at the gymnasium at $8 for adults and $4 for youths under sixteen. Daily permits are also available at $2 for the first day and $1 a day thereafter.

NAS Meridian has some fishing rules slightly different from the state. On station, trotlines, jugs, bush hooks, nets, and traps are illegal. Likewise, area chumming is also not allowed. The creel limits on NAS Meridian are slightly different from the state as well. Anglers on the installation may not keep any largemouth bass between fourteen and eighteen inches in length. Bass fishermen can only keep three bass under fourteen inches and three over eighteen inches. Channel catfish on the installation also have a slot limit. Anglers after catfish can keep six fish under fourteen inches, none between fourteen and sixteen inches, and all they catch over sixteen inches.

Miscellaneous Gasoline engines are not allowed on any of the waters of NAS Meridian. No boats are allowed on Annette and Tant lakes. An adult over the age of eighteen must accompany children twelve and under in a boat at all times. Military and retiree dependents between twelve and sixteen may use a boat alone, provided they have written permission from their parents. All boats afloat on NAS Meridian must have a U.S. Coast Guard–approved flotation device for each person aboard.

Camping and ATVs are not allowed on the installation. Additionally, some roads are closed to privately owned vehicles. Hunters and fishermen wanting to cross the runways must have a ramp pass from flight operations.

NAS Meridian is covered by the Lauderdale, NAS Meridian, Lynville, and Joe Williams Field (formerly Bravo Field) quadrangles.

For more information, contact: Game Warden, MWR Code 22, Naval Air Station Meridian, MS 39309, phone (601) 639-2666/2528 (8:00 A.M. to 4:30 P.M., weekdays).

MISSOURI

Missouri is well known for its hunting and fishing. Though it covers almost 69,000 square miles and offers a little over 2.1 million acres of public land to hunt, nearly 90 percent of the land in Missouri is private. Getting permission to hunt or fish on these lands can be a real problem. Like most southern states, hunting leases in Missouri are the norm rather than the exception.

There are twelve military installations in Missouri. Four of those installations belong to the Army and seven belong to the Air Force. One installation is under the control of the Defense Mapping Agency. Unfortunately, of all those installations, only three are open to hunting and fishing.

Army Installations

FORT LEONARD WOOD

- In the Ozark Mountains
- Nearly surrounded by Mark Twain National Forest
- Recreation area at Lake of the Ozarks
- 53,000 acres open to hunting and fishing
- Installation permit required
- White-tailed deer, turkey, and small game
- Fishing
- Camping closed to the public

Hunting Fort Wood, as it's known locally, has exceptional hunting. Open to the public, it offers 53,000 acres of hunting territory. The hunting program on Fort Wood is managed as well as any on private land.

Hunters on Fort Wood may take white-tailed deer, wild turkey, cottontail rabbit, squirrel, waterfowl, quail, raccoon, opossum, red fox, gray fox, and coyote. All big game hunting on the base is under a daily quota system. Some small game hunting is also under a quota system, but not all. Fort Leonard Wood also offers a historic-weapons hunt for two days every year. The hunt is limited to black-powder weapons and archery.

Hunters between sixteen and sixty-five on Fort Leonard Wood must have a valid Missouri hunting license and an installation sportsman's permit before getting a post stamp for the different species. The permit and stamp costs are as follows: sportsman's permit, $5; spring turkey gun stamp, $2; fall turkey gun stamp, $2; fall deer and turkey archery, $2; fall deer gun stamp, $2; and trapping stamp, $2.

Weapons used for hunting on Fort Wood must conform to the Missouri Wildlife Code, with some additional restrictions. Centerfire rifles and centerfire or rimfire handguns are not legal. Shotguns shooting slugs or buckshot may be used for deer, with the exception of the .410 bore; .410s may be used for small game. Muzzleloading rifles and handguns conforming to the Missouri Wildlife Code may be used to take any type of game. Crossbows may only be used during the general firearms deer season.

Hunters are not generally required to sign in for a hunting area on Fort Leonard Wood. The only exception is during the historic-weapons hunt for deer. Hunters must then sign in and out for an area.

While hunters aren't usually required to sign for an area, the areas have caps on the number of hunters allowed into them. Hunters must check it with the Outdoor Recreation Center when going afield to make sure the area is not already full. All hunting area quotas are on a first-come, first-served basis. There is no quota system for archers on Fort Leonard Wood.

Hunter success rates for deer and turkey hunters on Fort Leonard Wood are pretty good. An average of 15 percent to 20 percent of those holding deer permits are successful, while turkey hunters scored higher at 15 percent to 25 percent.

Fishing The waters of Fort Wood are open to public angling. Fishermen must meet Missouri licensing requirements and have a post sportsmen's permit. An additional trout stamp at $2 is required for certain waters on the post.

The fort offers numerous fishing opportunities. Because of military training requirements, not all areas are open at all times. Certain areas of the post are open daily, but not all.

Anglers must follow all Missouri fishing laws while on Fort Leonard Wood. In addition, the installation has some special rules fishermen should be aware of. The Stone Mill Spring and Branch Fishing Area requires a Fort Wood trout stamp and has special tackle regulations. Anglers fishing Stone Mill are limited to a single fishing rod and must quit fishing when they have taken five trout.

Creel limits on Fort Wood also differ slightly from the state. Installation anglers may keep only five channel catfish a day from installation waters. Anglers after all species, in waters other than Stone Mill, may use up to three rods. Trotlines, bush hooks, jugs, and nets are not allowed.

Penn's Pond, Bloodland Lake, and Bloodland Pond also have special creel limits.

The largemouth limit at Penn's Pond and Bloodland Lake is four daily. Anglers at Bloodland Pond may keep up to six. At Penn's Pond and Bloodland Pond, largemouth bass under fifteen inches must be released. At Bloodland Lake, bass between twelve and fifteen inches must be released immediately.

The creel limits are also slightly different at Decker's Ridge Pond and Indiana Avenue Pond. There the limit is three channel catfish daily and no more than ten hybrid sunfish a day.

Anglers on Fort Leonard Wood may take largemouth bass, smallmouth bass, channel catfish, rock bass, bluegill, crappie, redear sunfish, hybrid sunfish, carp, and bullheads. Bow-fishing is allowed for carp.

Miscellaneous Camping is permitted on Fort Leonard Wood at Big Piney Campground on the northeast portion of the reservation. The camping fee is $2. Only military ID card holders are allowed to camp in the campground.

Fort Leonard Wood also manages a 350-acre recreation area at Lake of the Ozarks, roughly an hour from the post. The recreation area offers camping, boating, fishing, water-skiing, and a marina.

ATVs are allowed on Fort Leonard Wood in specially designated areas. All ATVs used on the reservation must be registered before use.

The topographic maps of Fort Leonard Wood are Waynesville Quadrangle, Bloodland Quadrangle, Roby Quadrangle, Winnipeg Quadrangle, Devil's Elbow Quadrangle, and Big Piney Quadrangle. All are in the 7.5-minute series.

For more information, contact: ATFT-PA-CCR-O, Outdoor Recreation Center, Bldg. 2355, Fort Leonard Wood, MO 65473, phone (314) 596-4033 (8:00 A.M. to 5:00 P.M., weekdays).

LAKE CITY ARMY AMMUNITION PLANT

- Near Independence
- 2,401 acres open to hunting and fishing
- Closed to the public
- White-tailed deer, small game, and turkey
- Fishing

Hunting Hunting on Lake City property is restricted and well controlled. White-tailed deer hunting for bucks only is allowed. Hunting for turkey and small game is also available on a limited basis.

Expect to see huge deer at Lake City. According to the latest statistics, hunter success was only 13.6 percent, but the average field-dressed weight of bucks taken on this installation was a whopping 158 pounds.

The only people cleared to hunt at Lake City AAP are military, retired military, and plant personnel. State licenses are required.

Because the hunting area is also used as a firing range or a camping and training ground for Boy Scouts and college students, Lake City is closed for hunting some weekends.

Fishing Fishing is also allowed at Lake City, but only for military personnel holding a Missouri state fishing license.

For more information, contact: Public Affairs Office, Lake City Army Ammunition Plant, Independence, MO 64051-0330. To find out if the plant is open for hunting on a specific weekend, call (816) 796-7156.

Air Force Installations

WHITEMAN AIR FORCE BASE

- 65 miles east of Kansas City
- 2 lakes
- Installation permit required
- Fishing

Fishing There are two lakes on Whiteman Air Force Base, both stocked with a variety of species found in this part of North America. All Missouri licensing requirements apply to fishing on Whiteman. A base permit is required for fishing on this installation. Certain other restrictions apply to fishing on Whiteman.

For more information, contact: Outdoor Recreation Branch, 351 SMW, Whiteman AFB, MO 65305-5000.

MONTANA

Montana is one of our largest states, covering more than 147,135 square miles. With Alaska, it is one of the best states in North America to hunt big game. Montana is also famous for its fishing. Public land abounds in Montana, so finding a place to fish or hunt generally isn't a problem.

Montana doesn't have a large military presence. There are only five installations in the state. Three of those are less than 150 acres in size. The remaining two are fairly large but offer only fishing. Since Malmstrom Air Force Base is home to the 341st Strategic Missile Wing, public access is restricted for security reasons.

Army Installations

FORT WILLIAM HENRY HARRISON

- Near Helena
- 700 acres
- Fishing

Fishing Fort Harrison offers roughly 700 acres of public access for fishing. There are no special regulations for the post, and an installation permit is not required. All Montana fishing laws apply, including licensing requirements. All creel limits and fishing methods are as set by the state. The only species of fish available on the fort is brook trout.

There is no requirement to sign in or out for fishing on the fort. The only restriction is that no vehicles are allowed on the post except those with a post sticker.

For more information, contact: Montana Department of Fish, Wildlife, and Parks, 1420 East 6th Avenue, Helena, MT 59620.

Air Force Installations

MALMSTROM AIR FORCE BASE

- Recreation area on the border of Glacier National Park
- 29,100 acres
- Closed to the public
- Fishing
- Camping

Fishing   To fish on Malmstrom AFB, anglers must already have access to the base, that is, they must be active duty or retired military members or their dependents or base employees.

Compared to the rest of Montana, fishing on Malmstrom is rather limited. The only species available is stocked hybrid rainbow trout, and the limit is two. All anglers on the installation must meet state licensing requirements, but no special base permit is required. All Montana fishing laws, with the exception of the creel limit, apply to the base.

Miscellaneous   The only camping allowed on Malmstrom proper is in the base FAMCAMP for military members only. The base operates a recreation area on the border of Glacier National Park. The Saint Mary's Recreation Camp is on Saint Mary's Lake, 165 miles southeast of the base. The recreation camp is open June 1 to September 15. It offers excellent fishing but no marina or boat launching.

For more information, contact: 840 CSG/SSRO, Malmstrom AFB, MT 59402-5000, phone (406) 731-2903 (8:00 A.M. to 4:30 P.M., weekdays).

NEBRASKA

Situated in the middle of America's breadbasket, Nebraska is a state of many contrasts. The eastern part of the state is made up of Missouri River bottomlands and rolling hills covered in grain. The western part features badlands covered in scrub oak and sagebrush. Nebraska covers 77,277 square miles, 97 percent of which are privately owned.

There is not a large military presence in Nebraska. The U.S. Army maintains an ammunition plant at Grand Island and a National Guard facility in Mead. The Air Force has six installations in the state. Offutt Air Force Base, Strategic Air Command headquarters, offers fishing but no hunting.

Air Force Installations

OFFUTT AIR FORCE BASE

- Near Omaha
- 3,884 acres
- Closed to the public
- Fishing
- Camping
- Boating

Fishing   The base lake at Offutt Air Force Base offers some exceptional fishing to those fortunate enough to be able to fish it. It is not open to the public. Only those authorized unrestricted access to the base may fish the lake.

The lake was created several years ago when the runway at Offutt was extended for modern jets. Today it is a medium-sized impoundment stocked with rainbow trout, largemouth bass, catfish, bluegill, crappie, bullhead, and walleye. The lake is open year-round and offers a boat and bait shop with boat rentals.

Anglers at Offutt's base lake must have a valid Nebraska fishing license if they are over sixteen. No base permit is required and anglers do not need a trout stamp. Trout anglers must obtain a waiver form from the boathouse, however. All state rules and creel limits apply at the base lake.

I've had the pleasure of fishing the base lake on numerous occasions and can testify that the fishing is quite good here at certain times of the year. During the summer, channel catfish can be readily taken at night with cut bait or shrimp. During the spring, some large bass are taken from around the shorelines.

Miscellaneous The base offers an excellent trap and skeet range and an outdoor recreation branch. Boats are allowed on the lake without restrictions.

Primitive camping is allowed at the base lake for $2 a night. There are no hookups at the lake.

For more information on the fishing at Offutt AFB, contact: Outdoor Recreation, 55 CSG/SSRO, Offutt AFB, NE 68113, phone (402) 294-4978 (8:00 A.M. to 5:00 P.M., weekdays).

NEVADA

Nevada covers 110,000 square miles. Most of the state is publicly owned, so getting access to hunt is rarely a problem. Getting a tag is. Most of Nevada's hunting for big game is on a limited-entry permit basis. Competition is keen for the few tags every year and nonresidents are at a real disadvantage in the drawing.

There is a large military presence in this desert state, at least in terms of land ownership. The Department of Defense controls over 3,510,574 acres of mountains and desert in Nevada. Unfortunately, out of all that land, only 147,431 acres on one installation are open to the public for hunting and fishing.

Army Installations

HAWTHORNE
ARMY AMMUNITION PLANT

- 125 miles southeast of Reno
- 78,000 acres open to hunting
- Installation permit required
- Big game and small game
- Fishing

Hunting   Seventy-eight thousand of Hawthorne AAP's 147,431 acres are open to hunting. The plant is home to some monster mule deer as well as chukars, sage hens, and rabbits. Access to the plant is strictly controlled at all times.

Deer tags at the Hawthorne AAP are controlled by the Nevada Department of Wildlife. Tags are issued on a drawing basis, with Nevada residents receiving the bulk of the tags. All Nevada hunting regulations and licensing requirements apply on the plant's grounds.

In addition to state licenses, hunters on the Hawthorne AAP must have either an annual permit at $5 or a daily permit at $3 for military members, $4 for plant civilian employees, or $5 for the public.

Hunters must check in and out through the plant security office before going afield and upon returning.

Hunter success was not high during the 1988 season—only 10 percent of hunters were successful. The average field-dressed weight of yearling bucks taken on the plant was 100 pounds, normal for the mule deer found here.

Fishing Fishing is authorized at the Hawthorne Army Ammunition Plant. According to information available, the plant has a small reservoir of sixteen and one-half acres, fifty miles of stream, and a total of eight miles of shoreline. Only the sixteen-and-one-half-acre pond is open to fishing.

All Nevada fishing laws apply on this installation. Licensing requirements are as set by the state. Additionally, fishermen must have a daily permit. The daily fishing permits are the same price as the daily hunting permits.

For more information, contact: Public Affairs Office, Hawthorne Army Ammunition Plant, Hawthorne, NV 89415.

NEW HAMPSHIRE

Access to land is good in New Hampshire and hunting pressure is relatively light. Since it is such a small state, the military influence here is not large. There are only four installations and one of them, Pease AFB, is scheduled to close in 1991. Of the remaining installations, only New Boston Air Force Station offers any type of hunting and fishing.

NEW BOSTON AIR FORCE STATION

- West of Manchester
- 2,400 acres open to hunting and fishing
- Closed to the public
- Installation permit required
- White-tailed deer and small game
- Fishing
- Camping

Hunting New Boston Air Force Station offers hunters over 2,400 acres of prime wildlife habitat to hunt white-tailed deer, waterfowl, grouse, and rabbits. Hunting for deer and other species should be fair to good.

New Boston is open daily to military ID card holders, those officially authorized base support, and their guests. Hunters are not required to check in or out for a hunting area. Hunters on New Boston must meet all New Hampshire licensing requirements and purchase a base permit before going afield. All New Hampshire hunting regulations apply on the installation.

134

Hunters may use archery tackle, muzzleloading weapons, and shotguns to hunt on this installation. Crossbows, centerfire rifles, and handguns are not allowed. Still, due to the terrain in this area, hunters are at no disadvantage with the weapons allowed. Hunters must meet state hunter safety requirements on this installation. There are no additional requirements. There are also no age restrictions on young hunters.

Fishing Five ponds on New Boston offer everything from largemouth bass to pickerel to trout. The kids have one pond stocked with trout all to themselves. Fishing access is restricted. Anglers must have a military ID card and be authorized military privileges. Authorized fishermen may have up to three guests a day on installation waters.

All anglers on the installation must meet New Hampshire licensing requirements prior to purchasing an installation permit. The permits are available from the outdoor recreation branch at $5 for an individual fishing permit, $6 for a family permit, and $5 for a guest permit. All New Hampshire fishing regulations apply to New Boston Air Force Station. There are no deviations from state laws regarding fishing methods, creel limits, and slot limits.

Miscellaneous Camping is allowed at New Boston but only for military ID card holders and their guests. ATVs are legal on this installation but must stay on designated trails.

For more information, contact: John B. Mitchell, DEEV, New Boston Air Force Station, Amherst, NH 03057, phone (603) 472-3911, ext. 381 (8:00 A.M. to 4:30 P.M., weekdays).

NEW JERSEY

This small eastern seaboard state has been a subject of the outdoor media quite a bit lately. Antihunters have targeted it as the first state to attack in their effort to ban hunting. Fortunately, the hunters of New Jersey have joined together to stop them.

Still, antihunters protest every year during the Great Swamp deer hunt held in this state. They always attract a lot of attention. So does the Great Swamp. In a state the size of New Jersey (only 7,836 square miles) public hunting land is at a premium.

The Garden State has a long and colorful tradition of supporting the U.S. military. That tradition continues today. There are fifteen military installations in New Jersey. Although most of those installations are small, four are large enough to support hunting and fishing programs. Together, they contribute 56,171 acres of land for hunting and fishing.

The U.S. Army has the largest presence in New Jersey, with eight installations. They range in size from 31,110-acre Fort Dix to the 6-acre Oakhurst Area Research and Development Activity.

Naval installations in New Jersey cover 18,642 acres. Fortunately, most of these acres are open for hunting and fishing.

Army Installations

FORT DIX

- 17 miles southeast of Trenton
- 15,000 acres open to hunting and fishing
- Installation permit required
- White-tailed deer, turkey, and small game
- Fishing
- Camping closed to the public

Hunting Fort Dix lies in a heavily populated area between the cities of Wrights-town, Browns Mills, and Pemberton. Hunting pressure on the fort is less than in surrounding areas because of the hunter quota system used on the installation. Like most installations, no more than a certain number of hunters are allowed in the field at a time. This practice enhances both hunter safety and the quality of the hunt.

Game found on Fort Dix are the white-tailed deer, eastern wild turkey, cottontail rabbit, squirrel, pheasant, quail, grouse, waterfowl, and fox. The seasons for all game animals follow those of the state. Fort Dix also hosts a special muzzleloader hunt every year.

Hunters on Fort Dix must have proof of having completed a state-certified hunter safety course before purchasing a Fort Dix permit. Hunters must also meet the licensing requirements of the state of New Jersey. Hunters must be at least ten years of age to hunt on the fort and those between the ages of ten and thirteen must be accompanied by a licensed hunter over twenty-one.

Fort Dix, like New Jersey, has certain weapons restrictions. Hunters on the fort may not use centerfire or rimfire rifles, handguns, or crossbows. The only weapons legal on the fort are shotguns using slugs or buckshot for deer and shot for small game, muzzle-loaders of .45 caliber or larger, and archery tackle that conforms to state regulations.

Hunters are required to sign in at the hunter registration office for the day they would like to hunt. They may sign for up to two areas but must report back before moving to any other areas. Hunters must physically sign out at the hunter registration office (Range 14) upon completing their day afield.

All bag limits on Fort Dix match those of the state. Hunter success can be good on the fort. Hunter success rates approach 25 percent during special seasons for deer. No figure was available for hunter success rates on small game.

Fishing Like hunting, fishing on Fort Dix is open to the public. Fishermen must have the required New Jersey licenses before purchasing a post fishing permit from the outdoor recreation branch. All methods of fishing legal in the state of New Jersey are legal on Fort Dix. Fishermen on the post may use live bait, artificial lures, and multiple lines to take fish on the installation.

The waters of the post are stocked with trout, bluegill, pickerel, yellow perch, crappie, catfish, and largemouth bass. All creel limits are the same as the state.

Miscellaneous No ATVs are allowed on Fort Dix. All vehicles must stay on established roadways. A driver without a post sticker must obtain a visitor's pass from the main gate prior to going fishing or hunting.

Primitive camping is allowed at the Brindle Lake Camping Area. The area has ten sites available but is only open to military members, their dependents, retirees, their dependents, and Department of the Army civilians. It is not open to the public.

Maps of Fort Dix are available from the 1204th Engineer Company, ARNG Slocomb, Alabama. The map hunters and anglers need for this installation is the Fort Dix Special Edition, 1-1203D, 1984.

For more information on hunting and fishing at Fort Dix, contact: ATZD-GAC-CR, Outdoor Recreation, Bldg. 5201, Maryland Avenue, Fort Dix, NJ 08640, phone (609) 562-2358/6667 (8:00 A.M. to 5:00 P.M., weekdays).

PICATINNY ARSENAL

- Near Dover
- 3,600 acres open to hunting and fishing
- Closed to the public
- Installation permit required
- White-tailed deer, turkey, and small game
- Fishing

Hunting   Since Picatinny Arsenal is so close to New York City, it would seem that hunting pressure on this installation would be intense. It isn't. Picatinny is not open to the public, so hunting pressure is kept under control. There are 3,600 acres open to hunting on Picatinny Arsenal.

The only people allowed to hunt on Picatinny Arsenal are active duty military members, their dependents, military retirees, their dependents, and arsenal employees. All hunters must have a valid New Jersey hunting license and an arsenal permit. Yearly permits are $6, or $5 for daily permits.

Hunters on Picatinny must follow all New Jersey game laws. Weapons restrictions apply on the reservation, and all state bag limits are also enforced. All hunters must check in at the security office before going afield and check out after hunting.

Hunting is well managed on Picatinny Arsenal. Hunters on the installation may take white-tailed deer, eastern wild turkey, river otter, beaver, cottontails, and water-fowl. During the 1988 season, deer hunters took twenty-six bucks and twenty-two does from Picatinny Arsenal. Overall hunter success was 32.4 percent.

Fishing   Fishing at Picatinny Arsenal is also restricted to authorized individuals, who must meet the same eligibility criteria as hunters. All New Jersey fishing regulations apply on the arsenal. Fishermen must have an arsenal fishing permit, available at $5 a year for authorized individuals and $5 a day for guests.

Picatinny Arsenal has seven and four-tenths miles of stream, 330 surface acres of ponds, and eight miles of shoreline for angling. Trout, bluegill, pickerel, yellow perch, crappie, catfish, and largemouth bass can all be caught in Picatinny waters.

Miscellaneous   No camping or ATVs are allowed on arsenal lands. All people on the grounds must check in with the security office before going anywhere on the arsenal.

For more information on Picatinny Arsenal, contact: Public Affairs Officer, Picatinny Arsenal, NJ 07806-5000.

Naval Installations

NAVAL AIR ENGINEERING CENTER LAKEHURST

- 5,000 acres open to hunting and fishing
- Installation permit required
- White-tailed deer and small game
- Fishing
- Camping closed to the public

Hunting   Lakehurst is open to the public for hunting. All hunters must have a valid New Jersey hunting license and an NAEC hunting permit.

There are several types of permits available. The license fees for DOD personnel are $10 for an annual hunting permit, $20 for a first-deer permit, $5 for additional-deer permits, and $10 for a station pheasant permit. Private citizens must pay $20 for an annual hunting permit, $30 for a first-deer permit, $10 for additional-deer permits, and $35 for station pheasant permits. Daily permits are available to both DOD personnel and private citizens at $1 for small game permits, $2 for deer permits, and $15 for pheasant permits. Annual permits are valid from March 1 through February 28 each year.

Game found on this installation are white-tailed deer, cottontails, squirrels, waterfowl, pheasant, quail, grouse, raccoon, and fox. Deer hunting is reported as fair. Small game hunting is fair to poor, depending on species.

All New Jersey hunting seasons, bag limits, and general hunting regulations apply. Archers' equipment must meet the standards set by the state. The only firearms allowed on the installation are shotguns and muzzleloaders. Deer hunters using shotguns must use slugs. Muzzleloaders must be at least .45 caliber. Modern weapons, including rifles and handguns, are not allowed.

All hunters must sign in for their hunting areas before going afield. The sign-in sheet is posted on a bulletin board in front of the rod and gun club. Additionally, hunters not authorized normal access must stop at the main gate for a sportsman's vehicle pass. The pass must be surrendered at the main gate upon completion of hunting.

All hunters on the installation must have proof of a hunter safety course prior to obtaining a station hunting permit. Additionally, hunters must attend an annual hunting orientation before obtaining a station permit. The briefing is held on the second and fourth Tuesdays of August and September. Other briefings may be arranged. The briefings are held in Building 525.

Youngsters over ten may hunt on Lakehurst with a juvenile license. They must be accompanied by an adult at all times while afield. Those over fourteen must have a regular hunting license.

Hunting permits for Lakehurst are available from the center's rod and gun club. There is also a sportsmens' association on the installation. Membership in either can reduce hunting license fees.

Fishing   Lakehurst is also open to public fishing. Fishermen must have all necessary state licenses before purchasing a station permit. Annual fishing permits cost $10 for DOD personnel and $20 for the public. A daily permit is available at no cost. Fishing permits must be obtained from the test department on the installation. Members of the center's sportsmen's association and rod and gun club may buy station permits at the DOD price.

The waters on the center are stocked with largemouth bass, smallmouth bass, brown bullheads, pickerel, several types of sunfish, as well as brook and brown trout. All New Jersey creel limits and fishing regulations apply, and fishermen may use any method of fishing legal in New Jersey.

Miscellaneous   Camping is permitted at Lakehurst, but it is only open to DOD personnel and retirees. No ATVs are allowed on the installation and all vehicles must stay on existing roadways.

The Cassville and Lakehurst topographic maps cover this installation.

For more information on hunting and fishing on NAEC, Lakehurst, contact: John Joyce, Public Works Dept., Naval Air Engineering Center, Lakehurst, NJ 08733-5051, phone (201) 323-2911 (7:30 A.M. to 4:00 P.M., weekdays).

NAVAL WEAPONS STATION EARLE

- 8,000 acres open to hunting
- Closed to the public
- Installation permit required
- White-tailed deer and small game
- Saltwater fishing

Hunting Earle is open for hunting only to military members and civilian employees who work on the installation. Due to security constraints, it is not open to others, military or civilian. Approximately 8,000 acres of the station are open to hunting.

Hunters on Earle must have valid New Jersey licenses and station permits. They must also have completed a state-certified hunter safety course and must attend an annual hunter orientation prior to hunting.

The primary game animal hunted on Earle is the white-tailed deer. Small game is found on the station, but their numbers are limited. The seasons on Earle follow those of the state, with the same bag limits and opening and closing dates for all species.

Hunters on the weapons station may use only shotguns, muzzleloading weapons, and archery tackle. Crossbows, centerfire or rimfire rifles, and handguns are not allowed. Shotgunners must use slugs while hunting deer and shot for all other game. Black-powder weapons used for deer must be at least .45 caliber. Archery tackle must meet state guidelines.

All hunters on Weapons Station Earle must sign in before going to their hunting areas and sign out in person upon completion of hunting. Hunters should check in with the shore patrol/security office when signing in or out.

Fishing There are no freshwater fishing opportunities at Earle, but saltwater fishing is allowed along the waterfront area in Middletown. The species found are all of those native to this part of the New Jersey shoreline.

Access to fishing at Naval Weapons Station Earle is severely restricted. The same access requirements exist for fishing as for hunting. All New Jersey fishing license requirements must be met, and all New Jersey creel limits and methods of take apply.

Miscellaneous As one would expect on an installation of this type, camping and ATVs are not allowed.

Access is severely restricted here, but hunting and fishing should be good as a result.

The Marlboro, Sandy Hook, Farmingdale, Long Branch, and Asbury Park topographic maps cover this installation.

For more information, contact: Naval Weapons Station, Earle, Conservation Executive Committee, Colt's Neck, NJ 07722-5000, phone (201) 577-2000 (7:30 A.M. to 4:00 P.M., weekdays).

NEW MEXICO

New Mexico is famed as a big game hunter's paradise. This 121,666-square-mile state has produced more than its share of record-book elk and mule deer.

There are many military installations in the state, which range in size from the 1,746,720-acre White Sands Missile Range to the 1-acre Silver City Radar Site. White Sands is open to hunting from time to time, and its hunting is controlled by the New Mexico Department of Game and Fish. All other installations in New Mexico are closed to hunting and fishing except Fort Wingate Depot Activity.

FORT WINGATE DEPOT ACTIVITY

- West of Gallup
- Pronghorn antelope
- Fishing closed to the public

Hunting The only big game found on Fort Wingate is the pronghorn antelope. Hunting for these beautiful animals is strictly controlled by the state of New Mexico and the U.S. Army. The state issues up to forty-five antelope tags in a lottery for Fort Wingate's 8,100 acres of open hunting area.

Hunters who draw an antelope tag on Fort Wingate must report to the main gate on the weekend they are scheduled to hunt. There a security guard and state wildlife officer admit hunters through the gate and transport them to their assigned hunting areas. Due to the weapons stored here, security is tight.

The only hunting weapons authorized on the depot are shotguns, muzzleloaders, and archery tackle. Modern firearms are not allowed. Hunter success is high, at 30 percent, considering the weapons used.

No small game hunting is allowed on the installation.

Fishing Fishing at Fort Wingate is restricted to civilian employees of the installation and military members. All New Mexico licensing requirements must be met. No depot permit is required. The only species available on the depot are trout and catfish, and fishing areas are limited in size.

Miscellaneous No camping or ATVs are allowed on Fort Wingate. Security is very tight, but getting an antelope permit may be one of the best ways to harvest one of these desert speedsters.

For more information on hunting at Fort Wingate or the White Sands Missile Range, contact: New Mexico Department of Game and Fish, State Capitol, Villagra Building, Santa Fe, NM 87503. For information on fishing at Fort Wingate, contact: Frank O'Donivan, Fort Wingate Depot Activity, Gallup, NM 87316, phone (505) 488-5411 (8:00 A.M. to 4:00 P.M., weekdays).

WHITE SANDS MISSILE RANGE

- 1,746,720 acres
- 30 miles north of Las Cruces
- Limited hunting
- Oryx, deer, and antelope

Hunting White Sands Missile Range (WSMR), which occupies 1,746,720 acres near Las Cruces, has severe restrictions on hunting availability. Therefore, the New Mexico Department of Game and Fish works in a cooperative effort with the missile range to clear sites for hunting.

Hunters wishing to use WSMR must apply to the New Mexico Department of Game and Fish (located in Santa Fe) by April 27 of each year. The department has a drawing for hunting permits in which approximately 100 names are chosen. The chosen hunters are notified by the New Mexico Department of Game and Fish about times, limits, and where check-in stations are located. All hunts are planned in advance.

Three major varieties of game at WSMR are oryx, deer, and antelope. Trapping and bird hunting are not controlled by the New Mexico Department of Game and Fish; they must be cleared by the military.

In addition to the New Mexico state licensing requirements, hunters at WSMR must pay a fee for a user stamp when they arrive on the site.

For further information, contact: New Mexico Department of Game and Fish, ATTN: Game Management, State Capitol, Villagra Building, Santa Fe, NM 87503, phone (505) 827-7885.

NEW YORK

Upstate New York is renowned for its deer hunting. The patchwork of farmlands and wood lots yields huge whitetails every year. Thousands of hunters and fishermen enjoy the outdoor opportunities this state offers.

New York covers 47,377 square miles. Unfortunately, most of it is privately owned. Still, the Department of Environmental Conservation manages roughly 3 million acres of land for public hunting and fishing.

There is a large military presence in New York. With thirty-six installations, the Department of Defense is one of the major landowners in the state. While most of the installations are small, averaging less than 1,000 acres, there are three major Army installations in the state that total almost 134,000 acres. Two of these are open to the public for hunting and fishing. One is open to military members and DOD civilians only. None of the Air Force installations in New York offer hunting or fishing.

Army Installations

FORT DRUM

- Northeast of Watertown
- 82,265 acres open to hunting and fishing
- Big game and small game
- Fishing
- Camping closed to the public

Hunting At Fort Drum, 82,265 acres are open to the public for hunting. Although the hunting seasons and licensing requirements necessary to hunt on Fort Drum are managed by the state, all hunters must check in with the range control office in Building 928 before going afield. Proof of having taken a hunter safety course is not necessary on this installation but may be required by the state. Hunters must be at least sixteen. Handguns are not allowed for hunting on Fort Drum, but all other means legal in New York are acceptable.

Big game hunters on Fort Drum may take white-tailed deer and black bear in accordance with state regulations. The seasons for both are concurrent with state seasons. Small game found on the installation are cottontail, squirrel, pheasant, waterfowl, grouse, and snowshoe hare. Fort Drum also has healthy populations of coyote, bobcat, and red and gray fox.

The latest hunter success rates on Fort Drum are 12 percent for whitetail hunters, 2 percent for bear hunters, and 50 percent overall for small game hunters.

Fishing Fort Drum offers anglers 660 surface acres of freshwater. The waters of the post are stocked with rainbow, brown and brook trout, bass, walleye, northern pike, perch, and assorted panfish.

All anglers on Fort Drum must meet New York licensing requirements. No installation permit is required and all fishing regulations are the same as those of the state. Creel limits also are governed by the state, as are fishing methods.

Miscellaneous Camping is allowed at Remington Pond on Fort Drum. Camping is open only to military ID card holders and is controlled by the outdoor recreation branch. ATVs are not allowed on this installation but snowmobiles are permitted in the winter.

The USGS maps covering Fort Drum are Hammond, Antwerp, Theresa, Alexandria Bay, Lake Bonaparte, and Gollveneur.

For more information on hunting and fishing at Fort Drum, contact: Game Warden Section (LEA), Bldg. T-9, Fort Drum, NY 13602-5000, phone (315) 772-6105/5413/6806 (7:30 A.M. to 4:00 P.M., weekdays).

SENECA ARMY DEPOT ACTIVITY

- Near Romulus
- 10,661 acres
- Closed to the public
- Installation permit required
- White-tailed deer and small game
- Fishing
- Camping

Hunting All of the installation is open to hunting, but the only people authorized to hunt on the Seneca Army Depot are active duty and retired military members and depot civilian employees. Hunters on the installation must meet all New York licensing requirements and purchase an installation permit for $4 a year.

All seasons and bag limits on the depot match those of the state. There are weapon restrictions on this installation, however, that differ from those set by state law. Hunters on Seneca may use shotguns, muzzleloaders, and archery tackle to take big and small game. Modern rifles, either centerfire or rimfire, and handguns are not allowed. Age restrictions on the installation match those of the state. All hunters must be at least sixteen.

White-tailed deer are the only big game on the installation. Hunting for whitetails is excellent, probably the best in the Northeast. The last hunter success figures available indicate 16 percent of archers were successful on the installation, while 87 percent of gun hunters filled their deer tags.

Deer hunting on the installation is under a guide system. Hunters are required to check in with the hunter control office where they are assigned a guide to escort them to their assigned stands. Hunters must stay in their assigned stand area until picked up by their guide.

Small game hunting on the installation should be good, as well. Small game hunters must check in with the security police prior to going afield. Seneca offers to the small game hunter cottontail rabbit, squirrel, waterfowl, ringneck pheasant, and grouse. Coyote can also be found on the installation. Small game and predator regulations match those of the state.

Fishing Fishing is restricted on the depot, and fishermen must meet the same stringent access requirements as hunters. For those who can fish on this installation, the waters contain bass, catfish, and bullheads.

All state fishing license requirements and creel limits are enforced on the installation. Anglers must have an installation fishing permit before wetting a line. They may use either artificial lures or live bait but cannot use more than one hook and line. Fishermen must check through the security police office prior to fishing and upon returning.

Miscellaneous Camping is allowed on the installation but is limited to those eligible to use the Army Travel Camp. Reservations may be made by calling (607) 869-1211. ATVs are not allowed on this installation.

The Ovid, Romulus, Dresden, and Geneva South topographic maps in the 7.5-minute series cover the depot.

For more information, contact: Director of Engineering and Housing, Seneca Army Depot, Romulus, NY 14541, phone (607) 869-1309 (7:00 A.M. to 4:30 P.M., weekdays).

U.S. MILITARY ACADEMY WEST POINT

- 50 miles north of New York City on the Hudson River
- 9,000 acres open to hunting and fishing
- Installation permit required
- White-tailed deer
- Small game hunting closed to the public
- Fishing
- Camping closed to the public
- Boating

Hunting Of the 15,975 acres that make up West Point, 9,000 are open for hunting. The post is open to the public on a priority basis. All hunters on West Point must meet state licensing requirements before purchasing a USMA permit from the community recreation division administration office in Griffin Hall. For those eligible, permits are also available from the outdoor recreation area office at Round Pond.

Members of the public are allowed to hunt on academy grounds on a priority basis but are last in line when it comes to getting access to academy hunting. Additionally, the public can hunt only deer on the reservation.

Deer hunting on West Point is conducted in accordance with New York regulations as published by the State Department of Environmental Conservation. Season dates are as set by the state. There are separate deer seasons for archery and firearms.

During the archery season, hunters must have valid New York licenses and installation permits with them when afield. Bowhunters must sign in and out in person daily at the military police office at Washington Gate or at the hunt control center during the firearms deer season.

During the regular firearms deer season, all hunters with a valid installation deer permit are entered in a lottery for opening-day hunting areas. After the season opener, hunting areas are assigned on a first-come, first-served basis. To participate in the lottery and reserve an area for opening day, hunters need to register no later than ten days prior to the scheduled hunting orientation. Separate lottery drawings are held for each access category to determine the order and assignment of hunting opening-day areas.

Those entered in the opening-day lottery must attend a hunting orientation scheduled by the community recreation officer. Hunters must sign in and out in person with the hunt control center, including those hunting on opening day. When checking in at the hunt control center, hunters are given a hunting area identification badge that must be worn at all times while afield. All participants in the deer hunting program receive a hunting map, rules of the hunt, points of contact, dud and hazardous material information, briefing notes, and for non-DOD personnel, a liability-release statement.

There are forty-eight hunting areas managed by the deer hunting program. All have quotas for hunters afield at any given time. Eight of the areas are reserved for bowhunting-only, even during the regular firearms season. Four of the areas are restricted to shotguns only. The rest are open to any weapon legal for hunting in New York. Deer hunters during the regular firearms season, except for those hunting in the archery-only areas, must wear a minimum of 200 square inches of international orange visible from all sides.

Successful hunters must take their deer to the hunt control office immediately after they have field-dressed the animal. There, the hunters are required to weigh their deer, fill out forms, and remove the lower jaw from the animal and place it in the box provided. For those wishing to have their deer mounted, special arrangements can be made with the West Point forester. Hunter success for deer at West Point is roughly 10 percent.

Small game hunting is open to authorized individuals only, not the public. The small game hunting program administers forty-one hunting areas on which up to 169 hunters at a time may seek small game. Most of the areas allow no more than four to six hunters afield at a time.

Small game hunters must sign in and out of hunting areas in person at Washington Gate except during the regular firearms deer season. During the regular firearms deer season, small game hunters must check in and out through the hunt control center on Route 293. Since deer herd reduction is a major objective of the USMA hunting programs, small game season may be closed or reduced during the regular firearms deer season. Cottontails, squirrels, waterfowl, pheasant, grouse, and turkey can all be hunted on academy grounds.

The Point also manages a turkey hunt. Turkey hunters must have a valid New York small game license, a New York turkey permit, and a West Point hunting permit. Hunters are required to sign in and out for a hunting area with the military police at Washington Gate. A hunter may sign in for only one area at a time. There are forty-one hunting areas for turkey on the installation. All New York turkey hunting regulations and seasons apply on the reservation.

Fishing Fishing at West Point is also open to the public. There are more than thirteen lakes and ponds on the reservation and numerous miles of streams. Additional fishing is available in the Hudson River, along West Point's eastern border.

The waters of West Point contain bass, trout, panfish, walleye, perch, pickerel, and norlunge, a pike and muskellunge hybrid. All state regulations, licensing requirements, and creel limits apply to West Point. Fishermen must have an installation permit, as well. Children twelve and under must be accompanied by a licensed, responsible person over sixteen when fishing the Point.

Miscellaneous Each lake and pond on West Point has its own boating rules. Consequently, they are too numerous to list here. Basically nonpowered boats and boats with electric trolling motors are allowed on all waters except Lusk Reservoir and Long Pond. All watercraft used on the installation must meet USCG safety requirements.

The USMA has a camping area open to authorized individuals only. The campground fee is $7 per night. Additionally, the USMA offers an outdoor recreation area at Round Pond for authorized individuals. The Round Pond Outdoor Recreation Area offers to military members, retirees, dependents, and DOD civilians fishing, swimming, camping, boating, and hiking year-round.

ATVs are not allowed on the installation.

The U.S. Army Corps of Engineers Topographic Command's West Point and Vicinity, Series V82SP Special Purpose Map covers all of West Point's land.

For more information, contact: Dick Farley, Round Pond, Bldg. 622, West Point, NY 10996, phone (914) 938-2503.

NORTH CAROLINA

Generally, hunting in North Carolina is by lease arrangement. The state Wildlife Resources Commission manages nearly 2 million acres of land with public access, but hunting pressure on these lands is great.

Military land in the state totals 369,073 acres divided among two Army installations, two Navy installations, seven Air Force bases, and seven installations belonging to the Marine Corps. Fort Bragg, Camp Lejeune, and the Marine Corps Air Station Cherry Point offer hunting or fishing.

Army Installations

FORT BRAGG

- 13,500 acres open to hunting and fishing
- Installation permit required
- White-tailed deer, turkey, and small game
- Fishing
- Camping closed to the public
- Restricted boating

Hunting Hunters on Fort Bragg may take white-tailed deer, turkey, cottontail rabbit, squirrel, waterfowl, quail, dove, raccoon, opossum, bobcat, and fox. The post is open to the public for hunting, but hunting is allowed on a priority-and-quota basis. Those stationed at Fort Bragg, their dependents, other military members and retirees and their dependents, and Department of the Army civilians all have priority over the public for hunting.

All hunting areas except those used during the general deer season are assigned on a first-come, first-served basis. Openings during the general deer season are assigned on a quota basis. Eighty percent of the hunting slots are allocated for those mentioned above. The rest are reserved for the public. After 7:00 A.M. on the day of the hunt, all remaining slots are given out on a first-come, first-served basis.

All hunters must sign in prior to entering an open hunting area. Small game hunters and archery deer hunters are required to sign in for Areas I through IV or named danger areas when the danger areas are posted as open. Every adult hunter must personally sign in and out on sign-in sheets. Family members under sixteen sign in and out for hunting on the same line as their parent or guardian. Separate sign-in sheets are maintained for deer and small game. Hunters may hunt both deer and small game on the same day but may not sign in for both at the same time. Deer hunters may not sign in for more than one area at a time. Hunter registration opens daily during the hunting season no earlier than ninety minutes prior to sunrise. All hunters must be out of the field and signed out no later than ninety minutes after sunset.

Members of the public may hunt on Fort Bragg on all open hunting days except Sundays. Sunday hunting is reserved for the military. Other open hunting days are Thursday through Saturday, all federal holidays, and post down days.

On special occasions, such as opening days or holidays, registration and drawings for spaces may be held for safety, security, or fairness. Such drawings are planned, organized, and controlled by wildlife management personnel.

All hunters on Fort Bragg must meet North Carolina licensing requirements prior to purchasing a post permit. Additionally, all hunters on the installation must have completed a state-certified hunter safety course. An annual hunting permit is $15. A combination permit is available for $20 per year. Daily hunting permits cost $5.

Except for raccoon and opossum, game animals and birds may be hunted from Thursday through Sunday from one-half hour before sunrise until one-half hour after sunset. All hunting weapons legal in North Carolina are legal on Fort Bragg, but certain areas of the post may have weapons restrictions. All big game taken on the post must be checked at the wildlife check station.

Temporary tree stands are authorized for deer hunting on Fort Bragg but must not damage the tree in any way. Tree stands that require the use of bolts, nails, or anything else that must penetrate the bark of a tree are not allowed.

Hunter success varies considerably on Fort Bragg. Though the Fort has a respectable deer population, hunter success is less than 10 percent. Small game hunters do much better. The average is at least one quail per hunter for each hunting trip, and one duck per hunter for every three hunting trips.

Fishing Fishing on Fort Bragg is also open to the public. Like hunters, non-military anglers on the installation must meet North Carolina fishing license requirements before purchasing a post fishing permit. Military anglers using natural baits on the post need a post permit but no state license. All anglers on the post over sixteen must have a valid state license when using artificial lures and modern rods and reels. Fishing permits are $15 annually or $20 for a combination fishing and hunting permit. Daily permits are available for $5 each.

Anglers on Fort Bragg will encounter largemouth bass, bluegill, redear sunfish, redbreast, warmouth bass, channel catfish, and bullheads. Angling is permitted year-round, twenty-four hours a day unless otherwise posted. Certain areas may be temporarily closed or restricted and are listed at the hunting and fishing center and McKellars Lodge. Primary access roads to the closed areas are also posted.

The only pond where fishermen must sign in is McKeithan Pond. Written clearance from the Range Control Office must be obtained prior to fishing this pond.

Certain lakes on Fort Bragg have bait limitations that prohibit fishermen from using live minnows as bait. All lakes so restricted are posted. Fishermen on Fort Bragg may use trotlines and bush hooks on all waters except those managed for catfish. Trotlines may not be unattended and fishermen must remove them after fishing.

Fishing or boating within 100 meters of any dam, water plant, or sewage treatment plant on the Little River is prohibited. Andrews Church Lake and Wyatt Lake are closed daily from 6:00 A.M. to noon, and the Smith Lake Recreation Area is closed from May 15 through September 30.

Miscellaneous There are special boating regulations on Fort Bragg. Andrews Church Lake is closed to all boating. On all lakes and streams except McArthur and Mott lakes, boats may not have a motor in excess of twenty-five horsepower. There are no horsepower restrictions on McArthur Lake or Mott Lake. All boats must meet USCG safety requirements.

Camping is allowed on Fort Bragg for military members and retirees. Smith Lake Recreation Area offers thirteen RV hookups and eleven partial hookups.

All vehicles on Fort Bragg must be licensed to operate on North Carolina public roadways. No ATVs or three- or four-wheelers are allowed. Hunters may drive their vehicles on firebreaks if the vehicle is licensed for road use.

The Cliffdale, Southern Pines, and Fayetteville USGS topographic maps cover Fort Bragg.

For more information, contact: HQ, XVII Airborne Corps and Fort Bragg, ATTN: AFZA-DE-DW, Fort Bragg, NC 28307-5000, phone (919) 396-7507/7022/5720 (7:30 A.M. to 3:45 P.M., Monday through Saturday).

Marine Corps Installations

CAMP LEJEUNE

- Near Wilmington
- 14 miles of Atlantic Ocean shoreline
- Closed to the public
- Installation permit required
- White-tailed deer, turkey, and small game
- Freshwater and saltwater fishing
- Camping

Hunting   Camp Lejeune is not open to the public for hunting unless they are guests of authorized personnel. Authorized personnel are defined as military personnel, including retirees and their dependents, and civilians assigned to or employed on the base or living in base housing and their dependents, including retired civil service personnel.

All hunters over thirteen at Camp Lejeune must have valid North Carolina or Onslow County hunting licenses and the appropriate tags for the game being hunted. Additionally, hunters over thirteen must have Camp Lejeune permits, available from Building PT-4 on Parachute Tower Road, weekdays between 8:00 A.M. and 4:00 P.M. from one hour before sunrise until 9:00 A.M. on Saturdays and holidays. Hunting permits are also available from the John A. Lejeune Rod and Gun Club, Building 1938, Marine Corps Base, Camp Lejeune, prior to the firearm deer season.

Hunters under thirteen are not allowed to carry a weapon in the field but may accompany their parent or guardian while hunting. Those between thirteen and fifteen must be under the direct supervision of a parent or guardian at all times in the field.

The permits are reasonable, at $15 per year for a hunting permit or $20 for a combination hunting and fishing permit. A daily permit is available for $5. All applicants for base hunting permits or hunting-area passes must successfully complete the hunter safety test given at Building PT-4.

Hunters must get an area clearance from either of two hunter check stations. One station is in Building PT-4; the other is on Verona Loop. Check stations are open daily from the beginning of the season through January 1 each year.

When signing in at the check station, hunters pick the area they want to hunt that day. Up to 75 percent of the hunting-area passes may be checked out the night before the hunt. The remaining 25 percent of the passes may be checked out up to one hour before sunrise on the day of the hunt. The hunting pass must be in the hunter's possession while he or she is in the field. A duplicate pass must be left on the hunter's vehicle dashboard. All passes must be returned no later than one hour after the close of legal shooting hours, and all big game taken on the installation must be checked at one of the hunter check stations before being removed from Camp Lejeune.

There are three large firearms hunting areas on Camp Lejeune, as well as three smaller archery-only areas. All the areas are managed on a quota system to enhance the safety and quality of the hunt. Game and fur-bearing animals available on Camp Lejeune are white-tailed deer, squirrel, rabbit, fox, quail, dove, opossum, muskrat, skunk, raccoon, beaver, mink, otter, bobcat, and turkey. A trapping permit is necessary to take fur-bearing animals.

Camp Lejeune has weapons restrictions. Centerfire and rimfire rifles are not allowed on the installation. The only rifles allowed are muzzleloaders of .40 caliber or larger. Shotguns are also allowed, either modern or muzzleloading. Those having a shell capacity of more than three rounds must be plugged to hold no more than three. Deer may be taken with muzzleloading rifles, muzzleloading shotguns shooting slugs, or modern shotguns shooting slugs. Buckshot is not authorized except during special group hunts. Handguns and crossbows are not allowed in hunting fields on the installation.

Bowhunters must meet the requirements of the North Carolina game codes. All

archery tackle must be within state guidelines. No exploding broadheads, poison pods, or barbed broadheads are allowed.

Hunters afield after all animals except waterfowl, wild turkey, or dove must wear an international orange vest and cap. Bowhunters do not have to meet this restriction when hunting in an archery-only area or during the bow-only season.

All North Carolina bag limits apply to Camp Lejeune.

Fishing   Fishing on Camp Lejeune is open to the same people authorized to hunt on the installation. Anglers must meet all North Carolina licensing requirements. Those fishing in any of the installation's stocked ponds must have an installation permit prior to fishing. The fishing permits are available from the same office as the hunting permits and cost $15 annually or $20 in a combined hunting and fishing permit. Daily permits are available for $5 each.

Camp Lejeune offers both freshwater and saltwater fishing. There are eleven stocked ponds on the installation in addition to numerous streams. Some of the ponds contain channel catfish, but most are stocked with bluegill and bass. All the ponds have special restrictions beyond those of the state. Trotlines, setlines, and bush hooks are not allowed in any pond. Minnows may not be used as bait in any of the installation's ponds.

The streams on the base are managed under the laws of the state. All state regulations apply to the freshwater streams of Camp Lejeune including creel limits and methods legal for the taking of fish. No installation permit is required to fish the installation's streams.

No base permit is required for saltwater fishing on Camp Lejeune. Fishermen must meet any state or federal guidelines in effect including licensing requirements while fishing in saltwater. Saltwater species found at Camp Lejeune are any of those found in this part of the Atlantic.

Miscellaneous Camping is authorized on the installation but only for military ID card holders. ATVs are not allowed.

For more information, contact: Assistant Chief of Staff, Environmental Management Department, Camp Lejeune, NC 28542-5000, phone (919) 451-1690/2083 (7:30 A.M. to 4:00 P.M., weekdays); or Base Game Warden, Bldg. PT-4, Parachute Tower Road, Camp Lejeune, NC 28542-5000, phone (919) 451-2196 (7:30 A.M. to 4:00 P.M., weekdays).

MARINE CORPS AIR STATION CHERRY POINT

- Near Havelock
- 6,000 acres open to hunting and fishing
- Closed to the public
- Installation permit required
- White-tailed deer and small game
- Fishing
- Camping
- Restricted boating

Hunting MCAS Cherry Point is not open to the public for hunting. Those authorized to hunt unescorted on the installation are active duty military personnel and their dependents, retired military personnel and their dependents who live within a fifty-mile radius of MCAS Cherry Point, and civilian employees of MCAS Cherry Point, including the Naval Air Rework Facility.

Authorized individuals may have one or two hunting guests on the installation at a time. Sponsors must remain with their guests at all times.

All hunters on MCAS Cherry Point must meet North Carolina licensing requirements prior to purchasing an installation hunting permit. The permits cost $5 a year, or $7 a year for a combined hunting and fishing permit. Waterfowlers must have the appropriate federal duck stamps and deer hunters must have a valid North Carolina big game tag. All hunters over sixteen must take a hunter safety test when applying for an installation permit.

MCAS Cherry Point offers to hunters white-tailed deer, cottontail, squirrel, quail, dove, and waterfowl. All state seasons are in effect on the installation with the exception of bear and turkey seasons. Bear and turkey may not be hunted on the air station.

Hunters may use modern shotguns capable of holding no more than three shells for small game and deer. Deer hunters must use slugs in their shotguns and may not use either 28 gauge or .410-bore guns. Muzzleloading rifles are authorized for deer hunting if the bore diameter is at least .40 caliber. Muzzleloading shotguns may be used for both deer and small game. All shotgunners must use shot smaller than #2 for small game. Centerfire rifles and handguns are not allowed on the installation for hunting.

Archery hunting is also authorized on the installation. Archers must meet all state licensing and equipment requirements. Crossbows are not legal on the installation.

Cherry Point is divided into seven hunting areas. Several of those areas are bowhunting-only areas. The rest are open to gun hunting by both individual hunters and groups. Hunters must check in daily before going afield. The checkpoint is the game warden's office in Building 414. When checking in, a hunter will be given a hunting area pass and a vehicle placard. The hunter must have the area pass with him at all times. The vehicle placard must be placed on the dash of the hunter's vehicle in plain view.

Hunters may check in at the game warden's office up to one hour before sunrise to get a hunting area. All hunters must check back with the game warden upon completion of hunting or no later than one hour after sunset.

Dogs may not be used on the air station for hunting deer, but dogs may be used to take small game, upland birds, and waterfowl.

Hunter success at Cherry Point is 10 percent for whitetails. Small game hunter success ratios vary greatly depending on the species.

Fishing Fishing is allowed at MCAS Cherry Point. The same access restrictions apply to fishermen as to hunters. All fishermen on the installation must meet the licensing requirements established by the state. Additionally, fishermen over thirteen must have an installation permit. The permits are available for $3 per year or $7 per year for a combined fishing and hunting permit.

Anglers on Cherry Point may take largemouth bass, channel catfish, bluegill, and redear sunfish. Though state creel limits generally apply, certain ponds have special limits. Trotlines, set hooks, and bush hooks are not allowed on the installation. Additionally, anglers may not use minnows as bait in any of Cherry Point's ponds.

Fishing is permitted twenty-four hours a day on the installation. Anglers fishing at night must first check with the military police desk sergeant in Building 294 (phone 466-3615) before going out. Children under ten are not allowed to fish in any MCAS Cherry Point ponds unless they are under the direct supervision of an adult. The main gate pond is closed to fishing at all times.

Miscellaneous Outboard motors are prohibited in all installation ponds, but boats may be used in Bartlett, Catfish, and Duck ponds.

Primitive camping is allowed at Cherry Point. Restrictions that govern hunting and fishing access also apply to camping. All vehicles used on the installation must carry a valid state license, and ATVs are prohibited.

The Havelock and Cherry Point topographic maps cover this installation.

For more information on hunting and fishing at Cherry Point, contact: Wildlife Manager, NREA Dept. (Code LN), MCAS Cherry Point, NC 28533-5000, phone (919) 466-3242 (7:30 A.M. to 4:00 P.M., weekdays).

OHIO

Although it is a fairly large state, Ohio offers little in the way of public hunting lands. Of the state's 40,000-plus square miles, only 750,000 acres are open to the public for hunting and fishing.

Only one military installation is open to hunting and fishing.

RAVENNA
ARMY AMMUNITION PLANT

- 30 miles southeast of Cleveland
- 16,541 acres open to hunting and fishing
- White-tailed deer and small game
- Fishing

Hunting Hunting on Ravenna Army Ammunition Plant is jointly managed by the state of Ohio and the Department of the Army. There is no fee for hunting on the plant's grounds. All that is required is a valid Ohio license and the appropriate tags.

Of the plant's 21,000 acres, 16,541 acres are open to hunting. The plant, in conjunction with the Ohio Department of Natural Resources, issues 800 whitetail tags each year. The state is responsible for issuing 400 of those tags through a lottery system. The plant reserves the other 400 for plant employees and military personnel.

Small game hunting on the plant is limited. White-tailed deer, on the other hand, are well managed and offer excellent hunting opportunities. During the 1988 season, hunter success was 40 percent on whitetails, with 358 bucks and 351 does taken. The average body weight of yearling bucks taken that year was 113 pounds.

Civilian hunters interested in applying for one of the state-controlled permits at the plant can do so by sending a postcard with their name, address, and deer permit number to Ravenna Hunt, Division of Wildlife, Survey and Inventory, Fountain Square, Building G, Columbus, OH 43224-1329. Hunters may submit only one application, and all applications must be submitted during October of each year. Military personnel and plant employees should contact the plant directly at the address listed at the end of this section.

Fishing Ravenna offers fishing to local anglers and plant employees. A valid Ohio fishing license and any necessary tags are required.

The plant offers over sixty-two surface acres of stocked ponds, nineteen miles of stream, and a total of forty-four miles of shoreline for Ohio anglers. Species available are bass, sunfish, and catfish.

Miscellaneous Every year the Ravenna Army Ammunition Plant offers an excellent archery tournament on plant grounds. Camping and ATVs are not allowed on the plant.

For more information, contact: Public Affairs Division, Ravenna Army Ammunition Plant, 8451 State Route 5, Ravenna, OH 44266-9297.

OKLAHOMA

This midwestern state is actually the beginning of the West. Oklahoma covers 69,919 square miles and hosts three army installations and ten Air Force installations. Most are not open to the public for hunting and fishing, but those that are offer sportsmen 169,510 acres of outdoor opportunities.

Army Installations

CAMP GRUBER

- South of Muskogee
- 53,000 acres
- White-tailed deer and small game

Hunting Camp Gruber is under the control of the Oklahoma Army National Guard. Camp Gruber's lands are part of a larger wildlife management area managed by the state of Oklahoma, so all hunting on Camp Gruber is managed by the Oklahoma Fish and Wildlife Commission.

Camp Gruber Wildlife Management Area encompasses more than 53,000 acres and is divided into three hunting areas. Each area has its own regulations set by the state.

Big game hunting on Camp Gruber is limited to white-tailed deer. Small game animals include rabbit, quail, duck, and squirrel.

There are no special licensing requirements to hunt on Camp Gruber. All that is required is a valid Oklahoma hunting license. Hunters are not required to sign in or out on the installation, and there are no weapons restrictions. Anything legal in the state is legal on Camp Gruber.

There is no fishing on Camp Gruber.

The topographic maps covering the Camp Gruber area are the Hulbert 3-DMATC Edition, Series V783, Sheet 6955 I and the Webers Falls 3-DMATC, Series V783, Sheet 6955 II.

For complete details, contact: Oklahoma Department of Wildlife Conservation, Box 53465, Oklahoma City, OK 73152.

FORT SILL

• Near Lawton

• 70,000 acres open to hunting and fishing

• Closed to the public

• Installation permit required

• Big game and small game

• Fishing

• Restricted camping

Hunting Fort Sill offers eligible hunters some unique hunting opportunities. For one thing, it is one of the few places east of the Rockies where you can legally hunt elk. Fort Sill also offers excellent hunting for whitetails and turkeys.

Small game hunting on the installation is excellent. Hunters may take cottontail rabbit, dove, crow, waterfowl, quail, swamp rabbit, jack rabbit, squirrel, coyote, beaver, raccoon, bobcat, striped skunk, opossum, badger, rail, gallinule, common snipe, woodcock, prairie dog, and pheasant.

There are over 70,000 acres open to active duty and retired military members and their dependents, post employees and their dependents, and Department of the Army civilians and their dependents. All hunters on Fort Sill must meet Oklahoma licensing requirements and hunter safety course requirements. Additionally, hunters must have an installation safety briefing prior to purchasing their post permits. The post permits are available from the information center at the post's main gate.

Fort Sill has some safety regulations worth mentioning. Quail hunting parties can include no more than four people. International orange caps and vests are required for all gun deer and elk hunters. The orange fabric must total 500 square inches for each hunter. Orange camouflage is allowed, provided at least 400 square inches of the garment are orange. Hunters may not fire a weapon from a vehicle or within twenty feet of a vehicle. All weapons carried in a vehicle must be unloaded.

Fort Sill is divided into fourteen hunting areas. Like most installations, there is a hunter quota for each hunting area on the post.

All hunters must check in at the information center prior to going afield. At the information center, hunters register and pick up one parking pass and one hunting pass for the area selected. A hunting party of two or more may designate one member of the party to pick up the passes. Range and post-wide permits are issued for selected activities such as coyote, duck, and raccoon hunting, as well as small game hunting on the Quanah Range. Passes are usually available on a first-come, first-served basis after noon on the day prior to hunting.

Hunters must check back with the information center no later than one and one-half hours after sunset. Small game hunters and archery deer hunters may phone in after hunting. Gun deer hunters and elk hunters must check in at the information center upon completion of hunting. Small game animals taken must be reported to the information center. All big game animals must be brought to the information center.

Fort Sill limits the weapons that are legal to use on the installation. Hunters may use .22 rimfire rifles and pistols for hunting small game as well as shotguns shooting shot, muzzleloaders, and archery tackle. Big game hunters may use muzzleloaders, shotguns no larger than 10-gauge shooting slugs, and archery tackle. Centerfire rifles and handguns are not generally allowed but may be authorized on a special basis for deer and elk.

Night hunting for certain predators and fur-bearing animals is allowed on the fort. Hunters after raccoon and opossum must use shotguns loaded with shot no larger than #6. Predator hunters going afield at night must get clearance from the fish and wildlife branch prior to going out.

Hunter success at Fort Sill is good for both big and small game. Hunters willing to put forth an effort should have no problem taking game on this well managed installation.

Fishing Fort Sill is unique in that it requires fishermen to attend the installation's sportsman safety class before getting an installation permit. The reason is that Fort Sill is, after all, an artillery center. Consequently, many of the fishing and hunting areas lie along the boundaries of artillery firing ranges. It is important to know where those ranges are and when they are active.

Fishing on Fort Sill is restricted to those with the same eligibility as hunters. Many of the ponds lie within or are close to active ranges. Fishermen must obtain a range pass from the information center prior to fishing several of the ponds on Fort Sill. Those ponds requiring a pass are clearly designated on maps at the information center. Some ponds on the fort are closed during the duck and gun deer seasons. For a list of ponds that are open, check with the information center.

Fishermen on Fort Sill may generally use any method of fishing legal in Oklahoma to take fish from Fort Sill's waters. Trotlines may be used in the Fort Sill portions of Lake Elmer Thomas, Medicine Creek, and East Cache Creek. Trotlines may have no more than fifty hooks and be submerged no less than three feet. Jug-fishing and bush hooks are not allowed.

Fishermen may use gigs and bow-fishing equipment to take rough fish. Rough fish on Fort Sill are all species except trout, bass, channel catfish, and crappie. Spear guns may be used on the military side of Lake Elmer Thomas to take all species of fish except bass.

Creel limits on game fish at Fort Sill vary slightly from those of Oklahoma. Anglers may take no more than eight trout, thirty-seven crappie, and ten ten-inch channel catfish. Bass fishermen must adhere to a slot limit on largemouths and can take no more than five bass daily, only two of which may be sixteen inches or longer. All bass between twelve and sixteen inches must be released. Lake Elmer Thomas has its own bass regulations. It matches those of the state, with a ten-bass limit. Other species of fish on Fort Sill, such as bream, redear sunfish, warmouth bass, and other nongame species have no creel limit.

Miscellaneous Camping is not allowed on Fort Sill except in the Army Travel Camp in the main cantonment area. ATVs are not permitted on the post.

All sportsmen in the field on Fort Sill must be aware of the dangers of dud ammunition and unexploded ordnance. Fishermen and hunters finding such articles should mark their location, leave the area immediately, and report the find to the nearest MP or Army official.

Fort Sill is covered by the Arbuckle Hill, Fort Sill, Mount Scott, and Quanah Mountain, Oklahoma, topographic maps.

For information, contact: Sportsmen Services, Natural Resources Branch, Directorate of Engineering and Housing, Fort Sill, OK 73503, phone (405) 351-6050 (any time).

McALESTER
ARMY AMMUNITION PLANT

- 44,964 acres
- Installation permit required
- Big game and turkey
- Fishing

Hunting Hunting on McAlester is controlled jointly by the state and the plant. Only big game and turkey hunting are allowed on the installation. All hunters are selected by the state in a drawing.

Hunters are limited to using shotguns with slugs or archery tackle on McAlester. Archery hunters are further restricted to using traditional equipment. Longbows and recurves without attachments are all that are allowed. Compounds are illegal.

The bag limits on McAlester are liberal, with deer hunters allowed two deer a season. Hunters taking a doe first are often put in a drawing for any special hunts held later in the year. McAlester is literally overrun with whitetails! Hunter success on deer is 43 percent for hunters using shotguns and 15.6 percent for archers. The hunter success for archers is exceptional, considering the equipment limitations.

Hunters selected for the McAlester deer hunts must attend a plant briefing on the Thursday preceding their hunt. Check-in for the briefing is 8:00 A.M. Hunters failing to attend the briefing will have their reservations cancelled and will not be allowed to hunt. All hunts on the plant end at 2:30 P.M. on the last day of the plant season.

Hunting permits cost $15 a year and are available to the plant's civilian employees and the public. The permits are divided equally between the two groups.

Turkey hunters also fare well on the plant, with a 33 percent hunter success rate. Equipment restrictions for turkey hunters are the same as those for deer hunting, except that turkey hunters must use shotguns shooting shot.

The average weight of yearling white-tailed bucks taken on McAlester Army Ammunition Plant during the 1988 season was only seventy-three pounds, an indication of overpopulation. During the 1988 season, hunters took 217 bucks and 225 does from the plant.

Fishing Fishing is allowed on the plant's waters. The plant is blessed with about five miles of shoreline, eleven miles of stream, and a total of 1,042 surface acres of water.

All fishing regulations on the plant follow those of the state. Fishermen must meet all state licensing requirements and follow state creel limits for all species. The species found on the plant are all those found in Oklahoma with the exception of striped bass.

Miscellaneous Camping and ATVs are not allowed on the installation. Hunters and fishermen must check in at the security office prior to going afield or afloat.

For more information, contact: Wildlife Manager, McAlester Army Ammunition Plant, McAlester, OK 74501.

Air Force Installations

VANCE AIR FORCE BASE

- Near Enid
- White-tailed deer
- Installation permit required

Hunting Technically, Vance AFB itself is not open to hunting. The only hunting allowed is on Kegelman Auxiliary Airfield and is strictly controlled.

All hunters using the Kegelman area must have a Kegelman Wildlife Management Area hunting permit (Vance TW Form 71) available from the Vance Air Force Base

Rod and Gun Club for $15. All hunters must also comply with Oklahoma licensing requirements.

In order to hunt on Kegelman, hunters must make a reservation for the area the weekend before they want to hunt. No more than eight hunters are allowed into the Kegelman area at a time.

While the seasons and bag limits on the Kegelman Wildlife Management Area follow those of the state, there are weapons restrictions. Hunters on Kegelman may use shotguns with slugs, muzzleloaders, and archery tackle. No breechloading rifles, handguns, or crossbows may be used on the installation.

Whitetail hunting on the installation is fair, but hunter success figures are not available.

For more information on hunting the Vance AFB/Kegelman AAF area, contact: Vance Rod and Gun Club, Vance Air Force Base, OK 73705-5000.

PENNSYLVANIA

This northeastern state is renowned for both the huge white-tailed deer it produces and the sheer number of whitetails available.

Pennsylvania has a long tradition of deer hunting. The state encompasses over 45,000 square miles and offers about 4.5 million acres of land for public hunting. Unfortunately, the state also has a large population, so all public lands are hunted hard.

There are twenty-two DOD installations in the state. Not all of these installations are open for hunting and fishing, of course, but those that are offer 36,345 acres of well-managed hunting area. The installations offering hunting and fishing in Pennsylvania all belong to the U.S. Army.

Army Installations

FORT INDIANTOWN GAP

> • 23 miles east of Harrisburg
> • 15,958 acres open to hunting and fishing
> • Installation permit required
> • White-tailed deer and small game
> • Fishing

Hunting Fort Indiantown Gap offers 15,958 acres of land for northeastern hunters. The terrain is mostly rolling foothills covered in hardwoods, with some meadows. Hunters may take white-tailed deer, cottontail, squirrel, pheasant, grouse, varying hare, and groundhogs on this installation.

Fort Indiantown Gap is open to the public for hunting. A valid Pennsylvania hunting license and a daily hunting permit are all that are required. No special permit other than the daily permit is necessary. All rules and regulations, including bag limits and legal weapons, match those of the state.

Hunters are required to check in and out daily at the wildlife office. As at most installations, the number of hunters afield at any time on installation property is strictly controlled. When checking in with the wildlife office, hunters are allowed to choose a hunting area and pick up a pass for that area. All passes must be returned to the wildlife office at the end of the day.

Hunters must be at least eighteen to hunt on Fort Indiantown Gap. There is no requirement for completing a hunter safety course prior to hunting on the installation, but attendance is still a good idea.

Hunter success on Fort Indiantown Gap for deer is only about 5 percent. Small game hunters fare much better, with an average success of about 30 percent.

Fishing Fort Indiantown Gap has several ponds and streams stocked with trout, bass, various panfish, and pickerel. Fishing is open to the public, but anglers must check in and out at the wildlife office before going out.

There are no special licenses required for Fort Indiantown Gap. Anglers need only a valid Pennsylvania fishing license. All state regulations are in effect on Fort Indiantown Gap. All creel limits apply, as do legal methods of taking fish.

Miscellaneous Camping and ATVs are not allowed on Fort Indiantown Gap. All vehicles must remain on roadways.

The topographic map that covers this installation is the 2-DMA, Series V7315, Indiantown Gap Sheet.

For more information, contact: Pennsylvania Army National Guard, Fort Indiantown Gap, Annville, PA 17002, phone (717) 865-5444, ext. 2322 (8:00 A.M. to 4:00 P.M., Monday through Friday).

LETTERKENNY ARMY DEPOT

- Near Gettysburg
- 12,000 acres open to hunting and fishing
- Installation permit required
- White-tailed deer and small game
- Fishing and camping closed to the public

Hunting Letterkenny is divided into two hunting zones. Zone I includes 12,000 acres and is open only to Letterkenny employees, local military personnel, and retired military members, their dependents, and their guests. Zone II covers 5,000 acres and is open to the public.

Getting permission to hunt on Letterkenny Army Depot is a fairly involved process. All hunters must have a valid Pennsylvania license and all the appropriate tags for the season and weapon with which they are hunting. In addition, hunters must have a valid Letterkenny hunting permit. The permit costs $10 for all hunters and is available at Building S-617 for Zone I hunters. Zone II hunters must apply by mail to: Letterkenny Army Depot, ATTN: SDSLE-BAR (Hunting), Chambersburg, PA 17201-4150.

The applications must contain the hunter's name and address, his or her Pennsylvania hunting license number, seasons desired to hunt, and all applicable tag numbers (e.g., archery and muzzleloader). The applications must also contain a certified check, cashier's check, or money order in the amount of $10. Applications must be submitted no later than September 6 each year. Zone II permits are good in Zone I during certain special hunts.

Like most installations, hunters on Letterkenny must check in and out when going afield. Members of the public participating in Letterkenny hunts must check in at Boundary Gate 10. Hunters authorized to hunt in Zone I may check in at boundary gates 7, 10, or 11 during the week. Zone I hunters must also check in with Post 2 prior to going afield for the first time.

Hunting is well controlled on Letterkenny. All hunters must have completed a hunter safety course and must also attend an installation hunting briefing. No more than a certain number of hunters are allowed in the field at a time. Hunter orange is required during the shotgun and muzzleloader seasons.

Deer hunters on Letterkenny may use shotguns that are 20-gauge or larger shooting slugs. Flintlock muzzleloaders and archery tackle are also allowed. Centerfire rifles, handguns, and crossbows are banned.

Small game hunters may use bolt-action, single-shot, or pump .22 rimfire rifles. Revolvers in .22 rimfire are also legal. Shotguns used for small game season must be plugged to hold no more than three shells.

All seasons on Letterkenny are controlled. They change from year to year, so a current copy of the installation's hunting regulations are a must.

Hunter success on Letterkenny is impressive. During the 1988–89 season, hunters averaged 48 percent success on antlered deer and a 68 percent success on antlerless. Small game hunters also fared well.

Fishing   Fishing on Letterkenny is restricted to those authorized to hunt in Zone I. Fishermen must abide by Pennsylvania licensing requirements and have an installation permit as well.

Letterkenny offers good bass and trout fishing. There are several streams on the installation for trout fishermen, and Letterkenny Lake is periodically stocked with trout, bass, panfish, and catfish. The lake formed by the Letterkenny Dam in Horse Valley is periodically stocked by the Pennsylvania Fish Commission.

Miscellaneous   Camping is allowed on Letterkenny but is open only to authorized military members, their families, and retirees. ATVs are not allowed on the installation.

The Upper Strasburg, Fannetsburg, Chambersburg, and Scotland topographic maps cover Letterkenny Army Depot.

For more information, contact: Natural Resources Manager, SOSLE-EMN, Letterkenny Army Depot, Chambersburg, PA 17201-4105, phone (717) 267-8438 (8:00 A.M. to 4:00 P.M., weekdays); or Community Recreation Branch, SOSLE-B19, Letterkenny Army Depot, Chambersburg, PA 17201-4105, phone (717) 267-8674 (8:00 A.M. to 4:00 P.M., weekdays).

TOBYHANNA ARMY DEPOT

- 1,293 acres
- Closed to the public
- Installation permit required
- Fishing

Fishing Angling on Tobyhanna is open only to military and civilian employees of the installation. Anglers on Tobyhanna must have a valid Pennsylvania fishing license and a Tobyhanna Army Depot fishing permit. All Pennsylvania fishing laws apply to the installation.

Species available on Tobyhanna are trout, pickerel, and assorted panfish.

Miscellaneous Camping is not allowed on Tobyhanna. ATVs are allowed in specified areas in the winter.

For more information, contact: Community and Family Activities Division, Tobyhanna Army Depot, Box 5044, Tobyhanna, PA 18466-5044, phone (717) 894-7584 (weekdays, 8:00 A.M. to 4:40 P.M.).

SOUTH CAROLINA

This southern state covering 31,055 square miles has about 1.6 million acres open to public hunting. Though not known for its hunting and fishing, South Carolina provides some of the best hunting and fishing east of the Mississippi.

South Carolina hosts a sizable military population. From the Army's Fort Jackson to the Marine Corps's Parris Island, there are nineteen DOD installations in the state. Not all are open to hunting and fishing, but those that are offer more than 65,000 acres for East Coast sportsmen to enjoy.

Army Installations

FORT JACKSON

- Near Columbia
- 49,000 acres open to hunting and fishing
- Closed to the public
- Installation permit required
- White-tailed deer, turkey, and small game
- Fishing
- Camping
- Restricted boating

Hunting The hunting program on Fort Jackson is one of the best managed in the Department of Defense. It offers quality hunting and safety on 49,000 acres of prime wildlife habitat to those eligible to hunt on the installation.

Fort Jackson is not open to the public for hunting, but members of the public may hunt on Fort Jackson as guests of eligible personnel. Those authorized to hunt on Fort Jackson are active duty military personnel and their dependents, military retirees and their dependents, Department of the Army civilian employees and their dependents, post civilian employees and their dependents, National Guard and Reserve members on active duty, and 100 percent disabled veterans.

All hunters on Fort Jackson sixteen and over must have a Fort Jackson hunting permit prior to going afield. Hunters must also meet South Carolina licensing requirements, with some exceptions. According to Fort Jackson Regulation 28-4, those exceptions are as follows:

1. Military personnel on leave who are legal residents of South Carolina and stationed at installations outside South Carolina are not required to purchase a South Carolina or Richland County hunting or fishing license or a Fort Jackson permit. A big game permit for deer and turkey and a duck stamp is required when applicable. Dependents must purchase a resident South Carolina or a Richland County hunting and fishing license and a Fort Jackson guest permit or annual permit.

2. Military personnel on leave who are not legal residents of South Carolina and are stationed at installations outside South Carolina must purchase a South Carolina or Richland County hunting or fishing license and a Fort Jackson hunting or fishing permit. In addition, a nonresident big game permit is required for hunting deer and turkey.

3. Persons 65 years of age or older or 100 percent service-connected disabled veterans authorized to hunt or fish at Fort Jackson who have a South Carolina gratis or disability license are required to complete a sportsman locator card only.

4. Youth under sixteen may hunt only when accompanied by a properly licensed parent or authorized hunter with written permission from the child's parent or guardian.

Post hunting and fishing permits are valid from July 1 through June 30 of the following year. The permits are available from the Heise Pond Hunting and Fishing Center. Hunting permits are available on an annual basis at $15. An annual combination hunting and fishing permit is $20. Fort Jackson also offers a short-term combination license valid for ten days at $10. A special limited-stay permit is available at $3 per day.

Guest permits are only issued on a daily basis. A combination large-and-small-game hunting permit is $12 daily, while a small-game-only permit costs $5 per day. Guests may be brought on to Fort Jackson to hunt no more than fifteen times a year, no matter how many sponsors they have.

All hunters on Fort Jackson must check in and out at the Heise Pond Hunting and

Fishing Center. They must also sign in at the center when doing preseason scouting. Hunters signing in for a scouting expedition must include name, permit number, areas, and time in and out. Individuals may sign for no more than three of the six hunting areas, and areas must be signed for in order of preference and time of use. No weapons are allowed during scouting trips.

Hunters signing in for scouting must also complete a vehicle control form to be left on the dash of their vehicle while they are in the field. All hunters checking in or out at the Heise Pond Hunting and Fishing Center must also complete a sportsman locator card that will be kept on file in case of an emergency.

The only big game on Fort Jackson is the white-tailed deer. Deer hunting on the post is managed in a unique manner. Post wildlife management authorities and the civil engineering branch have constructed numerous permanent tree stands on the installation. These stands are constantly maintained and repaired. They are located in prime whitetail feeding and travel areas and offer an excellent opportunity to take a deer.

Most days, deer hunters are selected by a drawing. Hunters report to the Heise Hunting and Fishing Center around 4:45 A.M. and attend a briefing. After the briefing, hunters fill out a daily hunting card that is their ticket for the lottery drawing. Hunters are selected for stands around 5:30 A.M. and may go to their stand sites after being selected. Stand hunters may hunt from the stand only during morning or evening hunts. Another stand selection is held around 1:00 P.M. for the afternoon hunt.

Fort Jackson also allows still-hunting and deer drives, with and without dogs. Still-hunters are allowed to hunt only in certain areas, not in the same areas as hunters using tree stands. Drives with and without dogs are organized through the hunting and fishing center.

A still-hunter may stay in his or her assigned area all day. Still-hunters are selected by a random drawing after attending a safety briefing. Deer drives, on the other hand, are organized by the hunting and fishing center after enough hunters sign up to participate.

Some of the hunting areas on Fort Jackson are reserved for archery hunting. Tree stands and still-hunting areas are both available to archers. Although other deer hunters must wear hunter orange above the waist, including a hat, archers hunting in an archery-only area may hunt in full camouflage.

Fort Jackson has some unique firearms restrictions. Deer hunters may use centerfire rifles and handguns to take deer, but only from elevated tree stands. Shotgunners may use slugs to take deer, but again, only from elevated stands. Muzzleloaders are also restricted to tree stands. Shotgunners still-hunting or participating in a drive must use at least #1 buckshot. Archers may hunt from either tree stands or the ground.

Small game hunters on Fort Jackson have a smorgasbord of animals to hunt. Fort Jackson has impressive numbers of cottontail rabbit, squirrel, quail, raccoon, and waterfowl. All small game seasons coincide with those of the state, as do the big game seasons.

Small game hunters may use shotguns with shot no larger than #4, rimfire rifles, handguns, and archery tackle to pursue small game. There is no lottery for small game hunting but hunters must still check in and out at the Heise Hunting and Fishing Center before going afield.

Waterfowl hunters on the installation have a choice of hunting on their own or from one of the post's permanent duck blinds. They may reserve a blind up to one day in advance. Either way, they must check in and out at the Heise Center.

Turkey hunting is also a favorite on this installation. The post offers both a spring and fall turkey season for hunters using shotguns and archery tackle.

Hunter success on Fort Jackson is excellent. Deer hunters averaged a 54.5 percent success rate, while small game hunters did even better at 85.2 percent.

Fishing Fishing is excellent at Fort Jackson. There are numerous ponds on the post, as well as some natural bodies of water. All contain fish of one type or another and some are intensely managed for trophy fish.

Access to fishing on Fort Jackson is restricted to those who have hunting access. Members of the public may fish on the installation as guests of authorized personnel, and anglers under fourteen must be accompanied by an adult at all times. All anglers must meet South Carolina fishing licensing requirements and purchase a post permit if fifteen or over. The post fishing permits are available from the Heise Hunting and Fishing Center and cost the same as hunting permits.

During certain times of the year, anglers must check with the Heise Hunting and Fishing Center before going out. Many of the ponds lie within range boundaries or in active hunting areas, so it's for the angler's own safety that the sign-in requirement exists.

There are eleven intensely managed ponds on the installation. In these ponds, the creel limits differ from those of the state. For bass and catfish, the creel limit is five per day; for other species, thirty per day. There are no creel limits on non game fish in these ponds. All intensely managed ponds have slot limits, as well. Bass must be at least fifteen inches in length, while catfish must meet a twelve-inch minimum. These ponds are closed to set hooks, jug-fishing, trotlines, bow-fishing, spears, gigs, nets, seines, and fish traps, including tires.

Other waters on the installation, except Weston Lake, fall under the guidelines established by South Carolina. Weston Lake has the same restrictions on methods of taking fish as do the intensely managed ponds.

Miscellaneous Camping is allowed on Fort Jackson. The fort operates the Weston Lake Recreation Area eight miles from the main post. The area offers eligible campers RV, tent camping, and cabins. A military ID card is required to use the area.

ATVs are not allowed on the installation. Hunters may use normal, street-legal four-wheel-drive vehicles but must stay on roads and firebreaks unless retrieving game. Special concessions are made for handicapped hunters.

Boating is allowed on some Fort Jackson waterways. The post imposes restrictions on outboard motor horsepower and other methods of propulsion.

The 2-DMA V746SFTJACKSMIM topographic map, available from the Defense Mapping Agency, covers Fort Jackson.

For more information, contact: Outdoor Recreation Branch, ATZJ-PA-CFA-CR (ATTN: Mr. Berry), Bldg. 3392, Fort Jackson, SC 29207-7150, phone (803) 751-4948 (10:00 A.M. to 6:30 P.M., Thursday through Monday).

Air Force Installations

SHAW AIR FORCE BASE

- Near Sumter
- 11,450 acres
- Closed to the public
- Installation permit required
- Fishing

Fishing   Fishing on Shaw is limited to military members, retirees, dependents of military members and retirees, and base civilians. Anglers must meet the licensing requirements of South Carolina before purchasing a Shaw AFB fishing permit. All South Carolina fishing laws apply to the base, including creel limits and legal methods of taking fish. The ponds on Shaw are stocked with bream, crappie, bass, and catfish.

Miscellaneous   Camping and ATVs are not allowed on Shaw.

For more information, contact: 363CSG/SSS, Shaw AFB, SC 29152-5000, phone (803) 668-2204 (7:30 A.M. to 4:30 P.M., weekdays).

Marine Corps Installations

MARINE CORPS AIR STATION BEAUFORT

- On the north side of Port Royal Sound
- 7,000 acres
- Closed to the public
- White-tailed deer and small game
- Freshwater and saltwater fishing

Hunting   The only people eligible to apply for a permit to hunt on MCAS Beaufort are active duty military members, retired military members, civilian government employees, and dependents and houseguests of authorized personnel.

Hunters must fulfill the following requirements.

1. Complete a permit application.
2. Complete a statement of understanding of regulations.
3. Complete a government liability release (unless on active duty).
4. Attend a base hunter safety lecture (given only on Tuesday evenings).
5. Schedule and attend an ordnance hunter safety briefing for all ordnance areas (given by appointment only).
6. Have a valid state and county license for the game to be hunted.
7. Register weapons with the MCAS Provost Marshal's Office Consolidated ID Card Center (9:00 A.M. to 3:00 P.M., weekdays).
8. Purchase a permit from the game warden's office (Wednesdays and Fridays only, 1:00 to 4:00 P.M.).

All seasons on MCAS Beaufort follow those of South Carolina. The only major difference on the air station is the size of white-tailed deer that may be taken. No spotted fawns or deer under fifty pounds live weight may be taken on the installation.

Beaufort also has restrictions on the types of weapons that may be used. Centerfire rifles and handguns and rimfire rifles and handguns may not be used on Beaufort. Crossbows are also illegal. The only weapons that may legally be used are shotguns shooting slugs for deer and shot smaller than #4 for all other species, black-powder rifles over .44 caliber, shotguns, and archery tackle. Archery tackle must conform to state regulations.

Hunters must check in with the duty game warden or MP desk sergeant when the duty game warden is not present prior to entering and upon exiting any hunting area. MCAS Beaufort uses a badge-exchange system to register hunters. When a hunter checks in, he or she exchanges the individual hunting permit for two hunting area badges. One badge is placed on the dashboard of the hunter's car; the other is carried by the hunter. When a hunter quits for the day, he or she returns the two passes to the duty game warden or MP desk sergeant in exchange for the hunting permit.

Between August 15 and December 31 the maximum number of hunters allowed into any hunting area at a time ranges from three to five, depending on the hunting area. Between January 2 and March 15 five to eight hunters are permitted per area.

Although there are no hunter age restrictions on the installation, those under sixteen must be accompanied by someone over the age of eighteen at all times while afield.

While big game hunters are limited to pursuing white-tailed deer, small game hunters may take cottontail, squirrel, quail, dove, woodcock, snipe, fox, raccoon, opossum, and marsh hen.

Hunter success rates on the installation vary. During the 1989–90 season, seventy-eight whitetails were killed during the 140-day season. Small game hunters took home 100 small game animals during the same period.

Fishing Marine Corps Air Station Beaufort offers eligible anglers both freshwater and saltwater fishing. There are nearly sixteen acres of freshwater ponds available on the installation and miles of saltwater frontage. Freshwater species available on the installation include bluegill, red-breasted sunfish, striped and white bass hybrids, largemouth bass, and channel catfish. Saltwater fishermen may run into any species normally found along this part of the Atlantic Seaboard.

Eligibility requirements for fishing on MCAS Beaufort are the same as for hunting. In addition, all anglers on the installation must meet South Carolina licensing requirements, sign a statement verifying that they understand the installation's regulations, complete a waiver of damages form, and purchase a station permit. The station permit is available from the game warden on Wednesdays and Fridays between 1:00 P.M. and 4:00 P.M.

Anglers under sixteen must be accompanied by an adult over eighteen when fishing. Fishermen fishing at night must check with the duty game warden or MP desk sergeant.

All fishing rules and regulations, including creel limits, applicable in South Carolina are in effect on the reservation. MCAS Beaufort also restricts the use of live fish for bait in any of the station's ponds and limits the number of lines and hooks that may be used.

Miscellaneous Camping and ATVs are not allowed on the installation.

The topographic maps covering MCAS Beaufort are #5968 through #6004, available from the U.S. Army Corps of Engineers.

For more information, contact: S-4 Department, Natural Resources Environmental Affairs Office, Game Warden Office, Bldg. 601, MCAS Beaufort, SC 29904, phone (803) 522-7372 (7:30 A.M. to 11:30 A.M. and 1:00 P.M. to 4:00 P.M., weekdays).

Naval Installations

NAVAL WEAPONS STATION CHARLESTON

- 10,000 acres open to hunting and fishing
- White-tailed deer, turkey, and small game
- Freshwater and saltwater fishing

Hunting Not everyone is allowed to hunt on all parts of NWS Charleston. There are three categories of hunter as follows:

Category A. Military and civil service employees of the weapons station, POMFLANT, Navy Submarine Torpedo Facility, and military members attached to the weapons station marine barracks who have security badges. Authorized dependents of these people are also eligible.

Category B. Active duty military personnel and their dependents who hold ID cards.

Category C. The public, retired military personnel, and all people not included in Categories A or B. Applicants may be screened for criminal records before their applications are approved.

The procedure for applying for a permit on NWS Charleston is rather involved. Hunters wishing to hunt on the installation must submit an application to the morale, welfare, and recreation director, Building 708, between 8:00 A.M. and 4:30 P.M. on weekdays or between 10:00 A.M. and 2:00 P.M. on Saturdays.

When submitting their applications, hunters must provide sufficient identification to ensure that they are placed in the proper category. They must also prove that they hold all the appropriate state and federal licenses and tags. Dependents eighteen and over may purchase a permit and hunt on their own. Dependents fourteen and older may purchase a license but must be accompanied at all times by an adult while afield. All applicants must provide proof of having completed a state-certified hunter safety course.

Once selected to participate in weapons station hunts, hunters must sign up at designated assembly areas the day of the hunt. Hunters after small game are allowed to hunt in small groups. Hunters seeking big game follow an entirely different set of rules.

The only big game on the installation is white-tailed deer. There are three methods of hunting them allowed on NWS Charleston—stand hunting, driving, and dog driving. The rules for each are different.

Deer hunters preferring to hunt from tree stands must show up on time at the designated muster points listed below. Generally, morning hunts are from one and one-half hours before sunrise until 10:00 A.M., and afternoon hunts are from three hours before sunset until thirty minutes after. The muster points for the different hunting areas on NWS Charleston are: Southside Area, Redbank Club westside parking lot; Northside Area, MWR parking lot; Marrington, front gate on Redbank Road; and WPNSTA South, security building, WPNSTA South. Once assembled at the muster points, all hunters must present their badges and licenses. After the duty game warden checks participants' licenses, hunters are transported to their tree stands by government vehicles. Hunters must stay in their stands until picked up at appointed times.

Tree-stand hunters may use shotguns shooting slugs, black-powder rifles between .38 and .44 caliber, and archery tackle. Centerfire rifles, handguns, and crossbows are not allowed on the installation.

Hunters participating in deer drives with or without dogs must follow the same general rules, with the exception that the only weapons authorized during drives are shotguns with buckshot.

Small game hunters may use only shotguns shooting shot smaller than #4. They may take rabbit, possum, raccoon, gray squirrel (fox squirrels are protected on the installation), dove, waterfowl, turkey, quail, fox, and bobcat.

All small game seasons and bag limits on the installation match those of the state, as do the big game seasons. Hunter success at NWS Charleston is high, at 50 percent for big game and 70 percent for small game.

Fishing The same eligibility restrictions apply to fishing as to hunting. Anglers must meet all state licensing requirements and purchase a weapons station permit.

Although fishermen aren't required to assemble at a muster point prior to going fishing, some areas on the installation are restricted. Anglers wishing to fish these areas must check with the security office.

NWS Charleston offers both freshwater and saltwater fishing. The station's 226 acres of freshwater ponds are stocked with bass, bream, catfish, and crappie. Saltwater fishermen may encounter any species of fish found along this section of the Atlantic Coast.

All state fishing laws and creel limits apply on the installation. Fishermen may use any method legal in South Carolina to take fish on the installation.

Miscellaneous Camping is not allowed at NWS Charleston. ATVs and off-road driving are prohibited.

For more information, contact: Naval Weapons Station, Ticket Office, Bldg. 708, Code 15, Charleston, SC 29408-7000.

TENNESSEE

Tennessee abounds with excellent hunting and fishing opportunities. This 42,187-square-mile state has a deer herd rapidly approaching 500,000 animals as well as wild turkey and small game galore. Unfortunately, less than 5 percent of the state is public land. Although getting access to hunt on private land has historically not been a problem, hunting leases and posted land is becoming the rule rather than the exception.

Tennessee hosts twelve military installations around the state. They range in size from the 12-acre Alcoa Air National Guard Station to the 39,081-acre Arnold Air Force Base. Not all the installations are open for hunting and fishing, but those that are offer 75,088 acres of public land to sportsmen.

Army Installations

HOLSTON
ARMY AMMUNITION PLANT

- Near Kingsport
- 3,000 acres open to hunting
- Installation permit required
- White-tailed deer
- Small game hunting closed to the public

Hunting The wildlife management program at Holston is comanaged with the Tennessee Wildlife Resources Agency. This agency is responsible for issuing installation permits for hunting deer and small game, which is open to the public. Because the deer herd on Holston is intensely managed and because biologists from the state and the plant are constantly monitoring and evaluating the herd, all hunts are short and strictly controlled.

Hunters selected to participate in any of the deer hunts are met at the plant's main gate by members of the Holston Army Ammunition Plant Conservation Club. They must pay a daily $10 fee to hunt on the reservation. After receiving their passes, hunters are taken by government vehicle to their assigned stands and must remain there until picked up by the hunt controllers.

There are three deer seasons on the plant. A short archery-only deer season is held during October of each year, followed by a one-day youth-only deer season in early November. A shotgun season is held in late November or early December. No more than 150 tags are issued for any of the seasons.

Holston also offers dove and duck hunting. The seasons are the same as state seasons. Access during the small game seasons is limited to plant employees and other designated individuals. Upland game hunters must pay special fees for hunting on the plant.

Hunter success is high at Holston. During the 1988–89 season, 120 bucks and 110 does were taken from installation property for an overall hunter success rate on deer of 38 percent. Upland game hunters took 765 doves and 385 ducks.

Miscellaneous No privately owned vehicles are allowed on the installation. All transportation is provided by either the plant contractor or government vehicles. No camping is allowed.

For more information, contact: SMCHO-XO, Holston Army Ammunition Plant, Kingsport, TN 37660, phone (615) 247-9111, ext. 3753 (8:00 A.M. to 5:00 P.M., weekdays).

MILAN
ARMY AMMUNITION PLANT

- 20,543 acres open to hunting and fishing
- Installation permit required
- White-tailed deer and turkey
- Small game hunting closed to the public
- Fishing closed to the public

Hunting Altogether, the plant's grounds provide 20,543 acres of hunting territory. White-tailed deer and turkey are the only big game species on this installation. The plant has a separate permit system for each style of hunting. Military members and plant employees hunting with shotguns or bow and arrow pay a $10 yearly permit fee. Civilians pay $50 annually. Daily permits are available at $10 for civilian hunters. All hunters must meet the licensing requirements of the state of Tennessee before purchasing their plant permits.

All hunters on the installation must check in and out with the hunter control point or security office before going hunting and upon returning. Deer hunting is strictly controlled, and all hunters using shotguns for deer must wear hunter orange in accordance with state law. Hunters must also abide by Tennessee regulations concerning hunter safety courses.

Only military members and plant employees may hunt small game on the installation. The small game license is $10. A combination fishing and small game hunting license is available for an annual fee of $15.

During the 1988 season, hunters took 160 antlerless deer and 111 deer with antlers on the installation. The average dressed weight of yearling bucks taken was 124.6 pounds, indicating a well-fed herd. Hunters also took six turkeys during the 1988–89 season. Hunter success on big game was low overall, at 12.5 percent.

Fishing   Milan AAP's waters are open only to military members and civilian employees. While there are no rivers or streams on the reservation, Milan does have thirty acres of ponds, which are stocked with sunfish, bass, and catfish. All Tennessee licensing requirements and fishing laws apply.

Miscellaneous   Camping is not generally allowed on the installation. There is a nature trail along the plant's boundaries. ATVs are not authorized on the installation.

For more information, contact: Wildlife Management Office, Milan Army Ammunition Plant, Milan, TN 38358.

VOLUNTEER ARMY AMMUNITION PLANT

- Near Chattanooga
- 4,300 acres open to hunting
- White-tailed deer

Hunting   There are 4,300 acres of land open to hunting on the Volunteer facility. The hunting program is managed jointly by the Tennessee State Wildlife Resources Agency and Volunteer AAP officials, and the hunting seasons are short and well controlled.

Volunteer AAP offers only deer hunting. A two-day hunt for archers takes place the first weekend of October. A shotgun hunt is held the first weekend of November. The hunter quota for each of these hunts is 150.

Volunteer AAP also offers a special "Young Sportsman Only" hunt the last weekend in October every year. It, too, has a limited hunter quota, with seventy-five hunters allowed afield. Interested young hunters must apply in person the first Sunday in September in the plant's parking lot. All other hunts are applied for through the state.

Hunter success is high on Volunteer Plant's grounds. During 1988, hunters took seventy-eight bucks and seventy-one does for a hunter success rate of 43.4 percent. The average dressed weight of yearling bucks taken on the installation was 88.6 pounds.

Miscellaneous Fishing, camping, and ATVs are not allowed on the installation.

For more information, contact: Tennessee Wildlife Resources Agency, Ellington Agricultural Center, Box 40747, Nashville, TN 37204, phone (615) 781-6500 (8:00 A.M. to 5:00 P.M., weekdays).

Air Force Installations

ARNOLD AIR FORCE BASE

- Near Manchester
- Woods Reservoir Recreation Area
- 26,000 acres open to hunting and fishing
- Closed to the public
- White-tailed deer, turkey, and small game
- Fishing
- Camping
- Boating

Hunting Arnold offers excellent hunting to those with access to the installation. All hunters must be either military members assigned to Arnold or civilians employed there.

The only big game on Arnold are whitetails and wild turkey. They can be found over most of the installation, but only 26,000 acres are open to hunting.

All hunters on Arnold must meet Tennessee licensing requirements before purchasing their base permits at $10 each. Hunters must also follow all Tennessee laws concerning hunter safety courses, hunter orange, seasons, and bag limits.

Hunters on Arnold may not use modern rifles, either centerfire or rimfire. All handguns are also banned for hunting. Hunters may use archery equipment, shotguns, and muzzleloaders to take deer and turkey.

Small game is abundant on Arnold Air Force Base. Hunters must meet the licensing requirements of the state and follow all state seasons and bag limits. Small game hunters may use shotguns or archery tackle to take their prey.

Hunter success varies on Arnold. Bowhunters average 10 percent a year on deer, while hunters using shotguns and muzzleloaders do much better.

Fishing Fishing is also good at Arnold, but access is restricted to service members assigned to Arnold and civilian employees. Those allowed to fish on Arnold Air Force Base can expect to find bass, crappie, sunfish, catfish, and maybe a few trout. All Tennessee fishing laws, including licensing requirements, methods of take, and creel limits apply on the installation.

Miscellaneous Arnold offers camping, but it is limited to the camping area reserved for military travelers. The base operates a military recreation area on Woods Reservoir along the base's southern boundary. The Woods Reservoir Recreation Area offers eligible personnel a marina, RV and primitive camping, boat rental, waterskiing, and fishing.

ATVs are not allowed on the installation.

The topographic maps covering Arnold Air Force Base fall in the 8607, 7.5-minute series.

For more information on hunting and fishing at Arnold Air Force Base, contact: Wildlife Manager, AEDC/DEV, Arnold Air Force Base, TN 37388, phone (615) 454-4354/4066 (8:00 A.M. to 5:00 P.M., weekdays).

TEXAS

Texas has a world-wide reputation as being one of the best places to hunt. The huge private ranches spread throughout the state are home not only to American game such as the white-tailed deer but also to exotic species such as bluebuck, nilgai, roebuck, sika deer, and mouflon sheep. Unfortunately, it can cost you dearly to gain access to one of these ranches.

Fishing is also world-renowned here. With numerous natural lakes and hundreds of man-made reservoirs, Texas offers anglers a taste of heaven.

There are numerous military installations in the Lone Star State. Texas's 267,338 square miles are dotted with forty-five installations ranging in size from the 1-acre Hondo Auxiliary Training Field to 216,946-acre Fort Hood. Of course, not all these installations are open to hunting and fishing. Those that are, though, significantly enhance the outdoor opportunities available to Texas sportsmen.

Army Installations

FORT HOOD

- Near Killeen
- 198,000 acres open to hunting and fishing
- White-tailed deer, exotic game, turkey, and small game
- Installation permit required
- Fishing
- Camping
- Restricted boating

Hunting Fort Hood is open to the public on a limited basis and offers some unique hunting opportunities. It is one of the few military installations in the United States that has huntable populations of exotic game. In addition to the native white-tails and turkeys, hunters on Fort Hood may also take axis deer and blackbuck antelope during the season.

Hunters on Fort Hood are divided into two eligibility categories. Category 1 hunters have first crack at all hunting seasons and areas. They are defined by Fort Hood Regulation 210-25 as follows: active duty or retired military personnel and their family members; active or retired Department of the Army civilians and their eligible family members; and appropriated and nonappropriated fund civilian employees, including exchange personnel employed at Fort Hood for a minimum of twenty-four hours per week, and their eligible family members. Retirees over age sixty-five or with a 100 percent service-connected disability fall into special Category 1A. Category 2 hunters are defined as all other people, including Fort Hood employees working less than twenty-four hours per week, contractors, concessionaires, and their employees.

All hunters on Fort Hood must meet Texas licensing requirements before purchasing a Fort Hood hunting permit. The permits are available from the fish and wildlife branch in Building 1941. A Category 1 hunting permit costs $15; a Category 1A, $5; and a Category 2 hunting permit is $15. A special youth/small game permit is available free.

All small game seasons of Fort Hood follow those of the state of Texas. Hunters may take mournng dove, bobwhite quail, duck, geese, rabbit, squirrel, and furbearers in accordance with state seasons and regulations. Small game on the installation, with the exception of furbearers and squirrels, may be hunted only with shotguns using shot smaller than #2 and legal archery tackle. Furbearers and squirrels may be taken with .22-caliber rimfire rifles in certain areas during specified times.

Big game hunting on Fort Hood is a little more complicated. The hunting season and areas are separated into different categories based on types of weapons and hunting method. There are specific archery seasons and areas, guided rifle deer and turkey hunting seasons and areas, and special limited-range weapons hunting seasons.

The archery season generally coincides with the state's, and archery tackle restrictions are the same. All archery hunters must be registered with the Fort Hood Area Access Control Center (Building 56001) prior to going afield, and they must pass a shooting competency test held at the hunt control office (Building 1941) before hunting. Archers must requalify every two years, or two years after their last bow kill. The bow-qualification course consists of one arrow shot from five different shooting positions. To qualify, the archer must put a minimum of three of the five arrows in an eight-inch target.

Hunters must get an area clearance from the hunt control office during the archery deer and turkey hunt. Clearances are issued the day before each hunt by drawing. Areas not filled by drawing are filled on a first-come, first-served basis. No clearances are given or guaranteed by phone or mail any earlier than one day prior to the hunt. All clearances are issued in person at the hunt control office.

The drawings for area clearances are held at 11:00 A.M. each day, starting one day prior to the season opener. The drawings are all for the following day's hunts and are on a quota basis. Category 1 and 1A hunters are picked on a three to one ratio over category 2 hunters.

Hunting parties may be no larger than can be supported by the terrain of the hunting area. One member of the hunting party may sign the entire party in, but that member must present all the licenses belonging to the party.

All deer and turkey taken during the archery hunt must be tagged and taken directly to the fish and wildlife branch, Building 1938.

The guided rifle deer and turkey hunts are run much the same as the archery hunt. Hunters must be properly licensed and registered before applying for a permit/reservation for these hunts.

Permits are generally awarded on a three to one ratio. Hunters are selected for the first two days of the guided hunt by drawing. The drawing is conducted the last Friday of October and the results posted the following Monday at the hunt control office. All other hunt days are open for reservations, beginning at 7:30 A.M. at the hunt control office on the Monday following the drawing. Reservations must be made in person and a valid Fort Hood hunting permit must be presented when the reservations are made. The reservations must be made no later than 5:00 P.M. two days prior to the desired hunt days. A hunter may have only one reservation at a time.

Hunting areas not filled on the day of the guided hunt will be filled by "pot luck" drawings at 3:00 A.M. and 2:00 P.M. at the hunt control office. Only hunters present for the drawing are eligible to hunt.

All hunting during the guided rifle deer and turkey hunt is from assigned stands and blinds. Hunters are transported to their assigned positions by government vehicle under the direction of a hunting area guide. At the conclusion of the morning or evening hunt, hunters are transported back to the hunt control office by their assigned guide. No stalking or other movement is allowed around the stands.

The limited-range weapons deer and turkey hunts are conducted much like the archery hunts except hunters are limited to 20-gauge shotguns or larger using slugs, and .45-caliber muzzleloaders or larger. Archers may also participate in the limited-range weapons deer and turkey hunts but must abide by all regulations for those hunts.

Hunters participating in the firearms big game hunts on Fort Hood, whether hunting with guns or not, are required to wear at least 400 square inches of hunter orange above the waist. Additionally, all hunters on the post must have completed a state-recognized hunter safety course.

Hunter success is only fair at Fort Hood. Big game hunters averaged 17 percent during the last season. Figures for small game hunter success are not maintained. Fort Hood publishes an excellent guide for each year's hunting season. The address is listed at the end of this section.

Fishing Fishing is good at Fort Hood. The installation is bordered by Belton Lake and the Leon River and contains portions of Cowhouse Creek. There are also numerous natural and man-made lakes and ponds that dot the post. All Texas fishing regulations and licensing requirements apply on the post. All fishermen over sixteen must have a post fishing permit, as well.

The waters of Fort Hood contain largemouth bass, channel catfish, sunfish, crappie, and, during the winter, rainbow trout.

Fishermen are not generally required to check with the range access office prior to going out, as are hunters. Yet, certain ponds on the reservation do require a range clearance. Check with the range control office in Building 56001 to be sure.

While the fishing regulations and creel limits of the state generally apply on Fort

Hood, there are some differences. Trotlines, yo-yo devices, throwlines, and jug-fishing are banned. No live bait may be released in any of the installation's lakes or ponds. Shad trawls, wire loop or gigs, spear guns, and spears are all prohibited.

Miscellaneous There are two designated camping areas on Fort Hood. One is the travel camp on the post proper. The other is the Belton Lake Outdoor Recreation Area. The travel camp offers RV-style camping, while Belton Lake offers both RV and primitive camping.

No gasoline-powered boats are allowed on any of the post's lakes, ponds, or streams.

ATVs are allowed on the installation in specified areas. They are generally not allowed in the hunting fields.

The topographic maps covering Fort Hood are from the U.S. Geological Survey in the 7.5-minute series. They are Bland, North Fort Hood, Fort Hood, Shell Mountain, McMillian Mountain, and Post Oak Mountain.

For more information on hunting and fishing at Fort Hood, contact: Community Recreation Division, Hunt Control Office, Bldg. 1941, Fort Hood, TX 76544, phone (817) 287-5742/532-4552 (weekdays, 10:00 A.M. to 6:00 P.M.; weekends, 8:00 A.M. to 6:00 P.M.).

LONE STAR ARMY AMMUNITION PLANT RED RIVER ARMY DEPOT

* 18 miles west of Texarkana
* 34,500 acres
* Closed to the public
* Deer and small game
* Fishing
* Camping

Hunting Since the Lone Star Army Ammunition Plant and the Red River Army Depot are actually one installation, I'll refer to them as the Red River facility.

This part of eastern Texas features rolling, pine-covered hills combined with oak and brush bottomlands and marshy areas. It is an excellent place to hunt both deer and small game—if you can get access.

The Red River facility is not open to the public. According to Red River Army Depot (RRAD) regulations, the following personnel are authorized to hunt on the facility: active duty U.S. military personnel and their immediate families; RRAD and Lone Star Army Ammunition Plant (LSAAP) DA civilians, nonappropriated fund employees, prime-contract civilian employees and their immediate families; retired U.S. military personnel and their immediate families; retired RRAD and LSAAP DA civilians and their immediate families, and retired employees of the prime operating contractor; others when authorized by the RRAD or LSAAP commanders.

All hunters on the Red River facility must meet Texas licensing requirements, including hunter safety course completion, where applicable. Additionally, all hunters over seventeen must have a RRAD hunting permit before going afield. Children between the ages of eight and seventeen are allowed to hunt on the installation but must be accompanied at all times while afield by a licensed hunter over eighteen.

Hunting seasons on the Red River facility and bag limits for all game generally follow those of the state. There are weapons restrictions on the Red River facility not found in the Texas hunting laws.

Hunters after small game on the facility may use shotguns loaded with shot smaller than #2 or archery tackle. Deer hunters using guns are restricted to shotguns of 20 gauge or larger shooting slugs, and muzzleloaders .45 caliber or larger. Bowhunters after deer during the archery season must comply with Texas archery hunting equipment regulations.

Hunting is strictly controlled on the Red River facility. Due to the nature of the work done here, it would not pay to have anyone wandering around in an explosives area who isn't supposed to be there. Consequently, all hunters are required to sign for and remain in specified areas. Small game hunters generally have larger areas to hunt in than do deer hunters. All deer hunting on the installation is done from stands and blinds. Hunters are not permitted free run of the facility for stalking or still-hunting.

Whether after deer or small game, all hunters must check in at one of the hunt control points before going afield. When checking in, the hunter surrenders his facility permit and receives a hunting area badge that must be worn at all times while hunting. Upon quitting for the day, the hunter must return the badge to the hunt control point to get his permit back.

The hunt control points are at the main gate to the Red River Army Depot, Gate 7 at the Lone Star Army Ammunition Plant, and in Building 1451 at Elliott Lake. The Elliott Lake hunt control point is the primary check-in location for most of the hunting done on the facility. All deer taken on the Red River facility must be checked at Elliott Lake.

Most of the hunts for big game on the Red River facility are on a first-come, first-served reservation basis. Hunters may generally make reservations for a hunting area up to two days in advance, with the exception of opening weekends. Opening weekend hunts are conducted by lottery, with hunters applying for desired areas.

Some of the deer hunting on the Red River facility is done in active work areas. For this reason, transportation to and from the stands is by government vehicle. These hunts are exceptionally restricted and all hunters must check in and out at the Elliott Lake hunt control point only.

I believe the hunter success rates given for the Red River facility belie the actual success hunters have there. Officially, the hunter success rate on deer is only 15 percent, but that is a combined rate for all methods of hunting. I suspect that the success rate for deer hunters using guns may be closer to 35 or 40 percent. No figures were available for small game hunter success rates.

Fishing Fishing is allowed on this installation. Like hunting, angler access to the reservation is limited. Only those meeting the eligibility requirements for hunting may fish here.

All anglers on the installation must meet the licensing requirements set by the state of Texas. Additionally, anglers over sixteen must have a valid RRAD fishing permit. All state fishing regulations apply on the Red River facility. Anglers may use any method legal in Texas to take fish here. There are no special restrictions.

The waters of the reservation contain largemouth bass, crappie, sunfish, and catfish. Anglers may also catch the occasional alligator gar, carp, freshwater drum, or buffalo. State creel limits apply to all species.

As always, there are exceptions. At Elliott and Caney lakes, the creel and possessions limits differ from those of the state. Anglers at these two lakes may take up to five bass a day, ten in possession. Bass must be at least fourteen inches long. Catfish taken from these lakes must be at least nine inches long. The creel limit on catfish is eight, with sixteen in possession. Anglers may not take any white bass/striped bass hybrids from Caney and Elliott lakes. The creel limit on crappie is twenty-five, with a possession limit of fifty for these two lakes. All other species fall under state creel limits.

Miscellaneous Camping is allowed on the Red River facility. The installation runs the Elliott Lake Recreation Area, a 183-acre lake with established beach areas, recreational facilities, RV camping pads, tent sites, and rental cabins.

Camping is allowed at the Elliott Lake Recreation Area for up to seven days at a time. Reservations may be made in advance. ATVs are not allowed on the Red River facility.

For more information on hunting and fishing at the Red River Army Depot/Lone Star Army Ammunition Plant, contact: Bennie Murray, SDSSR-GB, Directorate of Engineering and Housing, Buildings and Grounds Div., Land Management Branch, Red River Army Depot, Texarkana, TX 75507-5007, phone (214) 334-2379 (Monday through Thursday, 6:45 A.M. to 5:15 P.M.).

LONGHORN ARMY AMMUNITION PLANT

- Near Marshall
- 7,197 acres open to hunting and fishing
- Closed to the public
- Big game and small game
- Fishing

Hunting Hunting is allowed on Longhorn Army Ammunition Plant located just outside Marshall. This 8,493-acre establishment has 7,197 acres available for

wildlife management programs, which are divided into thirty wildlife management areas. The plant is a closed installation with controlled public access, but military members and plant employees can hunt on the plant's grounds.

No information was available on small game hunting, but big game hunters managed a 45 percent hunter success rate, harvesting twenty-four bucks and eighteen does.

Fishing Fishing is allowed on Longhorn Army Ammunition Plant. There are six acres of ponds on the installation in addition to five and one-half miles of stream and six miles of shoreline. All state regulations apply.

Species available are bass, sunfish, crappie, and catfish.

For further information, contact: Public Affairs Division, Longhorn Army Ammunition Plant, Marshall, TX 75670.

Air Force Installations

DYESS AIR FORCE BASE

- Near Abilene
- Closed to the public
- Fishing

Fishing   Dyess has a one-acre pond stocked with bass and catfish. Angling in the base pond is limited to base personnel and their dependents.

Anglers on Dyess must meet all Texas licensing requirements and obey all state fishing laws. Any bait legal in the state of Texas may be used on Dyess, but anglers may not use multiple hooks and lines.

Miscellaneous   Camping and ATVs are not allowed on Dyess.

For more information, contact: 96 BW/DEV, Dyess AFB, TX 79607.

LACKLAND AIR FORCE BASE MEDINA ANNEX

- Near San Antonio
- 4,000 acres open to hunting and fishing
- Closed to the public
- White-tailed deer and small game
- Fishing

Hunting   Lackland's Medina Annex provides active and retired military personnel and their dependents with 4,000 acres of hunting territory. Hunting is not open to the public. The annex contains healthy populations of game, including white-tailed deer, cottontail, quail, feral hog, and javelina. Coyote and bobcat can also be found here.

All hunters must be at least seventeen years old, must comply with Texas licensing requirements, and must possess proof of having completed a hunter safety course. Bowhunters on the installation must also pass an archery competency test on the installation range before hunting.

All hunting seasons and bag limits match those set by the state, but Medina has some weapons restrictions not found in state regulations. Hunters on the annex are limited to using shotguns loaded with slugs or buckshot for big game and shotguns using shot smaller than #4 for small game. Rifles are not allowed on the facility. All handguns and crossbows are similarly banned. Archers must use bowhunting equipment that complies with state laws.

All deer hunting on the Medina Annex is done from blinds and stands. Hunters check in with the lease manager and game wardens at the main gate and are transported to their blinds and stands. Upon completing hunting for the day, hunters are picked up by government transportation and taken, with their game, back to the check-in point.

Hunter success isn't spectacular on the Medina Annex. During the last season, big game hunters logged a 5 percent success rate while those seeking small game averaged 50 percent.

Fishing   Fishing is limited on the Medina Annex. The amount of water on the installation is small but is stocked with bass and catfish. Angling, like hunting, is restricted. The only people authorized to fish here are active and retired military members and their dependents. All anglers must meet the licensing requirements set by the state. All state creel limits and regulations apply.

Miscellaneous   Camping is not allowed on the Medina Annex. There is a FAM-CAMP at nearby Kelly Air Force Base. ATVs are banned from the reservation. No privately owned vehicles are allowed on Medina Annex.

For more information on hunting and fishing on the Medina Annex or in this part of Texas in general, contact: Rod and Gun Club, SSYG, Bldg. 8174, Lackland AFB, TX 78236-5000, phone (512) 674-7831.

LAUGHLIN AIR FORCE BASE

- In western Texas near Del Rio
- 500 acres open to hunting
- Closed to the public
- White-tailed deer and small game
- Restricted camping

Hunting   Hunting on Laughlin is under the auspices of the Val Verde County Military Sportsmen's Association. The association manages about 500 acres of base property for the use of base personnel. The only people allowed to hunt on the Laughlin property are military and civilian personnel of Laughlin. Outsiders may hunt on Laughlin only as guests of authorized personnel.

Laughlin hunters must meet all state licensing requirements as well as have a hunter safety course for both the state and the base. Hunters must be at least sixteen, in accordance with state law. There are no weapons restrictions on Laughlin. Any weapon legal in Texas is legal on the base. All hunting seasons and bag limits at Laughlin coincide with those of the state.

Laughlin's hunting area contains cottontail, quail, waterfowl, jack rabbit, and stocked pheasant. Whitetails are the only species of big game found here.

Hunters are required to sign in and out on Laughlin. All hunters must report to the law enforcement desk with a valid Texas license and proof of having completed the required hunter safety courses. Hunters are required to sign for a specific area and game species when checking in.

Miscellaneous ATVs are not allowed on Laughlin. Camping is allowed, but only in the RV park on base.

For more information on hunting at Laughlin Air Force Base, contact: Mr. Charles Delaney, 47CES/DEF, Laughlin AFB, TX 78843-5000, phone (512) 298-5233.

SHEPPARD AIR FORCE BASE

- In northern Texas near Wichita Falls
- Closed to the public
- Fishing on Lake Texoma
- Camping
- Boating

Hunting Sheppard covers only 5,397 acres and offers no fishing and hunting on the base, but there are several state-run wildlife management areas nearby where hunting is available.

Fishing Sheppard Air Force Base has an outstanding recreation area that offers fishing on nearby Lake Texoma, which was formed when the Denison Dam was constructed on the Red River. Since the Red River is the border between Texas and Oklahoma, the lake lies in both states. That's how it got its name.

The Sheppard Air Force Base Recreation Annex lies on 488 acres of shoreline along the southwestern part of the lake and offers excellent fishing from shore. Anglers fishing from the shore need only a military ID card and a valid Texas license. Those using a boat at the recreation area must have a special Lake Texoma license.

Fishing at the annex is excellent. Lake Texoma is known throughout the South for its largemouth bass and striped bass fishing. Anglers here can also expect to catch bream, perch, white bass, blue catfish, channel catfish, yellow catfish, carp, freshwater drum, and alligator and spotted gar.

All Texas fishing laws apply on the Sheppard Recreation Annex. Anglers must meet all state licensing requirements and follow all state creel limits and size limits.

Miscellaneous The Sheppard Recreation Annex offers excellent services to those eligible. With a fully stocked mini-market, full-service marina, fishing dock, and camping area, it is a great place to spend a family vacation.

ATVs are not allowed on the recreation annex.

The Lake Texoma map includes the Sheppard Recreation Annex.

For more information, contact: Paul J. Leuschner, SSRO/219, Rt. 3, Box 151, Whitesboro, TX 76273.

Naval Installations

NAVAL AIR STATION CHASE FIELD ALTERNATE LANDING FIELD GOLIAD

- Near Beeville
- 1,500 acres open to hunting and fishing
- Closed to the public
- Installation permit required
- White-tailed deer and game birds
- Fishing

Hunting NAS Chase Field and ALF Goliad fall under the same wildlife management branch. Hunting is allowed on 900 acres of land at Chase Field and 700 acres at Goliad.

To hunt on either property, hunters must have a valid Texas hunting license and the appropriate tags, a military or government identification card, and a base hunting permit available from the NAS Chase Field Welfare and Recreation Department.

Like most installations, hunters on Chase Field and Goliad are required to sign in and out when going afield and upon returning. The exact sign-in procedures differ at each location.

Those hunting on Chase Field must check in with the main gate security office when coming aboard the installation. At the security office, the hunter presents his license, permit, and ID card and signs in for a specific area. The hunter may then drive to the hunting area along the field's perimeter road. After hunting, the hunter must check back with the security office and report any game taken.

At Goliad, hunters must also check in with the main gate security office. Here, though, all hunters are transported by government vehicle to their assigned hunting areas. At the completion of the hunting day, hunters are picked up at a prearranged place and time and transported back to the main gate. Again, all game taken must be reported.

Though all the seasons, legal game animals, and bag limits on both installations are the same as those established by Texas law, both Goliad and Chase Field have weapons restrictions. According to the information I obtained, the only legal weapons on both installations are shotguns and high-powered rifles. Handguns, archery tackle, muzzleloaders, and crossbows are all prohibited.

There is no hunter safety course requirement on either installation. All hunters under seventeen must be accompanied by a licensed adult. Keep in mind that even though the installation does not require a hunter safety course, Texas does for certain age groups.

Hunters at Chase Field and Goliad may take white-tailed deer, mourning dove, white-winged dove, quail, and pheasant. The hunter success rate is good at both locations. During the 1988–89 season, deer hunters hit a 25 percent hunter success rate and bird hunters averaged five to seven birds per hunting trip.

Fishing Fishing is allowed at the Chase Field/Goliad complex. The waters of the installations are stocked with largemouth bass, crappie, and channel catfish, and fishing is reported as good.

All fishing regulations established by the state of Texas apply to both installations. Anglers must meet all state licensing requirements and follow all state laws for methods of taking fish and creel limits. Anglers may not use live fish as bait on the installations. The only live bait allowed is worms.

Miscellaneous Camping and ATVs are not allowed at either installation.

The topographic maps covering Chase Field and Goliad are Skidmore (SW/4 Skidmore 15' quadrangle) N2815-W97375/7.5', Date 1979; and Berclair N2830-W9730/7.5, Date 1963.

For more information, contact: Security Department, NAS Chase Field, Beeville, TX 78103-5021, phone (512) 354-5412/5413.

NAVAL AIR STATION CORPUS CHRISTI

- On the Gulf of Mexico
- Closed to the public
- Saltwater fishing
- Camping
- Boating

Fishing There is no freshwater fishing available at NAS Corpus Christi. The saltwater variety more than makes up for it. All that's needed to take speckled trout, red drum, flounder, or other species found in the Upper Laguna Madre are a Texas fishing license and the appropriate saltwater stamp.

No reservation permit is required but ail anglers on the reservation must have a valid military or DOD ID card. The installation is not open to the public except on special occasions.

Miscellaneous Besides the fishing, NAS Corpus Christi is an excellent place to spend a family vacation. The installation offers RV camping at an inexpensive $7 per day. Boating is allowed along the shore of the installation, and beachcombing and suntanning are popular activities.

ATVs are not allowed on the installation and all motorcycles ridden on base must be street-legal.

For more information on the fishing and camping opportunities available at NAS Corpus Christi, contact: Marina, NAS Corpus Christi, Corpus Christi, TX 78419, phone (512) 937-5071 (7:00 A.M. to 5:30 P.M., daily).

VIRGINIA

Virginia is rich in both American and hunting history. Hunters rode to the hounds in this area long before the Liberty Bell rang. Today, it is one of the best states in the eastern United States for both big and small game hunting.

Army Installations

FORT A. P. HILL

- 40 miles north of Richmond
- 41,433 acres open to hunting and fishing
- Installation permit required
- White-tailed deer, turkey, and small game
- Fishing
- Camping closed to the public

Hunting By eastern standards, Fort Hill is a large installation. It covers more than 76,000 acres, 41,433 of which are open to the public for hunting.

Hunters on Fort Hill must have the appropriate state licenses and tags as well as any required federal tags and stamps before purchasing a Fort Hill hunting permit. They do not need a hunter safety course certificate to obtain a Fort Hill license. Proof of a hunter safety course is needed, however, to purchase the required Virginia state or county hunting license. Hunters on Fort Hill may take both big and small game in accordance with state guidelines, bag limits, and seasons. Hunters under seventeen may hunt on the installation but must be accompanied at all times by a licensed adult. Although youngsters do not need a state license to hunt, they must have a Fort Hill permit.

The only big game found on the installation are white-tailed deer and wild turkey. All deer and turkey seasons and bag limits coincide with those of the state. The only weapons legal for taking game on A. P. Hill are shotguns and archery tackle. Muzzleloaders, rimfire rifles and handguns, centerfire rifles and handguns, and crossbows are all prohibited.

Small game may be taken with shotguns and archery tackle. The small game animals on Fort Hill include cottontail rabbit, squirrel, waterfowl, quail, mourning dove, raccoon, and fox.

Each hunting day all hunters are required to go through the hunter check stations on the post before going afield and upon returning. At the check station, hunters must present all the required licenses and tags to receive a "bag card." All game taken must be noted on the bag card and the card returned to the check station at the conclusion of that day's hunting.

Although Fort Hill's quail and either-sex deer seasons vary slightly from those set by the state, the hunter-orange requirement does not. All hunters afield during any of the shotgun big game seasons must wear a minimum of 400 square inches of hunter orange.

Hunter success on Fort Hill is not what you would call outstanding. During the last season for which figures were available, 11,500 hunters took 460 deer; 3,000 hunters took 120 turkeys; and 1,700 hunters took 1,100 small game animals.

Fishing There are several lakes, ponds, and streams on Fort Hill open to fishing most of the time. Anglers must have the appropriate state license as well as a Fort Hill fishing permit.

Most of the fishing rules of Virginia are applicable on Fort Hill. The only major difference is the slot and creel limits on bass.

In addition to largemouth bass, Fort Hill anglers can expect to catch channel catfish, brown bullheads, chain pickerel, and bluegill.

Anglers are not required to sign in, but for your own safety it's a good idea to check with range control before going to certain ponds.

Miscellaneous Camping is allowed on Fort Hill. The post maintains an RV campground with forty-nine slots. All slots have hookups for water, electricity, and sewer. The campground has no bath or toilet facilities. Only those with valid military identification cards are allowed to use the campground.

For installation maps or more information, contact: Community Recreation Division, AFKA-FHA-CR, Fort A. P. Hill, Bowling Green, VA 22427-5000, phone (804) 633-8219 (8:00 A.M. to 4:30 P.M., weekdays).

FORT BELVOIR

- 12 miles from Washington in northern Virginia
- 8,650 acres
- Installation permit required
- Bowhunting only
- Deer and squirrel
- Fishing

Hunting   Fort Belvoir may very well be a bowhunter's paradise. The only legal weapon on the installation is bow and arrow. The installation is open to all, but has some qualification requirements.

All hunters on Belvoir must have the appropriate Virginia licenses and tags. They must also have proof of completing a state-certified hunter safety course. Prior to obtaining a Fort Belvoir permit, hunters must pass a shooting competency test sponsored by the outdoor recreation branch. There is no minimum age for this test. Archers must be able to place two out of three broadhead-tipped arrows in a nine-inch circle at twenty and thirty yards. Once they pass this test, hunters may purchase a Fort Belvoir hunting permit for $12. The permits are available from the outdoor recreation branch.

Over 3,000 acres are open to hunting on the installation, and hunters may take either deer or squirrel. The hunting areas are divided into stand and stalking areas and are assigned on a first-come, first-served reservation basis. Hunters may reserve a hunting area a week in advance by calling the outdoor recreation branch beginning on Monday of each week.

Hunters must check in with the outdoor recreation branch before going afield on the day of the hunt. All big game taken on the installation must be checked by post biologists. All seasons and bag limits on Fort Belvoir are the same as those established by the state.

Hunter success for white-tailed deer on Fort Belvoir may be the highest in the nation for archers. During the 1989–90 season, hunter success was just a hair over 68 percent. Squirrel hunters on the installation are even more successful.

Fishing   Fishing is authorized on Fort Belvoir. There are two free-flowing creeks on the post containing all the freshwater species found in this area of the nation. All licensing requirements, creel limits, and methods of fishing are the same as those established by the state. Any method of fishing legal in Virginia is legal on Fort Belvoir.

Miscellaneous   Camping and ATVs are not allowed on Fort Belvoir.

For Fort Belvoir hunting and fishing maps or more information, contact: Outdoor Recreation Branch, Bldg. 780, Fort Belvoir, VA 22060, phone (703) 664-3781 (weekdays, 7:30 A.M. to 4:30 P.M.).

FORT EUSTIS

- On the Chesapeake Bay
- 8,323 acres
- Installation permit required
- White-tailed deer and small game
- Freshwater and saltwater fishing

Hunting The exact amount of land open for hunting at Fort Eustis varies depending on current training activities. The hunting areas are divided into stalking and still-hunting areas. No stalking is allowed during the deer seasons, and the post is closed to hunting on Sundays and Mondays.

White-tailed deer on Fort Eustis may be hunted only from tree stands. Hunters may use shotguns or archery tackle to take deer, but all hunters must be in a tree stand before shooting.

Deer hunters must reserve a hunting stand before the day of their hunt. On the hunting day, hunters must report to the game warden's office between 4:15 A.M. and 5:00 A.M. to sign for a stand. Those stands not claimed by 5:00 A.M. may be assigned to another hunter. All hunters, including bowhunters, must wear hunter orange vests when moving to and from their assigned stands.

Shotgunners may use either buckshot or rifled slugs in 20, 16, 12, or 10 gauge. Bowhunters must use broadheads meeting state guidelines. Bows must be at least forty-five pounds draw weight.

Bowhunters on Fort Eustis must pass a competency test before getting a Fort Eustis archery permit. Archers must test at least every two years. Hunters whose last names begin with the letters A to M test in even-numbered years. Those whose names begin with the letters N to Z test in odd-numbered years. The archery test is fairly easy. Hunters must place nine out of fifteen arrows in the bull's-eye at various ranges. All shooting is done from an elevated platform and must be done with hunting gear, including broadheads.

In addition to white-tailed deer, hunters on Fort Eustis may also take gray and fox squirrel, quail, cottontail, mourning dove, raccoon, waterfowl, woodcock, and opossum. All game taken on Fort Eustis must be checked at the game warden's office.

Hunters may use shotguns, muzzleloading guns, and archery tackle to take small game on Fort Eustis. All other wildlife laws on the installation are the same as those set by the state. Small game hunters must check in with the game warden's office before going afield. Small game hunting areas do not generally require a reservation.

Hunter success rates on Fort Eustis are only fair. Big game hunters on the installation averaged 10 percent for the 1988–89 season. Small game hunters averaged only 5 percent.

Fishing Fishing is good at Fort Eustis and is open to the public. The post's waters contain largemouth bass, catfish, perch, striped bass, white bass/striped bass hybrids, crappie, bream, and sunfish.

While most post regulations follow those of the state, there are exceptions. All anglers on the post must have a valid post fishing license and must apply to the installation's outdoor recreation branch by letter at least two weeks before the desired date. Anglers sixteen or older must also have all the appropriate Virginia fishing licenses in their possession.

The creel limits enforced on Fort Eustis vary significantly from those set by the state. On Fort Eustis, anglers may have no more than twenty-five fish in their possession. That twenty-five-fish limit is for a combination of all species, of which no more than eight may be largemouth bass. Bass must also be at least ten inches long.

Fort Eustis offers saltwater fishing on the James and Warwick rivers. Again, all state fishing laws apply.

Miscellaneous Camping and ATVs are not allowed on Fort Eustis. Privately owned vehicles may be operated only on paved roads.

For maps and more information, contact: Outdoor Recreation, Game Warden Office, Bldg. 841, Fort Eustis, VA 23604, phone (804) 878-2684 (off-season, 8:00 A.M. to 5:00 P.M., weekdays; hunting season, 4:00 A.M. to 9:00 P.M., Tuesday through Saturday).

FORT LEE

- Near Prince George
- 5,633 acres
- Installation permit required
- Bowhunting only
- White-tailed deer and turkey
- Camping closed to the public

Hunting Only bowhunting is permitted on Fort Lee. Although the hunting program caters primarily to military members, retirees, military dependents, and Department of Defense civilians, it is open on a limited basis to the public.

All hunters on the fort must have the appropriate state hunting licenses, including a Virginia archery permit. After obtaining the state licenses, hunters may purchase a Fort Lee recreation permit and a Fort Lee archery permit. Like the other installations in Virginia, Fort Lee requires all bowhunters to pass a shooting competency test to qualify for a post archery permit. The test is conducted by the Fort Lee outdoor recreation branch and consists of shooting five arrows at a life-sized deer silhouette. Three out of the five arrows must hit the nine-by-fourteen-inch kill zone of the silhouette at twenty-five yards.

The only weapons authorized on Fort Lee are longbows, recurves, and compound bows. All must have a minimum draw weight of at least forty-five pounds. Arrows must be tipped with broadheads meeting Virginia specifications.

Hunters on Fort Lee may hunt from tree stands or still-hunt. If hunting from a tree stand, hunters must use a stand that does no tree damage. Any type of tree stand or step that causes tree damage is illegal.

Fort Lee sponsors an antlerless-only deer season every year in which the deer taken must be antlerless or have spikes less than three inches long. No antlered deer may be taken during this season.

All hunting on Fort Lee is by reservation only. Hunters wanting to hunt opening weekend must submit an application by the established deadline. The application should specify the desired primary hunting area plus an alternate in case the primary hunting area is filled. Applications for hunting on the opening weekend are selected by a drawing. Reservations for other than opening weekend may be made no later than 11:00 A.M. the day prior to the hunt. No hunting is allowed on Sundays.

Members of the public who wish to hunt on the post must apply by letter to: Director, Outdoor Recreation Branch, Community Recreation Division. The letter should contain the applicant's name, address, phone number, Virginia hunting license number, Virginia archery permit number, and the dates that the individual wishes to hunt. It's a good idea to include both primary and alternate dates in case the primary date is already filled. Fort Lee outdoor recreation branch employees try to accommodate all applicants.

All hunters on Fort Lee must check in at the military police station in Building P-8526 prior to going afield. Before that hunters must have completed all the required paperwork at the outdoor recreation branch. Hunters may fill out the paperwork for hunting on Fort Lee when they make reservations for a hunting area.

Hunters must also check out at the MP station when returning from the field. All game taken must be reported and all big game animals must be taken to the outdoor recreation branch to be checked by an installation biologist. All hunters must be out of the field by 6:00 P.M. on the day of the hunt.

Fishing Fishing is not allowed on Fort Lee.

Miscellaneous Camping is allowed in the Freedom Star Recreation Area. Camping is only allowed for those authorized military support.

ATVs are not authorized on this facility. Hunters must park their vehicles along the major roadways on the installation and walk to hunting areas. No vehicles are allowed on the installation's dirt roads or fire trails.

The Petersburg and Bermuda Hundred topographic maps cover Fort Lee.

For more information on hunting at Fort Lee, contact: Provost Marshal Office, Bldg. P-8526, Fort Lee, VA 23801, phone (804) 734-2072 (anytime).

FORT PICKETT

- Near Blackstone
- 40,000 acres open to hunting and fishing
- Installation permit required
- White-tailed deer, turkey, and small game
- Fishing
- Camping

Hunting Fort Pickett offers an outstanding hunting program. Altogether, more than 40,000 acres of this installation are open to hunting. The wildlife populations are exceptionally well managed. Hunters may take white-tailed deer, eastern wild turkey, cottontail rabbit, squirrel, quail, waterfowl, bobcat, fox, crow, raccoon, and opossum on the installation.

All hunters on Fort Pickett must meet the licensing requirements set by Virginia. Additionally, hunters must have a Fort Pickett hunting license, available at the game check station, in their possession. The Fort Pickett hunting license costs $12 a year and is valid from January 1 to December 31 each year. Hunters under eighteen must be accompanied by an adult while afield on Fort Pickett. All hunters on the installation must wear a minimum of 500 square inches of hunter orange while afield. Waterfowlers and bowhunters may remove their hunter orange once they are in their blinds.

Fort Pickett is divided into several hunting areas, with each area having a hunter quota depending on the season and type of game. Generally, more small game hunters will be allowed into a hunting area at a time than big game hunters. No more than 500 hunters are allowed on the post at any time.

Fort Pickett has two trophy deer management areas. The access rules and bag limits for these areas differ slightly from the rest of the installation. All deer hunting areas on Fort Pickett offer an antlerless season. The season is slightly different for each area and is closed when the quota is reached.

The hunting seasons on Fort Pickett generally follow those of the state, although opening and closing dates may vary slightly due to military training requirements. The installation is open to hunting Monday through Saturday during hunting seasons; no hunting is permitted on Sundays or Christmas Day. Bag limits on the installation are the same as those for the state.

Although military members, military retirees, and DOD-sponsored civilians generally have priority for hunting areas on Fort Pickett, the public may also hunt on the post. The big difference between military-sponsored hunters and members of the public is that military hunters may reserve hunting areas a day in advance. Members of the public are assigned hunting areas on a first-come, first-served basis.

All hunters must check in and check out at the game check station (Building T-420) daily. Each hunter is issued a daily bag card (Fort Pickett Form 1004) and assigned a specific hunting area when checking in. Hunters must remain within their hunting areas as outlined on the daily bag card and may change hunting areas only once daily. Hunting area changes can be made only after noon by returning the bag card and signing for a new area. Hunters must complete their bag cards whether game is taken or not. Hunters must have their daily bag cards in their possession at all times, except for the driver of the hunting vehicle. His bag card must be displayed on the dashboard of the vehicle on the driver's side.

Fort Pickett has weapons restrictions not found in the state hunting regulations. Deer and turkey on the installation may be taken only with archery tackle and shotguns. Small game may only be taken with shotguns except for raccoon and squirrel in certain areas where a .22-caliber rifle may be used. Small game hunters must use shot smaller than #2 and deer hunters must use buckshot. Slugs are not authorized installation-wide but may be used in certain special use areas.

During the 1989–90 season, hunters on Fort Pickett averaged 8 percent success on deer, 176 percent on quail, and 98 percent on rabbits.

Fishing Fishing is excellent on Fort Pickett. The post offers eleven ponds and lakes, ranging in size from 2 acres up to 384 acres. Total freshwater surface acreage on the installation is 564 acres. All those acres contain fish of one sort or another.

Anglers on Fort Pickett must meet all the licensing requirements of Virginia. Additionally, those over fifteen must have a post fishing permit, available from the outdoor recreation branch. A full year's permit costs $12, a daily permit is $2, and a five-day permit is $5. An additional $3 per day is charged for permits to fish in the stocked catfish ponds on the installation. Three ponds on the installation are managed strictly for channel catfish and require a special permit at a cost of $3 per day in addition to the basic post fishing permit. Anglers using boats must have a boating permit, also available at the outdoor recreation branch. The cost is $5 for boats without motors and $10 for boats with motors.

The lakes and ponds other than the catfish ponds contain a variety of both game fish and rough species. Game fish found on Fort Pickett include largemouth bass, bluegill, redear sunfish, red-breasted sunfish, pumpkinseed, black crappie, white crappie, and chain pickerel. Rough species found on the installation are carp and brown bullhead.

Anglers aren't required to sign in or out on Fort Pickett, but they are restricted to certain fishing methods. Trotlines, bush hooks, and jug-fishing are all banned on the installation. Fishermen may use up to two attended hooks and lines. There are no restrictions on live bait.

The fishing seasons and creel limits at Fort Pickett vary slightly from those of the state. Certain areas have a slot limit on bass and creel limits different from those set by Virginia. All the catfish ponds have their own creel limits.

Miscellaneous   Camping is allowed on Fort Pickett but is only open to authorized individuals. ATVs are not allowed.

Fort Pickett has some special boating regulations worth mentioning here. Most of the waters on the installation are off limits to gasoline engines. No motor over thirty-five horsepower may be used on any of the installation's waters. All boats must carry USCG-approved life preservers, and each person aboard must have his own life preserver.

The Darville, Dinwiddie County, Blackstone East, Danieltown, and Warfield quadrangles cover Fort Pickett.

For more information, contact: HQ U.S. Army Garrison, AFZA-FP-ACR (ATTN: Game Check Station), Fort Pickett, Blackstone, VA 23824, phone (804) 292-2618 (8:00 A.M. to 4:00 P.M., weekdays).

RADFORD ARMY AMMUNITION PLANT
NEW RIVER
ARMY AMMUNITION PLANT

- 2,089 acres open to hunting
- Installation permit required
- Limited public access
- White-tailed deer

Hunting   Radford AAP and New River AAP together offer 2,089 acres of hunting territory to Old Dominion hunters. There is limited public access at the New River unit.

The New River facility is located in Dublin and is also referred to as the loading plant. The main facility is located in Radford and is called the manufacturing plant.

To hunt at the New River unit, civilians must pay $3.50 for an application. They are chosen by lottery for a limited number of positions, and those who are chosen must pay a $10 permit fee. All hunters at both plants must have a Virginia hunting license and pay the $10 permit fee.

White-tailed deer and occasionally turkey may be hunted. Weapons allowed are bow and arrow and shotgun.

During the 1988 deer season, 349 hunters hunted on the facilities with an average hunter success rate of 37.63 percent for shotgunners and 12.5 percent for archers. The average dressed weight of yearling bucks taken on the facilities was eighty pounds.

Miscellaneous Fishing and camping are not allowed at Radford or New River. All public access is strictly controlled.

For more information, contact: Commander, Radford Army Ammunition Plant, ATTN: SMCRA-EN, Radford, VA 24121, phone (703) 639-7480.

Air Force Installations

LANGLEY AIR FORCE BASE

- On the Atlantic coast
- 400 acres open to hunting and fishing
- Closed to the public
- Installation permit required
- White-tailed deer
- Freshwater and saltwater fishing
- Restricted camping

Hunting Of the 3,440 acres that comprise Langley AFB, only 400 are open to hunting. Hunting at Langley is not open to the public. Only those holding valid military identification cards may hunt on the installation.

Small game hunting is not allowed on Langley. The only animal that may be hunted here is the white-tailed deer. Hunters must meet the licensing requirements established by the state of Virginia. Hunters must also have a Langley Air Force Base hunting permit (Form 5) available from the civil engineering directorate for $2 a year.

All deer hunting is done from permanent tree stands situated around the installation. The stands are assigned by a random drawing of all hunters' applications. Hunters must stay in their assigned stands until the end of the hunt.

The only weapons authorized for use on Langley are shotguns of 12, 16, or 20 gauge using slugs or buckshot and archery tackle meeting the specifications of Virginia law.

A hunter may not load his or her gun until firmly in place in the assigned tree stand. When going to or from the stand, hunters must open the action of the gun. All hunters afield during the shotgun hunt must wear a minimum of 400 square inches of hunter orange as specified under Virginia hunting regulations.

Both the bow and shotgun seasons follow those set by the state. Hunting is only fair at Langley but is well managed and safe.

Fishing   Langley has both freshwater and saltwater fishing. Anglers on the installation must meet the licensing requirements set by Virginia and the same eligibility requirements as hunters. No base permit is required to fish for saltwater species. Freshwater anglers, on the other hand, must have a Langley fishing permit. The permit is available from the civil engineering directorate.

Langley has a little over thirty acres of freshwater ponds stocked with bass, crappie, bluegill, catfish, pike, and sunfish. Watercraft are not allowed on the ponds but all other fishing regulations match those of the state.

Saltwater fishing along Langley's oceanfront is for flounder, speckled trout, spotted weakfish, croaker, catfish, bluefish, and eels. Saltwater regulations, including those concerning crabbing, match those of the state.

Miscellaneous   Camping is allowed on Langley, but only in the base's FAM-CAMP. ATVs are not allowed.

For more information on hunting and fishing at Langley AFB, contact: 1CSG/DEV, Langley AFB, VA 23665, phone (804) 764-3906 (8:00 A.M. to 5:00 P.M., weekdays).

Naval Installations

NAVAL SECURITY GROUP ACTIVITY NORTHWEST

- Near Chesapeake in both Virginia and North Carolina
- 4,118 acres
- White-tailed deer and small game
- Fishing
- Camping closed to the public

Hunting   NSGA Northwest is open to public hunting. There are no priority systems at this installation, so everyone stands the same chance of access.

The hunting areas on NSGA Northwest are in both Virginia and North Carolina and all hunting seasons are the same as those established by these states. Hunters on NSGA Northwest may take white-tailed deer, cottontail, squirrel, quail, and dove.

Hunters from Virginia must meet Virginia licensing requirements; North Carolinians must meet the licensing requirements of that state. When signing in to hunt on the installation, hunters must have all applicable state hunting licenses from either state and proof of having completed a certified hunter safety course. There is no minimum legal age for hunting on the installation, but hunters under eighteen must be accompanied by an adult at all times while afield.

There is no reservation system on this installation. All hunting areas and tree stands are assigned on a first-come, first-served basis at the game warden station, where all hunters must check in. When checking in, hunters must present their credentials, fill out a hunting request, and pay the applicable fees. Hunters are then assigned to stands or hunting areas and issued a hunting area badge. The hunter must leave his or her hunting license at the game warden station when the badge is issued.

The hunting area badge serves as a license while the hunter is in the field or on stand. Upon completing hunting for the day, the hunter reports back to the game warden station and exchanges the badge for the hunting license.

Hunters are not permitted to move around freely on this installation. Once a hunter is assigned to a stand or field, he or she must proceed directly to the assigned area and remain there until at least noon. Hunters may move from their stands between noon and 1:00 P.M. but must be back on the stand by 1:00 P.M. Afternoon hunts end one-half hour before sunset and all hunters must then go to the game warden station.

The only weapons allowed on NSGA Northwest are shotguns of 12 to 20 gauge and archery tackle meeting either Virginia or North Carolina requirements.

Hunting is only fair at this installation. Big game hunters averaged 3.5 percent for the 1989–90 season, while upland game hunters did better at 18 percent.

Fishing All fishing areas on NSGA Northwest are on the Virginia side of the reservation. Therefore, all anglers must meet the licensing requirements as established by Virginia.

The only species available at NSGA Northwest are largemouth bass and catfish. All state fishing rules apply, including creel limits and slot limits, if any.

Miscellaneous Camping is allowed on NSGA Northwest, but only military ID card holders may camp there. ATVs are not allowed on the installation. Hunters' and anglers' vehicles must be parked in designated areas on the installation.

The Moyock, Virginia and North Carolina; and Lake Drummond SE, Virginia and North Carolina, topographic maps cover the installation.

For more information, contact: Ms. Robin Heubel, Natural Resources Specialist, Naval Security Group Activity Northwest, Bldg. 8, Code 40N, Chesapeake, VA 23322-5000, phone (804) 421-8939 (7:45 A.M. to 4:15 P.M., weekdays).

NAVAL SURFACE WARFARE CENTER DAHLGREN

- 1,200 acres open to hunting and fishing
- Closed to the public
- Installation permit required
- White-tailed deer and small game
- Freshwater and saltwater fishing

Hunting Only military personnel, retired military personnel, active duty and retired dependents, and DOD civilians may hunt on Naval Surface Warfare Center (NSWC) Dahlgren. Members of the public may hunt on the installation, but only as guests of authorized individuals.

In addition to having all applicable state licenses, hunters on Dahlgren must have an installation permit. Before getting a permit, though, hunters must pass a written test on Dahlgren-unique hunting rules. Bowhunters on the installation must also pass at least annually a shooting test.

There are approximately 1,200 acres open to hunting on the Dahlgren military reservation. Those acres contain white-tailed deer, cottontail rabbit, squirrel, waterfowl, quail, and dove. All station hunting seasons follow those of the state.

Hunters are required to check in and out daily at the installation game check station. All game taken on the installation must be reported and checked, as required.

Fishing NSWC Dahlgren offers fishing to those same individuals authorized hunting access. All anglers must meet Virginia's licensing requirements.

Species available at NSWC Dahlgren are largemouth bass, pickerel, channel catfish, and bream in the freshwater impoundments of the installation. Saltwater species available are bluefish, rockfish, spotted weakfish, and channel catfish and white and yellow perch (in the brackish water). All state-set methods of take and creel limits apply on the installation.

Miscellaneous Camping and ATVs are not allowed on NSWC Dahlgren. The Dahlgren topographic map covers this installation.

For more information, contact: Dr. Thomas Wray II, Code C8305, Naval Surface Warfare Center, Dahlgren, VA 22448, phone (703) 663-8695 (8:00 A.M. to 4:00 P.M., weekdays).

NAVAL WEAPONS STATION YORKTOWN

- Northeast of Newport News
- 10,000 acres
- Installation permit required
- White-tailed deer

Hunting The only hunting allowed on NWS Yorktown is for white-tailed deer, and that hunting is excellent. During the 1989–90 season, deer hunters on Yorktown took one deer for every 56 hours spent hunting.

Hunting is strictly controlled at Yorktown. All hunters are taken by a guide to an assigned stand where the hunter must stay until retrieved by the guide. Due to security constraints, hunters are not allowed to stalk or still-hunt on the installation.

The only weapons allowed on Yorktown are shotguns shooting buckshot. The installation is open to hunting only on Saturdays and federal holidays. No hunting is allowed on Christmas Day.

To hunt on the installation, the prospective hunter must write a letter requesting permission to be included in the upcoming deer season and enclose proof of having completed a certified hunter safety course. The letter should be addressed to: Commanding Officer, ATTN: Game Warden, NWS Yorktown, VA 23691. The letter must be received by November 1 of each year. After the drawing, which is held the first week in November for that year's season, all selected hunters' names are posted at the gate near the security office. This list entitles the selected hunters to bring weapons on the station.

All hunters selected to participate in the annual deer hunt must have the applicable state licenses and must purchase a station permit for $10. On hunt days, hunters must meet at an assembly area where they are briefed and escorted to their stands.

Miscellaneous   Camping and ATVs are not allowed on this installation.

For more information, contact: NWS Game Warden, Code 09C2, Yorktown, VA 23691, phone (804) 887-4953 (6:00 A.M. to 2:30 P.M., weekdays).

Marine Corps Installations

QUANTICO MARINE BASE

- On the Potomac River near Washington
- 45,000 acres open to hunting and fishing
- Installation permit required
- White-tailed deer, turkey, and small game
- Fishing
- Camping closed to the public

Hunting   Approximately 45,000 acres in thirty-four hunting areas are open to hunting on Quantico. The hunting programs on Quantico are open to the public as well as to military members, military dependents, retirees, and DOD civilians.

Quantico hunters may take white-tailed deer, eastern wild turkey, cottontail, squirrel, waterfowl, quail, woodcock, dove, raccoon, bobcat, and both red and gray fox. The hunting seasons for all species generally follow those of Virginia, although dates may vary slightly.

All hunters on Quantico must meet the licensing requirements of Virginia before purchasing an installation hunting permit. All licensing requirements apply; bowhunters must have an archery tag issued by the state as well as the appropriate big game tags and waterfowl stamps. In accordance with state law, hunters must also prove they have completed an approved hunter safety course when purchasing a Virginia license for the first time. Hunters under eighteen are allowed to hunt on Quantico but must be accompanied at all times by an adult over twenty-one.

Quantico's hunting program has one unique aspect. Hunters can earn bonus priority points for hunting areas during the season. To accumulate "chits," hunters must put in a certain number of hours of volunteer work during the off-season. Hunters with chits, active duty marines, and certain other hunters may make reservations by phone or in person the day before hunting, earlier than other hunters. On opening days, the hunter must use the chits personally. During the rest of the season, the chits may be used for guests or for other members of the earner's hunting party.

Active duty military personnel and retirees may make reservations after noon the day before hunting. Others may make reservations after 2:00 P.M. the day before hunting. Any remaining hunting areas are assigned on a first-come, first-served basis the day of the hunt. Area assignments are made so that there are at least seventy-five acres available for each hunter.

Hunters on Quantico may use shotguns with slugs, muzzleloading rifles in .40 caliber or larger, and legal archery tackle to take deer. Small game may be taken only with shotguns shooting shot or archery tackle. Crossbows, modern rifles, and handguns are not allowed in the hunting fields on Quantico. Deer may not be hunted with dogs, but dogs may be used for all upland game except turkey.

All hunters must check in and out at the game check station when going afield on the installation. Any game taken must also be checked at the game check station.

Safety is paramount at Quantico, as it is at all installations. Hunters afield during the general deer season and either-sex deer season must wear a hunter orange garment displaying at least two square feet of orange front and back. Bowhunters afield during the archery-only season or hunting in an archery-only area are exempt from the hunter orange requirement. Small game hunters are not exempt. Waterfowl hunters may remove the orange garment when they are in their stands.

Hunter success is only fair at Quantico, but I suspect that may be due to a lack of effort rather than a lack of animals. Big game hunters took 700 deer during 12,000 trips and 40 turkeys in 1,000 trips during the 1989–90 season. Small game hunters averaged about a quail a trip and three squirrel per trip during the same season.

Fishing Fishing is excellent at Quantico. The base has numerous reservoirs, lakes, ponds, and creeks, which all contain both game fish and rough fish of one sort or another. Some of the reservoirs have special regulations.

Lunga Reservoir, entirely within the boundaries of the base, has horsepower restrictions on the size of motors used there. Anglers on Lunga Reservoir must have all applicable Virginia fishing licenses and an installation fishing permit.

R-6 Pond is in an artillery impact area, so anglers wanting to fish this body of water must first check with the range control office. It, too, requires a post fishing permit as well as the appropriate state licenses.

Aquia Reservoir, along Quantico's periphery, is primarily managed by Stafford County for drinking water. A base permit is not required here unless the angler is fishing from a portion of the shore within reservation boundaries.

Fishing limits on the installation vary slightly from those of the state. There is a five-fish creel limit on largemouth bass as well as a slot limit. No angler may take more than five bass, and all bass between twelve and fifteen inches must be released unharmed. Quantico anglers may also take up to four striped bass over twenty inches, eight chain pickerel, and six trout. There is no size limit on trout or pickerel. Anglers taking crappie and sunfish may take as many fish as they desire. Quantico officials request that anglers take as many of these species as possible to prevent overpopulation.

The methods of taking game fish on the base generally are the same as those for the state. Trotlines, setlines, bush hooks, and jug-fishing are prohibited on the base. Anglers may use more than one hook and line to take all species of fish except trout. Trout anglers may use only one hook and line. Anglers may also take frogs by gigging and gar and carp with bow and arrow. Seines are generally not authorized on the installation.

Miscellaneous Military ID card holders may camp on Quantico Marine Base. ATV and ORV use is strictly forbidden on the installation.

The Nokesville, Joplin, Quantico, Stafford, Somerville, and Independent Hill topographic maps cover Quantico Marine Base.

For more information on hunting and fishing at Quantico, contact: Public Works Branch, ATTN: Game Checking Station, Box 1855, Quantico, VA 22134-0855, phone (703) 640-5523/29 (8:00 A.M. to 4:30 P.M., weekdays).

WASHINGTON

Washington's diverse terrain is home to a variety of big and small game, including three types of deer and two types of elk. Excluding Alaska, Washington offers the best hunting in North America for mountain goat and black bear.

Washington also hosts twenty-two military installations. Due to its spectacular coastline, most of those installations belong to the U.S. Navy, but two of the largest, including Fort Lewis, belong to the Army.

Army Installations

FORT LEWIS

- Outside Tacoma
- Hunting
- Limited fishing
- Camping closed to the public

Hunting Although Fort Lewis covers 86,000 acres of land, available hunting acreage varies with weekly training requirements.

Hunting is open to the public as well as military personnel, and all hunters must abide by Washington state registration and seasonal requirements. All hunters must sign in and out at the main gate.

Hunters will find waterfowl, small game, deer, and a limited pheasant population at Fort Lewis.

Fishing Fishing access is limited to certain lakes. The varieties of fish at Fort Lewis include trout, perch, and other spiny-rayed fish.

Miscellaneous Camping is limited to military personnel.

For more information, contact: Morale Support Activities, Outdoor Recreation, Building 2409, Fort Lewis, WA 98433, phone (206) 967-7788 (7:45 A.M. to 4:00 P.M., weekdays).

Naval Installations

NAVAL AIR STATION WHIDBEY ISLAND

- Near Oak Harbor on Puget Sound
- 70,000 acres
- Closed to the public
- Installation permit required
- Upland game and waterfowl
- Saltwater fishing
- Camping

Hunting Hunting opportunities are very limited on Whidbey Island. The only animals available are upland game and waterfowl. Hunting access is restricted to military members, military retirees, DOD civilians, and their dependents and guests.

Hunters on the installation must meet all state and federal licensing requirements before receiving a station permit. The station permits are available at no cost from the station's security department in Building 220.

Hunters are required to check in and out of the security department when going hunting and upon returning. The weapons that can be used are restricted to shotguns shooting shot smaller than #2. No other weapons are allowed in the hunting fields.

There are three major hunting areas on Whidbey Island. All have the same access restrictions and sign in/out requirements.

Fishing The only fishing available at the Whidbey Island station is for saltwater species. Anglers may take any species of fish found in Puget Sound, but the premier species is sea-run cutthroat trout and steelhead.

Anglers must meet all state licensing requirements for fishing on the installation. All Washington fishing laws and regulations apply and all creel limits are the same as the state.

Miscellaneous Camping is allowed on the installation, but only military ID card holders are allowed to camp here. ATV use is also authorized, but the vehicle must have a station registration and the rider must have insurance.

For more information, contact: NAS Whidbey Island Security, Code SE, Bldg. 220, Oak Harbor, WA 98278, phone (206) 257-3122 (daily).

NAVAL SUBMARINE BASE BANGOR

- 13 miles south of Bremerton on the Hood Canal
- 6,691 acres
- Closed to the public
- Installation permit required
- Deer
- Freshwater and saltwater fishing
- Restricted boating

Hunting Deer are the only game available for hunting at Bangor Submarine Base, which includes the Indian Island and Keyport facilities. Deer hunting is open only to active duty military personnel, retired military personnel, dependents sixteen and over of retired and active duty personnel, DOD civilians and their dependents over sixteen, retired DOD civilians, and all contract employees of Bangor Submarine Base.

The base is divided into ten hunting areas. With the exception of Area 3, all areas are restricted to bowhunting-only. Area 3 is open to both bowhunting and shotgun hunting. Rifles, muzzleloaders, handguns, and crossbows are not allowed on the installation. Hunting in nine of the base's hunting areas is allowed only on weekends and federal holidays. Area 10 is open daily to hunting. Except for Area 10, each area is open to a maximum of four hunters at a time. Area 10 is open to a maximum of five hunters at a time.

Bowhunters on Bangor must qualify with their weapon every year. Hunters may call (206) 396-4192 at Bangor and (206) 385-0100 at Indian Island for qualification schedules. Shotgunners aren't required to qualify every year but must present proof of having completed a hunter safety course before receiving an installation hunting permit.

Bowhunting equipment used on Bangor must meet some pretty stringent requirements. Bows must be at least forty pounds in draw weight. Broadheads must be at least seven-eighths-inch wide and unbarbed. The back of the broadhead must be completely closed by a smooth, unbroken surface starting at maximum blade width, forming a smooth line toward the opposite end of the shaft. The back of the broadhead may not angle into the shaft toward the point.

Shotgunners must use rifle slugs in 10, 12, 16, or 20 gauge. Buckshot is not allowed.

All hunters on the installation must have fulfilled Washington licensing requirements before applying for a base permit. The base hunting permits are issued by random drawing before each hunting weekend. Hunters wanting to hunt on the installation must fill out a registration form at Building 1004 on the Bangor Submarine Base or at the main gates at the Keyport and Indian Island facilities.

Hunters assigned to hunting Areas 1 to 9 on the Bangor Base must check in and out with the game warden at the operations area gate on Trigger Avenue. Hunters hunting in Area 10 will receive specific sign-in and sign-out instructions from the game warden. When checking in, hunters are issued a parking pass to be displayed on the dash or window of their vehicle. Hunters have their own parking areas next to all the hunting areas and must park in these areas or run the risk of losing their hunting privileges. Hunters may not go afield earlier than one hour prior to legal shooting time and must be out of the field one hour after the end of legal shooting time.

All game bagged on the installation must be checked by the game warden before being taken off the base. Bag limits for deer on Bangor Submarine Base are the same as those for the state. Albino deer and partial albino deer are protected on the installation.

Fishing Fishing is allowed on Naval Submarine Base Bangor, but is restricted to personnel who meet the requirements detailed in the hunting section. Anglers on the installation must meet all Washington licensing requirements for both freshwater and saltwater fishing.

The fishing and general recreation areas on Bangor Submarine Base are in two permanent zones and several temporary zones. Each recreation area has its own rules posted at the entrance to the area.

Anglers on the installation must check in with either the pass and identification branch or through the operations area gate before going fishing.

Miscellaneous Camping and ATVs are not allowed on the installation.

Bangor offers a saltwater launching facility at Floral Point for anglers wanting to fish the waters of Puget Sound. The base's Cattail Lake allows freshwater canoe and nongasoline-powered boating.

For more information on hunting and fishing at the Naval Submarine Base Bangor or the Keyport or Indian Island facilities, contact: Game Warden Section, Naval Submarine Base Bangor, Bremerton, WA 98315-5000, phone (206) 396-4192 (weekdays, 8:00 A.M. to 4:00 P.M.).

WISCONSIN

This northern tier state supports healthy populations of white-tailed deer and other game. It is one of the best states in the nation for bowhunting white-tailed deer with the world record whitetail taken here in 1914.

Wisconsin does not have a large military presence. There are only six installations in the entire state; two of which are Army, and the other four, Air Force. The installations range in size from the 100-acre General Billy Mitchell Field in Milwaukee to 59,779-acre Fort McCoy. None of the Air Force installations in the state offer fishing or hunting; the Army installations do.

Army Installations

BADGER
ARMY AMMUNITION PLANT

* In south-central Wisconsin near Baraboo
* 3,000 acres open to hunting, a 7-acre pond
* Closed to the public
* White-tailed deer
* Fishing

Hunting Hunting on Badger Army Ammunition Plant is limited to white-tailed deer. The plant has 3,000 acres open to hunting. No charge is made for hunting on the plant's grounds, but all hunters must meet the licensing and tag requirements of Wisconsin.

The plant is managed under a cooperative agreement with the state, so expect state seasons and bag limits to apply. Access to the plant is strictly controlled, with hunting access limited to military members, civilian employees of the plant, and their guests.

The Badger Army Ammunition Plant has weapons restrictions that limit hunters to using shotguns with slugs or buckshot and archery tackle for taking deer. No exact details were available.

Hunter success rates during the 1989–90 season were below the state average. Hunters took 116 bucks and 98 does for a hunter success rate of 8.04 percent. The good news is that the average dressed weight of a yearling buck taken from the plant was 131 pounds. That's a large whitetail by anyone's standards!

Fishing Badger Army Ammunition Plant has a seven-acre stocked pond for fishing.

For more information, contact: Security Office, Badger Army Ammunition Plant, Baraboo, WI 53913.

FORT McCOY

- In southwestern Wisconsin near Sparta
- 50,000 acres open to hunting and fishing
- Installation permit required
- White-tailed deer, turkey, and small game
- Fishing
- Camping closed to the public

Hunting Fort McCoy has up to 50,000 acres open to hunting at any given time. A few areas may be closed due to training requirements from time to time. Fort McCoy is open to the public for both big and small game hunting.

The only big game animal found on Fort McCoy is the whitetail. Black bear may also inhabit the fort, but they cannot be hunted there. Small game animals found on the fort are cottontail rabbit, squirrel, grouse, turkey, woodcock, duck, geese, and assorted waterfowl.

Fort McCoy offers up to four deer seasons ranging from archery to a special muzzleloader season held from time to time. All hunters on the installation must be properly licensed in Wisconsin, but no hunter safety course is required by the installation.

Fort McCoy is managed as a separate deer management unit and issues its own hunter-choice permits. Hunters who want to apply for a McCoy hunter-choice permit must fill out a Fort McCoy form AFZR-DE FORM 1161. A separate form must be completed by each hunter in a party. Up to ten forms may be mailed in one envelope. The completed forms and required remittance must be mailed to: Commander, Fort McCoy, ATTN: NRMD (Permit Sales), Sparta, WI 54656-5000.

Permits are issued by a classification/drawing system. The fort classifies hunters into three categories with slightly different odds of being drawn for each. The categories are as follows: category A—active and retired military, Reserve, and National Guard members and their dependents; category B—Fort McCoy DOD and non-appropriated-fund civilians and their family members; and category C—members of the public.

Before applying for a Fort McCoy tag, hunters must have a valid Wisconsin license for the game to be hunted. The costs of the Fort McCoy hunting permits are as follows and are the same for all hunters: small game, $6; archery (deer), $9; gun deer, $12; muzzleloader, $8; and combo (includes fishing, small game, and gun deer permits), $20.

Unlimited quantities of category A and category B permits are available for gun deer and muzzleloader seasons each year. Category C permits are limited for these seasons. All category C applications for combo, gun deer, and muzzleloader permits are processed according to the postmark date. If there are more category C applications than there are slots available, a drawing is held to determine who will hunt. Unsuccessful applicants will receive a refund of their application fees. There is no quota for small game and archery permits in any category.

Small game hunters and archery deer hunters are not required to sign in and out when hunting on the post. Archery deer hunters must register all deer taken with post authorities at the provost marshal's office, Building 1760. Gun deer and muzzleloader hunters must sign in before going afield at one of three established checkpoints: Gate 19 on the north post, Coal Yard Gate on the south post, or Gate 48 on the south post. Hunters may check in before 5:00 A.M. but may not enter a hunting area prior to that time.

Hunters on the installation may not use handguns or crossbows to take any animal on the post. All other weapons are legal, including high-powered rifles. Some gun-deer areas may require the use of shotguns or muzzleloaders.

The minimum legal age to hunt on Fort McCoy without direct adult supervision is eighteen. Hunters as young as twelve may hunt on the installation provided they are under the direct supervision of a responsible adult over twenty-one.

Hunter success for deer on Fort McCoy is above the state average. Archery hunters average 17 percent, gun deer hunters average 51 percent, and muzzleloader hunters average 25 percent during the regular muzzleloader season and 39 percent during the special muzzleloader season. Those figures are indicative of a very well managed deer herd and well managed hunting program.

Fishing Fishing is excellent on Fort McCoy and is open to the public. There is no drawing for a fishing license, but there is still a category system. There are four categories of anglers on the post. Categories A, B, and C are the same as for hunters; all are charged $7 for a license. Category D is divided into two subcategories. The Category D $4 permit is for children under sixteen, disabled, people over sixty-four, and those anglers holding a four-day nonresident license. A Category D $1 permit is for children three to nine who are not fishing for or in possession of trout.

Anglers can apply for a Fort McCoy fishing permit on a Fort McCoy Form 161. Be sure to include all Wisconsin fishing license or sporting license numbers on the form. Mail applications to the same address for hunting permits. Fort McCoy permits are valid from August 31 for one year. The actual fishing seasons may vary from year to year. State trout stamps are required on the installation when fishing for trout.

The thirteen lakes and impoundments on the reservation range in size from 3 acres to 211 acres. All are stocked with fish of one sort or another. The species found on Fort McCoy include brook trout, rainbow trout, brown trout, largemouth bass, bluegill, pumpkinseed, and crappie.

There are also a couple of streams on Fort McCoy. All trout taken from any flowing water on Fort McCoy must be released.

The fishing regulations on Fort McCoy generally follow those of the state, but there are some differences in creel limits. Anglers on Fort McCoy may take no more than five trout of any species in one day. Live bait and artificials may both be used on the installation, but anglers may use no more than one hook and line.

Miscellaneous Camping is allowed on Fort McCoy. The fort runs a well kept camping area with 113 sites. Both tent and RV camping is allowed. Campers pay $6 a night for campsites without electric power and $8 a night for campsights with. Camping is authorized on the installation only for those with military ID cards.

ATVs may not be used on Fort McCoy, but there is a county-maintained snowmobile trail that stretches ten miles through post property.

The 7.5-minute topographic map quadrants that cover Fort McCoy are Tomah, City Rock, Millston, and Alderwood Lake.

For more information, contact: AFZR-DE-N, Permit Collection Officer, Fort McCoy, WI 54656-5000, phone (608) 388-2252/3337 (8:00 A.M. to 4:00 P.M., weekdays).

WYOMING

Wyoming is world-renowned for its hunting and fishing opportunities. This 97,914-square-mile state offers some of the best hunting and fishing in North America. With everything from white-tailed deer to mountain goats, hunters here can have the experience of their lives.

All three military installations in Wyoming belong to the Air Force. Two of them are too small to offer any hunting or fishing. The third, Francis E. Warren Air Force Base, is fairly large at 33,466 acres.

Air Force Installations

FRANCIS E. WARREN
AIR FORCE BASE

- In Cheyenne
- Closed to the public
- Installation permit required
- Fishing
- Camping

Fishing Fishing is allowed in two small lakes that are stocked with rainbow, cutthroat, brown trout, and channel catfish. The lakes are open to military members, retirees, dependents, and civilian employees of the base.

All anglers on the installation must meet Wyoming licensing requirements and

purchase a base fishing permit. Most of the base's fishing regulations follow those of the state, but there are differences in the creel limit. Base anglers may take only six trout and six catfish daily. No live fish may be used as bait, but worms, crickets, and other types of nonfish live bait may be used. Artificials are also authorized on the installation. Anglers may use no more than one hook and line.

Miscellaneous Camping is allowed on F. E. Warren. The Base FAMCAMP offers a modern campground for RV campers. The pads are complete with water and electricity as well as a laundry and restrooms.

No ATVs are allowed on the installation.

For more information, contact: 90CSG/DEV, F. E. Warren AFB, WY 82005, phone (307) 775-2213 (weekdays, 7:30 A.M. to 4:30 P.M.).

○ **Hunting open to the public**
● **Hunting closed to the public**

Loring AFB ○

ME

NCU Cutler ●

Fort Drum ○

VT **NH**

NY

New Boston AFS ●
○ Fort Devens

MA

Seneca AD ●

RI

USMA West Point ●

CT

MN

WI

MI

○ Fort McCoy

Badger AAP ●

PA

Picatinny Arsenal ●
Fort Dix
NWS Earle
NAEC Lakehurst

Fort Indiantown Gap ○

IA

Joliet AAP ○

Ravenna AAP ○

Letterkenny AD ○

NJ

Aberdeen Proving Ground
NATC Patuxent River
Fort George G. Meade

MD

DE

Fort Belvoir ●

Naval Electronic System Engineering Activity
NOS Indian Head

Joliet ATA ○

IN

OH

Chanute AFB ●

WV

VA

Iowa AAP ○

NWSC Crane ○

Jefferson Proving Ground ○

Quantico Marine Base ●
NSWC Dahlgren ○

Langley AFB
Fort Eustis
NWS Yorktown

MO

IL

Indiana AAP ○

Fort A. P. Hill ○

Naval Security Group Activity Northwest

○ Lake City AAP

○ Fort Knox

Fort Lee ○

Fort Pickett ●

MCAS Cherry Point ●

KY

Radford AAP ●

Fort Leonard Wood ○

Fort Campbell ○

Holston AAP ○

NC

Fort Bragg ○

Volunteer AAP ○

TN

Camp Lejeune ●

○ Fort Chaffee

Milan AAP ○

Arnold AFB ●

GA

SC

AR

Redstone Arsenal ○

Anniston Army Depot ●

Fort Jackson ●
NWS Charleston ○
MCAS Beaufort ●

Little Rock AFB ●

Camp McCain ○

Fort Gordon ●

Pine Bluff Arsenal ○

Columbus AFB ○

Fort McClellan ●

○ Fort McPherson

Fort Stewart ●

AL

NAS Meridian ○

Fort Rucker ○

Fort Benning ●
○ MCLB Albany

Kings Bay NSB ●

○ Barksdale AFB

Moody AFB ●

NAS Cecil Field ●

MS

Tyndall AFB ○

LA

○ Fort Polk

Eglin AFB

FL

○ Avon Park AFR

Mississippi AAP

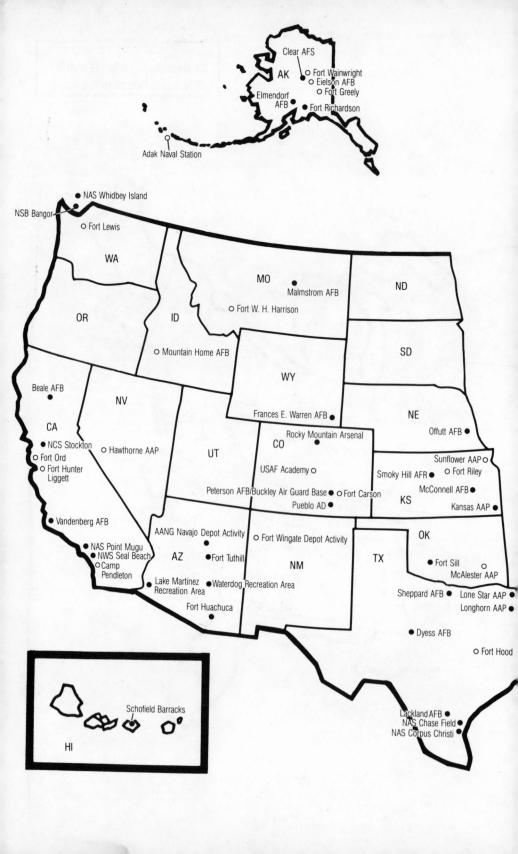

○ **Fishing open to the public**
● **Fishing closed to the public**

○ Loring AFB

ME

NCU Cutler ○

K. I. Sawyer AFB ○   Fort Drum

VT   **NH**

○   **NY**   ● New Boston AFS
       ○ Fort Devens

MN

WI   ● Seneca AD   **MA**   **RI**

USMA West Point ●   **CT**

Picatinny Arsenal ○

MI   **PA**   Fort Dix

○ Fort McCoy   Tobyhanna Army Depot ●   NWS Earle ○

Badger AAP ●   Fort Indiantown Gap   ○ NAEC Lakehurst

Joliet AAP ●   Ravenna AAP ○   Letterkenny AD ○   **NJ**   Aberdeen Proving Ground

IA   Joliet ATA ●   **IN**   **OH**   **MD**   NATC Patuxent River

Iowa AAP ○   Chanute AFB ●   **DE**   Fort George G. Meade

       NWSC   **WV**   **VA** ○   Naval Electronic System Engineering Activity

       Crane ○   Jefferson Proving   Fort Belvoir ○   NOS Indian Head

IL   Indiana AAP ○   Ground ○   Quantico Marine Base ●   Langley AFB ●

MO   NSWC Dahlgren ○   Fort Eustis

○ Lake City AAP   ○ Fort Knox   Fort A. P. Hill ○

○ Whiteman AFB   **KY**   Radford AAP ○   Fort Pickett ○   Naval Security Group Activity Northwest

Fort Leonard Wood   Fort Bragg ● MCAS Cherry Point

○   Fort Campbell   **NC**   ○

      ○

TN   ● Camp Lejeune

○ Fort Chaffee   ○ Milan AAP   ● Arnold AFB   **SC**

AR   **AL**   **GA**   ● Shaw AFB

     Redstone ●   ● Anniston Army Depot   ○ Fort Jackson

Little Rock AFB ●   Camp McCain ○   Arsenal   ●   NWS Charleston

      Columbus ○   Fort McClellan ○   Fort Gordon ●   MCAS Beaufort ●

Pine Bluff Arsenal ○   AFB   ○ Fort McPherson ○ Fort Stewart

      NAS ●   Maxwell AFB ●   ● Fort Benning

○ Barksdale   Meridian ○   Fort Rucker ○   ● MCLB Albany ● Kings Bay NSB

AFB   **MS**   NAS Pensacola ●   Moody AFB ○   ● NAS Cecil Field

LA   ●   ○ Tyndall AFB

○ Fort Polk   ● ●   ○   **FL**

        Eglin AFB

      NAS Whiting Field   ○ Avon Park AFR

Index